Mastering Cybersecurity: "MCQs to Test and Expand Your IT Security Knowledge" (Volume- I)

Rajasekar V.R.
Rajkumar S

ISBN: 9798850466626

To our beloved family members

Special Thanks to

Ms. Shahana R
&
Mr. Dhyaneshwaran R

.

The page was left intentionally blank.

CONTENTS

The page was left intentionally blank.

Chapter 1
Information Security Basics

This chapter includes questions from the following topics:
- Information Security Strategies.
- Functional Requirements for Security.
- Fundamental Design Principles for Security.
- Information Security Techniques.
- Combating Cybercriminals and Cyber Attackers.

1. **Which of the following may occur due to the failure of standard security controls?**
   a. System-specific risks.
   b. Risk to the organization as a whole.
   c. Risk specific to subsystems.
   d. Risk to a specific location of the organization.

2. **Which information security concept is Alice concerned with when she wishes to send a private e-mail to Bob and does not want anyone else to be able to read it except Bob, hence maintaining privacy?**
   a. Confidentiality
   b. Integrity
   c. Non-repudiation
   d. Authentication

3. **Fancy Bears and Anonymous are examples of what?**
   a. Types of malware.
   b. Cryptographic ciphers.
   c. Popular computer security blogs.
   d. Hacking organizations.

4. **An individual harassed repeatedly by being followed, called, or written is a target of what?**
   a. Bullying
   b. Phishing
   c. Stalking
   d. Identity theft.

5. **Which of the following are possible security threats?**
   a. Illegitimate use.
   b. Backdoors
   c. Masquerading
   d. All of the above.

6. **In Cybersecurity, authenticity is defined as what?**
   a. The first or original copy of a document or message.
   b. The property of being genuine and verifiable.
   c. It is being able to apply financial management to a process.
   d. It is being able to map an action to an identity.

7. **Suddenly, your phone begins to receive unsolicited messages; this might be an example of what?**
    a. Packet sniffing.
    b. Blue-snarfing
    c. Blue-jacking
    d. Geotagging

8. **What is the term used to describe an action or technique to identify and eliminate a threat or attack to mitigate it?**
    a. Threat
    b. Countermeasure
    c. Vulnerability
    d. Risk

9. **Which scenario indicates an integrity breach? Alice sends a message to Bob that Trudy intercepts.**
    a. Trudy cannot read it because it is encrypted, but it can be delivered to Bob in its original form.
    b. Trudy changes the message and then forwards it on.
    c. Trudy reads the message.
    d. Trudy deletes the message without forwarding it.

10. **What is defined as accountability in Cybersecurity?**
    a. It is being able to map an action to an identity.
    b. The first or original copy of a document or message.
    c. The property of being genuine and verifiable.
    d. It is being able to apply financial management to a process.

11. **Which computer security principle may be violated if a computer system is not accessible whenever needed?**
    a. Access Control.
    b. Confidentiality
    c. Availability
    d. Authentication

12. **Which aspect of a comprehensive approach to Cybersecurity includes these items: policies, procedures, standards, user education, incident response, disaster recovery, compliance, and physical security?**
    a. Security program.
    b. Administrative controls.
    c. Asset management.
    d. Technical controls.

13. **Which aspect of a comprehensive approach to Cybersecurity includes these items: classification, implementation steps, asset control, and documentation?**
    a. Security program.
    b. Asset management.
    c. Administrative controls.
    d. Technical controls.

14. **A flaw or weakness in the system is called what?**
    a. Risk
    b. Threat
    c. Vulnerability
    d. Impact

15. **Select the entity that can pose a threat to an information asset.**
    a. Employees
    b. External Parties.
    c. Natural Disasters.
    d. All of the above.

16. **The threat "disclosure" will affect which of the following?**
    a. Confidentiality
    b. Integrity
    c. Availability
    d. All of the above.

17. **Which of the following can be considered a threat to information security? (Select all that apply.)**
    a. Unauthorized access and data collection.
    b. Piracy and copyright infringements.
    c. Password-protected PDF documents.
    d. Remote backup servers.

18. **Identify the attacks in the following scenarios: (1) The attacker collected credit card details by calling victims and using false pretexts to trick them. (2) The attacker sent out 100,000 random e-mail addresses with a message claiming that "Your Bank account has been locked out. Please click here to reset your password."**
    a. (1) Spearphishing and (2) Pharming.
    b. (1) Hoax and (2) Spearphishing.
    c. (1) Vishing and (2) Phishing.
    d. (1) Pharming and (2) Phishing.

19. **Which of the following is mitigated by administrative controls?**
    a. Assets
    b. Risk
    c. Vulnerabilities
    d. Threats

20. **Choose the measure that cannot prevent the exposure of sensitive data.**
    a. Discarding sensitive data as soon as possible.
    b. Avoid storing data as plain text.
    c. Disabling auto-complete on forms collecting sensitive data.
    d. Using weak cryptographic algorithms without proper key management.

21. **Which of the following is a part of Operational Controls?**
    a. Encryption and Decryption.
    b. Digital Signatures and Digital Envelopes.
    c. Contingency planning and physical securities.

    d.   Certification Authorities and Digital Certificates.

22. **What is the optimal order to consider the steps of the continuous data security process?**
    a.   Real-time monitoring and protection, Identification and baseline, Raise the Bar.
    b.   Raise the Bar, Identification & Baseline, Real-time Monitor & Protection.
    c.   Identification & Baseline, Raise the Bar, Real-time Monitor & Protection.
    d.   Identification & Baseline, Real-time Monitor & Protection, Raise the Bar.

23. **What is the term used to describe an inexperienced attacker who uses code written by others to attack a system?**
    a.   Man-in-middle.
    b.   Borrower.
    c.   Script Kiddie.
    d.   None of the above.

24. **How would an event in which a company's financial system was compromised, resulting in the deletion of payroll information, be classified?**
    a.   An occurrence with a low impact.
    b.   A high-speed collision.
    c.   An incident with a moderate impact.
    d.   Contingent upon the cost of recovery.

25. **How would the situation in which online banking customers cannot make third-party transfers since the occurrence of an incident be categorized?**
    a.   A low urgency event.
    b.   A medium urgency event.
    c.   A high urgency event.
    d.   An enhancement request.

26. **Which of the following statements regarding the advanced persistent threat (APT) is true?**
    a.   APT frequently targets a single organization.
    b.   APT is frequently motivated by business and political factors.
    c.   The operators continually monitor the interaction to achieve the specified goal.
    d.   APT targets only government assets.

27. **Which of the following statements regarding computer security is incorrect?**
    a.   Protecting a computer is critical even if no critical data is stored.
    b.   Malware infection is the sole cause of a computer's slow performance.
    c.   Anti-virus software is 100% effective.
    d.   Attackers do not only target individuals.

28. **Which is the significant technology included in endpoint detection and response?**
    a.   Continuous monitoring.
    b.   Zero-day OS updates.
    c.   One-Time patching process.
    d.   Automatic policy creation for endpoints.

29. **Which of the following is not a primary goal of computer-based information system security?**
    a.   It prevents system assets from being lost, damaged, or abused.

    b.   Control of data analysis.

    c.   Information and application processes are accessible.

    d.   The data's accuracy and the application processes' dependability.

30. **Which of the following is an organization's weakest link in terms of security?**
    a. Using a software firewall instead of a hardware firewall.
    b. Employees of the organization.
    c. Using free anti-virus software.
    d. Organization policies.

31. **Which report was the first to address the management and policy implications of the growing field of computer security?**
    a. Rand Report R-609.
    b. IEEE Report R-100.
    c. IETF Report J-120.
    d. IANS Report – 100.

32. **Which of the following is considered a security risk?**
    a. A document that is password protected.
    b. Unauthorized access and collection of data.
    c. Servers for remote backup.
    d. Authorized data modification

33. **Which of the following statements is not true regarding implementing computer security?**
    a. Selecting a location for defence mechanisms.
    b. Computer security is a relatively simple process.
    c. Computer security entails complex algorithms and the protection of sensitive data.
    d. Computer security is frequently an afterthought.

34. **Which of the following statement define a security attack?**
    a. An event identified by correlation and analytics tools as malicious activity.
    b. An event that has been reviewed by analysts and deemed worthy of deeper investigation.
    c. An event on a system or network detected by a device.
    d. None of the above.

35. **Non-repudiation is frequently used for what?**
    a. To ensure the confidentiality and integrity of the communication.
    b. To protect the system from backdoors and Trojan horses.
    c. To prevent the sender from denying that the communication has occurred.
    d. To protect the system from spoofing attacks.

36. **What is referred to as masquerading?**
    a. An attacker modifies data transmitted during communication.
    b. An attack is a fraudulent replication of a valuable piece of data.
    c. In communication, an attacker assumes the identity of another party.
    d. A hacker gains access to remote systems through an attack.

37. **Which of the following are assets of a computer system that must be protected?**
    a. Integrity, Confidentiality, Authenticity, Availability, and Immunity,

    b.   Attacker, Threat, Adversary, and Vulnerability.

    c.   Hardware, Software-based systems, data, and networks.

    d.   Intrusion Detection System, Firewall, Anti-Spyware, Anti-Virus, and Encryption Algorithms.

38. **What aspect of information security does the integrity objective focus on?**
    a. Verification that information is accurate.
    b. Verification that ethics are appropriately maintained.
    c. Establishment of direct access control of data.
    d. Verification that data is kept private and secure.

39. **What is the chief information officer's (CIO) responsibility?**
    a. Choosing the appropriate hardware.
    b. Locating appropriate software.
    c. Selecting the appropriate vendor.
    d. All of the above.

40. **Which of the following is not a physical asset?**
    a. On a piece of paper, a chart or graph is printed.
    b. Employees' experience and knowledge.
    c. Within an organization, network equipment is installed.
    d. Within an organization, servers and computers are used.

41. **What is the most effective method for preventing a logical security breach?**
    a. Architectural design of the network.
    b. Network layout.
    c. Design of distributed systems.
    d. System software, including the operating system.

42. **Which of the following qualifies as a Cybersecurity element?**
    a. Operational Security.
    b. Network Security.
    c. Application Security.
    d. All of the above.

43. **Which external users can access a genuine user's account by posing as an authentic user?**
    a. Masquerader
    b. Intruder
    c. Misfeasor
    d. Clandestine user.

44. **Which Cybersecurity principle is best exemplified when an employee requests root access to a UNIX system, and access is only granted if the employee performs work requiring specific rights or privileges?**
    a. Open Design.
    b. Least privileges.
    c. Separation of Privileges.
    d. None of the above.

45. **Which of the following is a term that refers to stealing another's idea or invention and exploiting it for one's gain?**
    a. Plagiarism
    b. Intellectual property rights.
    c. Privacy
    d. Documentation

46. **Which of the following is a false statement about "Information Security"?**
    a. Security is solely concerned with safeguarding information assets.
    b. A balance between security and usability is required.
    c. Security is a straightforward process.
    d. Security is a delicate balance of accessibility and protection.

47. **Locate the statement that has nothing to do with data integrity.**
    a. Manipulation or alteration of data without authorization.
    b. Extraction of data to share with unauthorized parties.
    c. Unauthorized data modification.
    d. The deliberate or unintentional substitution of data.

48. **What is the term for a legitimate user who gains access to an unauthorized system asset?**
    a. Masquerader
    b. Misfeasor
    c. Clandestine user.
    d. Outsider attacker.

49. **Which Cybersecurity standards require that the security mechanism be as simple and compact as possible?**
    a. Open-Design.
    b. Least privilege.
    c. Fail-safe Defaults.
    d. The economy of the mechanism.

50. **What is the term used for someone who takes control of a system's supervisory functions to bypass prevention, access, and detection controls?**
    a. External user.
    b. Intruder
    c. Masquerader
    d. Misfeasor

Answer Key

1. (b) Risk to the organization as a whole may occur due to the failure of standard security controls. If security controls fail, it can lead to unauthorized access, data breaches, or other security incidents affecting the entire organization. This can result in financial losses, damage to the organization's reputation, and legal or regulatory consequences. System-specific risks and risks specific to subsystems or locations may also occur, but the failure of standard security controls can have a broader impact on the organization.

2. (a) Alice is concerned with the concept of confidentiality when she wishes to send a private e-mail to Bob and does not want anyone else to be able to read it except Bob, hence maintaining privacy.

Confidentiality is the protection of sensitive information from unauthorized access or disclosure. In this case, Alice wants to ensure that the contents of the e-mail are kept confidential and only accessible by the intended recipient, Bob.

3. (d) Fancy Bear and Anonymous are well-known hacking groups known for their involvement in high-profile cyber-attacks and data breaches. They are not types of malware, cryptographic ciphers, or computer security blogs.

4. (c) The individual is a target of stalking.

5. (d) All of the above are possible security threats. Illegitimate use refers to unauthorized access or use of a system or data. Backdoors are secret ways of bypassing standard authentication or encryption in a computer system, and masquerading involves pretending to be someone or something else to gain unauthorized access or deceive a user.

6. (b) The property of being genuine and verifiable. Authenticity in Cybersecurity refers to the property of a message, document, or other information being genuine and verifiable, meaning that it can be trusted to be what it claims to be and not have been tampered with or altered.

7. (c) Blue-jacking is a technique in which an attacker sends unsolicited messages or spam messages over Bluetooth to nearby devices, such as mobile phones or laptops, without the user's consent. Blue-jacking often aims to advertise or promote a product, service, or website, but it can also be used for phishing attacks or to spread malware.

8. (b) Countermeasure.

9. (b) Trudy changes the message and forwards it, indicating an integrity breach because the original message was modified.

10. (a) It is being able to map an action to an identity.

11. (c) Availability.

12. (a) A security program is a set of management, operational, and technical controls to ensure information and systems confidentiality, integrity, and availability. A comprehensive security program should include all four types of controls and on-going risk assessments, audits, and testing to ensure effectiveness. Administrative controls are an essential component of a security program and provide the framework for implementing and maintaining all other types of controls.

13. (b) Asset management identifies values, organizes, and controls an organization's assets to ensure they are used effectively and efficiently. This includes classifying assets based on their criticality and sensitivity, implementing appropriate security measures to protect them, controlling and monitoring their access, and documenting all aspects of the asset management process.

14. (c) Vulnerability.

15. (d) All of the above can threaten an information asset. Employees may intentionally or unintentionally cause harm to the asset, external parties such as hackers or competitors may attempt to steal or damage the asset, and natural disasters such as floods or fires can physically damage the asset.

16. (a) Confidentiality

17. (a, b) Unauthorized access and data collection can compromise the confidentiality and integrity of information. Piracy and copyright infringements may also involve the unauthorized use or distribution of confidential information or intellectual property. Password-protected PDF documents and remote backup servers are not necessarily threats to information security in and of themselves.

18. (c) (1) The attacker collecting credit card details by calling victims and using false pretexts to trick them is an example of Vishing, a social engineering attack that uses phone calls or voice messages to deceive people into divulging sensitive information. (2) The attacker sending out 100,000 random e-mail addresses with a message claiming that "Your Bank of America account has been locked out. Please click here to reset your password" is an example of Phishing, which is a type of social engineering attack that uses fraudulent e-mails, texts, or websites to trick people into disclosing personal and sensitive information.

19. (b) Administrative controls are security controls that aim to reduce risk by establishing policies, procedures, and guidelines for people and organizations to follow. These controls help to manage the behaviour of individuals and groups within an organization and create a security-aware culture. They can include security awareness training, background checks, security policies, procedures and guidelines, access controls, and incident response planning. By implementing administrative controls, organizations can reduce the likelihood of security incidents and mitigate the risk of harm to their assets, systems, and data.

20. (d) Using weak cryptographic algorithms without proper key management can increase the risk of sensitive data exposure, as weak encryption can be easily cracked by attackers, compromising sensitive data. On the other hand, a, b, and c are measures that can prevent the exposure of sensitive data. Discarding sensitive data as soon as possible, avoiding storing data as plain text, and disabling auto-complete forms collecting sensitive data all help to limit the exposure of sensitive data and minimize the risk of data breaches or unauthorized access.

21. (c) Contingency planning and physical securities are a part of Operational Controls. Operational controls are a type of security control that focuses on the day-to-day processes, procedures, and activities necessary to ensure the on-going security of an organization's systems and data. These controls include contingency planning, access controls, physical security, and system maintenance. Encryption and decryption, digital signatures and envelopes, certification authorities, and digital certificates are all technical controls used to secure data and systems.

22. (c) Identification and baseline involve identifying and categorizing data assets, establishing a baseline of regular activity, and defining policies and procedures for data security. Raise the Bar involves implementing additional security controls, improving security awareness and training, and enhancing incident response procedures. Real-time monitoring and protection involves implementing real-time monitoring and protection measures to detect and respond to security incidents as they occur. Following this order allows for a comprehensive approach to continuous data security, beginning with establishing a baseline and policies, then implementing additional security controls and incident response procedures, and finally monitoring and protecting data in real-time.

23. (c) Script Kiddie is the term used to describe an inexperienced attacker who uses code written by others to attack a system. Script Kiddies typically do not have the knowledge or skills to develop their attack code, so they rely on pre-packaged exploit tools and scripts that are widely available on the internet.

These tools often come with user-friendly interfaces that make it easy for inexperienced attackers to launch attacks against vulnerable systems.

24. (c) An event in which a company's financial system was compromised, resulting in the deletion of payroll information, would be classified as an incident with a moderate impact. An incident is an event that has the potential to cause harm to an organization's systems or data. The severity of the harm caused determines the impact of an incident, the scope of the incident, and the resources required to respond to and recover from the incident. In this case, compromising the financial system and deleting payroll information would moderately impact the organization's operations and financial stability. The incident would require significant resources to investigate and recover from, but it is not a catastrophic event threatening the organization's survival.

25. (b) The situation in which online banking customers cannot make third-party transfers since an incident is categorized as a medium urgency event. While it is not an emergency or critical situation that requires immediate attention, it is still a significant issue that affects the functionality of the system and the user experience. The bank should prioritize fixing the issue promptly to minimize customer impact and prevent potential financial loss.

26. (b) While APT attacks may target government assets, they are not limited to government targets. APT is a long-term, targeted attack against a specific organization, typically to steal sensitive information or intellectual property. The attackers may be motivated by various factors, including financial gain, business competition, espionage, or political interests.

27. (c) Anti-virus software is essential in protecting a computer from malware and other threats, but it is not 100% effective. Attackers constantly develop new techniques and malware to evade detection, and anti-virus software must be updated regularly to keep up with the latest threats.

28. (a) Endpoint detection and response (EDR) is a technology that monitors endpoint devices such as laptops, desktops, servers, and mobile devices for security incidents. EDR solutions continuously monitor endpoint devices for unusual behaviour, malware, and other security threats. Continuous monitoring allows security teams to detect security incidents in real-time, investigate and remediate them quickly, and prevent them from spreading to other parts of the network. EDR solutions also provide forensic data, such as logs and alerts, which can identify the incident's root cause and prevent similar incidents.

29. (b) Control of data analysis is related to data management and analysis, which is a different aspect of information systems management. While information security plays a crucial role in ensuring data integrity, confidentiality, and availability, its primary focus is not on controlling data analysis.

30. (b) Even with robust security measures, employees can inadvertently or intentionally compromise an organization's security. This can happen through actions such as falling for phishing scams, using weak passwords, failing to update software or operating systems, or sharing sensitive information with unauthorized individuals.

31. (a) Rand Report R-609 was the first to address the management and policy implications of the growing field of computer security. Published in 1970, the Rand Report R-609, "A Proposed Standard Security System for Distributed Systems," was the first report to address computer security's management and policy implications. The report proposed a standard security system for distributed systems and emphasized the importance of management involvement in computer security.

32. (b) While password-protecting a document and using servers for remote backup can be security measures, they do not necessarily constitute security risks. On the other hand, unauthorized access and collection of data is a security risk as it can result in data breaches, theft of sensitive information, and compromise of systems and networks. Similarly, authorized data modification can also be a security risk if it is done without proper authorization or authentication, leading to data loss, corruption, or exposure to threats.

33. (b) Computer security is a relatively simple process that is not true regarding implementing computer security. Implementing computer security is not a simple process. It involves selecting and deploying a range of defence mechanisms and tools, such as firewalls, encryption, access controls, intrusion detection and prevention systems, and security policies and procedures. It also involves the development of complex algorithms and protocols to protect sensitive data, prevent unauthorized access and attacks, and ensure the confidentiality, integrity, and availability of information systems and resources. Furthermore, computer security must be implemented proactively as an integral part of the system design and development process rather than as an afterthought.

34. (c) An event on a system or network detected by a device.

35. (c) Non-repudiation is frequently used to prevent the sender from denying that the communication has occurred.

36. (c) In communication, an attacker assumes the identity of another party, which is referred to as masquerading.

37. (c) Hardware, Software-based systems, data, and networks are computer system assets.

38. (a) Information security's integrity objective focuses on verifying that information is accurate and has not been tampered with or altered without authorization.

39. (d) The chief information officer's responsibility is not limited to hardware, software, or vendor selection. The CIO is responsible for the overall management and strategy of the organization's information technology and digital assets, including data security, system performance, technology investments, and alignment with business goals. Therefore, option d. "All of the above" is not the correct answer.

40. (b) Employees' experience and knowledge.

41. (d) The most effective method for preventing a logical security breach would be system software, including the operating system. This is because logical security breaches often involve unauthorized access or data modification, which can be prevented or mitigated through secure software and access controls.

42. (d) All of the above qualify as cybersecurity elements. The external user who can access a genuine user's account by posing as an authentic user is called a Masquerader.

43. (a) A Masquerader is an unauthorized external user who pretends to be genuine to gain access to a system or network. They can do this by stealing the genuine user's login credentials, such as their username and password, or by using other methods like phishing attacks or social engineering. Once they gain access to

the system or network, they can perform malicious activities like stealing sensitive data, planting malware or viruses, or causing other types of damage.

44. (b) The principle of least privileges is a fundamental Cybersecurity principle that requires granting users the minimum level of access necessary to perform their job functions. By only granting root access to an employee when it is necessary for specific tasks, the organization can limit the potential damage resulting from a malicious or unintentional action taken by the employee. This is an effective way to mitigate the risk of insider threats and reduce the attack surface of a system or network.

45. (a) Plagiarism is using or presenting someone else's ideas, work, or words as one's own without proper attribution or permission. It is considered a form of intellectual theft often associated with academic misconduct or copyright infringement.

46. (c) Information security is not a straightforward process as it involves many complex and interrelated activities, such as risk management, threat analysis, access control, incident response, and security awareness training. It also requires continuous monitoring and updating to keep up with the evolving threat landscape and business requirements.

47. (b) is unrelated to data integrity. It is a data confidentiality issue where unauthorized parties are accessing data.

48. (b) A misfeasor is a legitimate user who misuses their access privileges to access or modify system assets without authorization. Misfeasance can be intentional or unintentional, and various factors, such as lack of training, carelessness, or malicious intent, can cause it.

49. (d) The economy of the mechanism is a fundamental principle of Cybersecurity that states that the security mechanism should be as simple and compact as possible to minimize the risk of errors or vulnerabilities. Simple security mechanisms are easier to design, implement, test, and maintain and less likely to contain errors or defects that attackers can exploit.

50. (b) An intruder is an individual or entity that gains unauthorized access to a system or network by circumventing security controls or exploiting vulnerabilities. In the context of the question, an intruder takes control of a system's supervisory functions to bypass prevention, access, and detection controls, also known as privilege escalation.

Chapter 2
The CIA Triad

This chapter includes questions from the following topics:
- The fundamentals of the CIA Triad.
- Data Confidentiality.
- Data Integrity.
- Data Availability.
- Authenticity
- Authorization

1. **What are the CIA Triad's components?**
   a. Confirmation, Integrity, Authenticity.
   b. Confidentiality, Information, Availability.
   c. Confidentiality, Integrity, Availability.
   d. Certification, Integrity, Availability.

2. **What does "Confidentiality" mean in the CIA Triad?**
   a. Identifies that the received data is accurate and has not been altered.
   b. It prevents unauthorized users from accessing data.
   c. It enables unauthorized data access.
   d. Ensures data is accessible to unauthorized users and is not accessed by authorized users.

3. **Mr John intercepts an unencrypted text message from Mr Sam, modifies the location of a meeting, and forwards the modified information to Mr Robert. Which two CIA Triad tenets were violated? (Select all that apply)**
   a. Confidentiality
   b. Authentication
   c. Availability
   d. Integrity

4. **What does "Integrity" mean in the CIA Triad?**
   a. It identifies the accuracy and intelligence of data.
   b. Prevents unauthorized users from accessing data.
   c. Assures that data is accessible to all.
   d. Ascertains that data is accurate and has not been tampered with by unauthorized entities.

5. **There are numerous advantages to maintaining comprehensive backups of essential data. Which component of the CIA Triad is most affected when a company is practising a proper backup practice?**
   a. Integrity
   b. Confidentiality
   c. Authorization
   d. Availability

6. **Alice sends an unencrypted message to Bob, intercepted by an attacker who reads the message but does not alter the content. Which principle of the CIA Triad would have been violated?**

a. Confidentiality
b. Integrity
c. Availability
d. All of the above.

7. **Alice sends Bob an encrypted communication; an attacker intercepts it, but she cannot read it. Outraged, she deletes it before it can reach Bob. Which principle of the CIA Triad would have been violated?**
   a. Confidentiality
   b. Integrity
   c. Availability
   d. All of the above.

8. **What does "availability" mean in the CIA Triad?**
   a. Ensures that data is accessible to authorized users.
   b. Prevents unauthorized users from accessing data.
   c. Ascertain that data is accurate and unaltered.
   d. Ensure that data is accessible to anyone at any time or location.

9. **Alice sends Bob a plain-text message intercepted by an attacker who does not interfere with its delivery. Which component of the CIA Triad was breached?**
   a. **Confidentiality**
   b. Integrity
   c. Availability
   d. All of the above.

10. **What is the purpose of Alice and Bob's fictional characters?**
    a. To demonstrate the ISO27000 standard.
    b. To carry out a distributed denial-of-service attack.
    c. To demonstrate the CIA Triad.
    d. To come into contact with Wi-Fi attacks.

11. **In the given figure, who is depicted as an attacker in Alice, Bob, and Mallory?**
    a. Bob
    b. Mallory
    c. Alice
    d. All three (Alice, Bob, and Mallory).

12. **An attacker intercepts a plain-text message between Alice and her boyfriend, Sam. The attacker is angered by the message, so he forwards it to Bob, making it appear as though Alice intended it for Bob. Which aspect of the CIA Triad has been breached by the attacker?**
    a. Confidentiality
    b. Integrity
    c. Availability
    d. All of the above.

13. **An attacker intercepts Alice's message to Bob; which of the following best describes the breach of confidentiality?**

    a. Without forwarding the message to Bob, the attacker deletes it.
    b. Although the attacker could not read the encrypted message, he forwarded it to Bob unchanged.
    c. The attacker read the message.
    d. The attacker altered and forwarded the message to Bob.

14. **An attacker intercepts Alice's message to Bob; which of the following scenarios best describes the integrity breach?**
    a. Without forwarding it, the attacker deletes the message.
    b. Before forwarding the message, the attacker modifies it.
    c. The attacker has read the message.
    d. Because it is encrypted, the attacker cannot read it; Bob receives it in its original format.

15. **When a student submits an assignment via a university's student portal, the hash value serves as a confirmation code. The above exemplifies which component of the CIA Triad?**
    a. Confidentiality
    b. Authorization
    c. Integrity
    d. Availability

16. **An attacker intercepts Alice's message to Bob; which of the following best describes the availability violation?**
    a. The attacker could not decipher the message but it was transferred to Bob intact.
    b. The attacker deletes the message without transmitting it.
    c. The attacker read the message.
    d. The attacker modifies the message and forwards it to Bob.

17. **Which aspect of Cybersecurity does the figure illustrate?**
    a. Establishment of a security mechanism to guarantee the privacy of data.
    b. Mallory can intercept Alice and Bob's encrypted communication.
    c. Implement a security mechanism to ensure Alice's and Bob's data availability.
    d. The danger posed by the use of dissimilar communication protocols by dissimilar users.

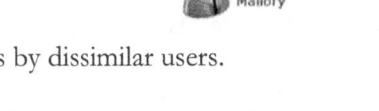

18. **A professor cannot alter a student's final grade once submitted without completing a document explaining the reasons for the adjustment. Which part of the CIA Triad is aided by this step?**
    a. Integrity
    b. Availability
    c. Authorization
    d. Confidentiality

19. **What is a Confidentiality Breach?**
    a. Unauthorized data destruction.
    b. Unauthorized data reading.
    c. Unauthorized resource use.
    d. Unauthorized data modification.

20. **Mr Bala received a message from Mr Ali but could not confirm that Mr Ali sent it or was untampered. Which two aspects of security are compromised in the scenario described above?**

    a. Confidentiality and Authentication.
    b. Confidentiality and Message Integrity.
    c. Authentication and Message Integrity.
    d. Authentication and Availability.

21. **All of the following are threats to confidentiality and result in unauthorized disclosure, except what?**
    a. Interception
    b. Inference
    c. Eavesdropping
    d. Interruption

22. **Which of the following is not a threat to confidentiality?**
    a. Interception
    b. Fabrication
    c. Inference
    d. Intrusion

23. **Which of the following is used to protect the confidentiality of data?**
    a. Cryptographic hashing techniques.
    b. Firewalls
    c. Encryption of sensitive data.
    d. Intrusion detection system.

24. **Which CIA triad component ensures "authorized constraints on information access and disclosure"?**
    a. Integrity
    b. Availability
    c. Confidentiality
    d. All of the above.

25. **"Only the sender and intended receiver can read the transmitted message content" is an example of what?**
    a. Authentication
    b. Confidentiality
    c. Availability
    d. Integrity

26. **What does OAuth provide?**
    a. Confidentiality
    b. Integrity
    c. Access delegation.
    d. Secure communications.

27. **Which fundamental security property assures the verification of the genuineness of a received message?**
    a. Confidentiality
    b. Authenticity
    c. Accountability

    d.   Availability

28. **An administrator failed to back up the data and dropped the laptop, breaking it into many pieces; in the above scenario, which aspect of the CIA Triad failed to preserve?**
    a.   Confidentiality
    b.   Integrity
    c.   Availability
    d.   All of the above.

29. **Triad Industries has not yet made public records of a potential merger with VRR Tech. If those records are made public, they may harm the stock prices of both companies, jeopardizing the transaction. Which security principle is most critical when classifying information in this scenario?**
    a.   Confidentiality
    b.   Availability
    c.   Integrity
    d.   Authenticity

30. **Which of the following is not a factor in maintaining data integrity?**
    a.   Wrenching data in order to share it with unauthorized entities.
    b.   Unauthorized data alteration.
    c.   Intentional or accidental data replacement.
    d.   Unauthorized data modification.

31. **What is service theft?**
    a.   The infringement consists of the unauthorized destruction of data.
    b.   The infringement entails the unauthorized modification of data.
    c.   The infraction entails the unauthorized utilization of resources.
    d.   The violation entails unauthorized data reading.

32. **From Sam's point of view, which aspect of the CIA Triad is violated by the attacker who intercepts an official message sent by Alice to him and forwards it to Bob, altering the message to make it appear as though Alice intended it for Bob?**
    a.   Confidentiality
    b.   Integrity
    c.   Availability
    d.   All of the above.

33. **What are the ramifications of the threat of "data disclosure"?**
    a.   Loss of Integrity.
    b.   Loss of Confidentiality.
    c.   Loss of Availability.
    d.   All of the above.

34. **When customers withdraw money from a bank, the teller requests their names and identification cards. After verifying the customer's identification cards, tellers issue cash and return the tokens. Which of the following categories best describes the work of bank tellers?**
    a.   Accounting
    b.   Authorization

    c. Authentication
    d. Availability

35. **Identify the type of violation in the following scenario. "A message sent from A to B and accidentally sent to many others"?**
    a. Message Integrity.
    b. Authentication
    c. Confidentiality
    d. None of the above.

36. **Which aspect of the CIA Triad can be accomplished via the organization's backup procedures?**
    a. Confidentiality
    b. Availability
    c. Integrity
    d. Authorization

37. **When students log into their university accounts, their grades should be visible. Which aspect of the CIA Triad is exemplified by the ability to view their grades?**
    a. Integrity
    b. Authorization
    c. Availability
    d. Confidentiality

38. **A university uses a clustered server to enable students to submit assignments even if the server is unavailable; server clustering enables which aspect of the CIA Triad?**
    a. Availability
    b. Confidentiality
    c. Authorization
    d. Integrity

39. **A university-enabled WPA2 encryption on the campus's Wi-Fi network, supporting an aspect of the CIA Triad?**
    a. Authorization
    b. Integrity
    c. Confidentiality
    d. Availability

40. **Students can access their grades through the Online Student Portal but cannot modify them. Which aspect of the CIA Triad does the preceding restriction support?**
    a. Authorization
    b. Availability
    c. Confidentiality
    d. Integrity

41. **Which aspect of the CIA would be jeopardized if a denial-of-service attack was successful?**
    a. Confidentiality
    b. Integrity
    c. Availability
    d. Authentication

42. **The sender and receiver of a message may identify one another as an example of what?**
    a. Integrity
    b. Availability
    c. Confidentiality
    d. Authentication

43. **Due to the high volume of students registering for courses concurrently through the Student Information System (SIS), students experience delays in displaying the web pages and cannot complete the registration process. Which of the following was violated in the scenario mentioned above?**
    a. Integrity
    b. Confidentiality
    c. Availability
    d. Accountability

44. **What is the term for ensuring that "the system would perform its intended function without being harmed by deliberate or accidental unauthorized manipulation"?**
    a. System Integrity.
    b. Data Integrity.
    c. Availability
    d. Confidentiality

45. **An employee travels to a conference containing sensitive product information on his laptop. Which techniques could be used to safeguard the laptop's data's confidentiality?**
    a. Ensure that all software is updated.
    b. Secure the laptop's BIOS with a password.
    c. Transfer the confidential documents to a USB flash drive.
    d. Use a Trusted Platform Module (TPM) and encrypt the hard drive.

46. **A company recently moved its web server to the cloud and behind a load balancer. Which CIA triad principle is the organization attempting to ensure by configuring a load balancer?**
    a. Confidentiality
    b. Installation
    c. Integrity
    d. Availability

47. **Which tools can encrypt an operating system's disk volumes (Hard Disk), ensuring data integrity and confidentiality?**
    a. Buffer Overflow Protection.
    b. Least Privilege.
    c. Malware Protection.
    d. Bit-Locker.

48. **Which aspect of the CIA Triad would the hashing be used to ensure?**
    a. Confidentiality
    b. Integrity
    c. Availability
    d. All of the above.

49. **What is the low-level change to Windows that allows for isolating different objects based on their level of trust?**
    a. Control of Integrity.
    b. Control of Confidentiality.
    c. Control of Availability.
    d. Control of Reliability.

50. **A student sees other students' completed assignments on a teacher's desk.**
    Which security perimeter was violated in the above incident?
    a. Validation
    b. Confidentiality
    c. Continuity
    d. Accessibility

Answer Key

1. (c) The CIA Triad stands for Confidentiality, Integrity, and Availability, a widely recognized information security model.

2. (b) In the CIA Triad, Confidentiality refers to protecting sensitive information from unauthorized access or disclosure. Only authorized individuals or systems should access the data and information, which should not be disclosed to others without proper permission.

3. (a,d) By intercepting and modifying the text message, Mr John has violated the confidentiality of the message by accessing it without proper permission. He has also violated the integrity of the message by altering its contents before forwarding it to Mr Robert.

4. (d) In the CIA Triad, Integrity refers to the assurance that data or information has not been tampered with, altered, or modified unauthorized. It ensures that the data remains accurate, consistent, and trustworthy over its entire lifecycle, from creation to disposal.

5. (d) Availability is the component of the CIA Triad most affected by a company's backup practices. Maintaining comprehensive backups of essential data ensures that the data remains available and can be restored in case of a system failure, disaster, or cyber-attack. It helps to ensure that the data remains accessible to authorized users when needed.

6. (a) Confidentiality would have been violated. By intercepting and reading the unencrypted message, the attacker has violated the confidentiality of the message by accessing it without proper permission. Since the attacker did not alter the content or delivery of the message, the integrity and availability of the message were not violated.

7. (c) Availability would have been violated. Since Alice deleted the encrypted communication before it could reach Bob, the attacker successfully denied access to the message, thus violating the availability of the communication.

8. (a) Availability means data is accessible to authorized users when needed. In the CIA Triad, availability refers to the assurance that authorized users can access data or information when needed, including

9. (a) Confidentiality was breached. By intercepting and reading the plain-text message, the attacker has violated the confidentiality of the message by accessing it without proper permission. Since the attacker

did not alter the content or delivery of the message, the integrity and availability of the message were not violated.

10. (c) The purpose of Alice and Bob's fictional characters is to demonstrate the CIA Triad. Alice and Bob are commonly used as fictional characters in cryptography and Cybersecurity to illustrate various scenarios and concepts related to security, including the CIA Triad. They are often used to explain complex ideas in a simple and relatable way.

11. (b) Mallory is depicted as the attacker in the given figure.

12. (a) The aspect of the CIA Triad that the attacker has breached in this scenario is confidentiality. The attacker has accessed and disclosed information (the message) intended to be kept private between Alice and Sam.

13. (c) Confidentiality is the property that ensures that information is not disclosed to unauthorized individuals or entities. In this scenario, the attacker intercepted the message and read its content, which means that the confidentiality of the message has been breached.

14. (b) Before forwarding the message, the attacker modifies it to the scenario that best describes the integrity breach. In this scenario, the attacker has changed the contents of the message, which means that the message has been tampered with and the integrity of the message has been compromised, violating the integrity aspect of the CIA Triad.

15. (c) The above scenario exemplifies the integrity component of the CIA Triad. The hash value serves as a confirmation code that ensures the integrity of the submitted assignment, as any changes made to the document will change the hash value, indicating that the document has been tampered with.

16. (b) The attacker deletes the message without transmitting it. In this scenario, the attacker has prevented the message from being delivered to Bob, violating the availability aspect of the CIA Triad.

17. (b) Mallory can intercept Alice and Bob's encrypted communication. The figure illustrates a Man-in-the-Middle (MITM) attack, where Mallory intercepts and alters the communication between Alice and Bob, a security threat to the data's confidentiality and integrity.

18. (a) The new step where the professor has to complete a document explaining the reasons for any adjustment to a student's final grade is related to the integrity aspect of the CIA Triad. By implementing this measure, the integrity of the student's final grade is maintained, and any changes must be documented, ensuring accountability and transparency.

19. (b) A confidentiality breach is the unauthorized reading or disclosure of sensitive or private information.

20. (c) Authentication is compromised because B cannot confirm the identity of sender A, i.e., whether the message was sent by A or not. Message Integrity is compromised because B cannot confirm whether the message has been tampered with or altered during transmission.

21. (d) Interruption is not a threat to confidentiality. It refers to a threat to availability, where authorized users cannot access the system or data.

22. (b) Fabrication is not a threat to confidentiality but rather a threat to integrity. Fabrication is the creation of false or fictitious data or information.

23. (c) Encryption of sensitive data is used to protect the confidentiality of data. Encryption is a technique that transforms data into an unreadable format, which can only be decrypted and read by those who have the necessary key or password. It ensures that the data remains confidential even if unauthorized entities intercept it.

24. (c) Confidentiality is the component of the CIA triad that ensures that information is not disclosed to unauthorized individuals or entities. It involves protecting data privacy by keeping it hidden from those who are not authorized to access it. This includes implementing encryption, access controls, and user authentication measures to limit access to sensitive information.

25. (b) This is an example of confidentiality, one of the three main components of the CIA triad. Confidentiality refers to the protection of sensitive or private information from unauthorized disclosure or access. In this case, the message content is protected and can only be accessed by the sender and intended receiver, ensuring the information remains confidential. This can be achieved through various means, such as encryption or access controls.

26. (c) OAuth provides access delegation, which allows users to grant third-party applications limited access to their resources without giving the applications their login credentials. This means that the user can grant access to the application without compromising their login details, maintaining the confidentiality of their credentials.

27. (b) Authenticity is the fundamental security property that assures the verification of the genuineness of a received message.

28. (c) In the scenario described, the aspect of the CIA Triad that failed to preserve is "Availability." The data is no longer available due to the failure to back up the data and the physical destruction of the device.

29. (a) Confidentiality is the most critical security principle in this scenario. Confidentiality protects sensitive information from unauthorized access, disclosure, or modification. The potential merger between Triad Industries and VRR Tech is a sensitive piece of information that could harm the stock prices of both companies if made public prematurely. Therefore, it is essential to classify this information as confidential and ensure that only authorized personnel can access it. By doing so, the organization can maintain the confidentiality of the information and prevent any unauthorized disclosure, which could lead to financial loss or damage to the reputation of both companies.

30. (a) Wrenching data to share with unauthorized entities is not a factor in maintaining data integrity. It is not a known security threat or vulnerability that could compromise data integrity. The other options mentioned, such as unauthorized data alteration, intentional or accidental data replacements, and unauthorized data modification, are factors that could compromise data integrity.

31. (c) Service theft is the infraction that entails the unauthorized utilization of resources. This refers to a situation where an attacker gains unauthorized access to computing resources, such as network bandwidth, processing power, or storage, and uses them for malicious purposes. The attacker may use these resources to launch attacks and store stolen data or mine cryptocurrency, among other activities. This type of attack can cause harm by degrading system performance, increasing operational costs, and reducing the availability of resources for legitimate users.

32. (d) Sam's point of view, the aspect of the CIA Triad that the attacker violates is confidentiality, integrity, and availability.

33. (b) The primary ramification of the threat of "data disclosure" is the loss of confidentiality. When sensitive or confidential data is disclosed to unauthorized individuals, it can have severe consequences for an organization or individual, such as financial loss, reputational damage, legal repercussions, and loss of trust. Data disclosure can also lead to the loss of integrity and availability, as unauthorized access to data can modify or destroy that data, making it unusable or unreliable.

34. (b) The work of bank tellers best fits into the category of Authorization, as they are responsible for ensuring that the customer is authorized to access the requested funds and involves verifying the customer's identity through their identification cards and ensuring they have the funds to withdraw. Accounting involves keeping track of financial transactions, authentication involves verifying the identity of a user, and availability involves ensuring that resources are accessible to authorized users.

35. (d) The type of violation in the scenario described is not listed among the options provided. However, the violation relates to confidentiality, as the message was intended for only one recipient, B, but was accidentally disclosed to other unintended recipients. The disclosure of the message to unintended recipients violates the confidentiality of the message, as it was not kept private and only shared with the intended recipient.

36. (b) Backup procedures can help ensure the availability of data and systems by allowing for the recovery of lost or damaged data in case of a system failure, natural disaster, or other unforeseen circumstances. Organizations can quickly restore access to essential resources during an outage or disruption by regularly backing up critical data and systems. However, backup procedures alone do not address the other aspects of the CIA Triad, such as confidentiality or integrity, which may require additional security measures to be implemented.

37. (d) The aspect of the CIA Triad exemplified by the ability to view grades when logging into a university account is "confidentiality." This is because grades are considered sensitive information and should only be accessible to authorized individuals who have been granted permission to view them.

38. (a) Server clustering is a technique used to improve the availability of a system by spreading the load across multiple servers. If one server goes down, another server in the cluster can take over, providing uninterrupted access to the service. Therefore, server clustering enables Availability in the CIA Triad, ensuring that the university's students can submit their assignments even if the server is unavailable.

39. (c) WPA2 encryption on the campus Wi-Fi network is an example of security control that provides confidentiality by ensuring that network traffic is encrypted and protected from unauthorized access, preventing attackers from intercepting and reading sensitive information transmitted over the network, such as login credentials or personal data.

40. (a) The preceding restriction that students cannot modify their grades supports the aspect of the CIA Triad known as Authorization. Authorization refers to granting or denying access to resources or actions based on an individual's identity and their level of privilege or authority. In this case, the students are authorized to view their grades but not authorized to modify them, which helps to ensure the integrity of the grades.

41. (c) The aspect of the CIA Triad that would be jeopardized if a denial-of-service (DoS) attack was successful is availability. A DoS attack aims to disrupt or restrict access to a particular resource or service, making it unavailable to legitimate users. This type of attack does not typically involve unauthorized

access or alteration of data, so confidentiality and integrity may not be compromised. However, the unavailability of a resource or service can still have significant consequences for the affected organization or individuals.

42. (d) Identifying the sender and receiver of a message is an example of authentication. Authentication is verifying a user's or system's identity, ensuring that the person or system is who they claim to be. In this case, the sender and receiver verify each other's identities, a form of authentication. Authentication is essential for maintaining security and preventing unauthorized access to systems and data.

43. (c) In the given scenario, students cannot access and use the SIS due to the high traffic volume, resulting in a denial of service, which violates the aspect of the CIA triad called availability, which refers to ensuring authorized users can access and use the resources and information they need when needed.

44. (a) The term for ensuring that "the system would perform its intended function without being harmed by deliberate or accidental unauthorized manipulation" is System Integrity.

45. (d) Using a Trusted Platform Module (TPM) along with hard drive encryption is a common technique for safeguarding the confidentiality of data on a laptop.

46. (d) By configuring a load balancer, a company attempts to ensure the principle of availability in the CIA triad. A load balancer distributes incoming network traffic across multiple servers to prevent a single point of failure and provide high availability. If one server goes down, the load balancer will redirect traffic to the remaining servers, ensuring that the application or service remains available to users.

47. (d) Bit Locker is a tool that can encrypt an operating system's disk volumes, ensuring data integrity and confidentiality.

48. (b) Hashing is primarily used to ensure data integrity, which is the accuracy and consistency of data over time and throughout the data lifecycle. Hashing algorithms can generate a unique digital fingerprint or hash of a message or file, which can be compared to the original hash to verify that the data has not been tampered with or modified. Therefore, the correct answer is (b) Integrity. However, it is worth noting that hashing can indirectly support confidentiality by making it more difficult for an attacker to tamper with data without being detected.

49. (b) The low-level change to Windows that allows for isolating different objects based on their level of trust is known as "Control of Confidentiality," or more specifically, Mandatory Access Control (MAC) implemented through the use of security labels and permissions. This technique separates objects on a system based on their security levels. It ensures that higher security objects cannot be accessed or modified by lower security objects, helps prevent unauthorized access or modification of sensitive data, and supports the confidentiality aspect of the CIA triad.

50. (b) The incident violates the confidentiality security perimeter as the student saw other students' completed assignments intended to be kept confidential between the teacher and the individual students. The incident did not affect the validation, continuity, or accessibility of security perimeters.

Chapter 3
Common Cybersecurity Acronyms

This chapter includes questions from the following topics:
* Various standard and essential acronyms in Cybersecurity

1. **What does the acronym "TRNG" stand for in Cybersecurity?**
   a. Thermal Noise Random Number Generator.
   b. Translation Noise Random Number Generator.
   c. True Rounded Number Generator.
   d. Test Random Number Generator.

2. **What does the acronym "CARO" stand for in Cybersecurity?**
   a. Computer Anti-virus Research Organization.
   b. Computer Algorithm Research Organization.
   c. Centre for Advanced Research of Objects.
   d. Centre for Algorithm Research and Occupation.

3. **What does the acronym "OWASP" stand for in Cybersecurity?**
   a. Open Web Association Security Protocol.
   b. Only Web Association Security Principle.
   c. Open Web Application Security Project.
   d. Open Web Access Security Protocol.

4. **What does the acronym "DHA" stand for in Cybersecurity?**
   a. DNS Harvest Attack.
   b. Directory Harvest Attack.
   c. Direct Harvest Attack.
   d. Dictionary Harvest Attack.

5. **What does the acronym "S/MIME" stand for in Cybersecurity?**
   a. Secure Multipurpose Intranet Mail Extensions.
   b. Secure Multipurpose Internet Message Extensions.
   c. Secure Multipurpose Intranet Message Extensions.
   d. Secure Multipurpose Internet Mail Extensions.

6. **What does the acronym "SSL" stand for in Cybersecurity?**
   a. Service Security Level.
   b. Secure Software Layer.
   c. Secure Socket Layer.
   d. Service Software Language.

7. **What does the acronym "CGI" stand for in Cybersecurity?**
   a. Common Gateway Interface.
   b. Communication Gateway Interface.
   c. Communication Gateway Information.
   d. Common Gateway Information.

8. **What does the acronym "GII" stand for in Cybersecurity?**
    a. Graphical Information Infrastructure.
    b. Graphical Institute of Information.
    c. Global Information Infrastructure.
    d. GUI Information Infrastructure.

9. **What does the acronym "EDoS" Stand for in Cybersecurity?**
    a. Electrical Denial of Service.
    b. Economic Denial of Sustainability.
    c. Extreme Denial of Service.
    d. None of the Above.

10. **What does the acronym "AKMC" stand for in Cybersecurity?**
    a. Automated Key Management Centre.
    b. Automated Key Merger Centre.
    c. Allocated Key Management Centre.
    d. Allocated Key Merger Centre.

11. **What does the acronym "CAPTCHA" stand for in the context of Cybersecurity?**
    a. Completely Automated Public Test to Tell Computers and Humans Apart.
    b. Completely Automated Program to Tell Computers and Humans Apart.
    c. Completely Automated Picture Turing test to tell Computers and Humans Apart.
    d. Completely Automated Public Turing Test to Tell Computers and Humans Apart.

12. **What does the acronym "TIMS" stand for in Cybersecurity?**
    a. Telecommunications Information Management System.
    b. Treaty Information Management System.
    c. Traffic Incident Management System.
    d. Time and Information Management System.

13. **What does the acronym "SPA" stand for in Cybersecurity?**
    a. Secure Password Authentication.
    b. Simplified Planning Approach.
    c. System Performance Analysis.
    d. Self-Promoting Attack.

14. **What does the acronym "L2TP" stand for in Cybersecurity?**
    a. Layer-2 Tunnelling Protocol.
    b. Lightweight 2 Transport Protocol.
    c. Light-2 Transparent Protocol.
    d. Layer-2 Transport Protocol.

15. **What does the acronym "M2FH" stand for in Cybersecurity?**
    a. Machine-to-Faith Human.
    b. Media-to-Fake Human.
    c. Machine-to-Fake Human.
    d. Media-to-Faith Human.

16. **What does the acronym "DRM" stand for in Cybersecurity?**

a. Dynamic Resource Management.
b. Document Relationship Management.
c. Distributed Reference Model.
d. Digital Rights Management.

17. **What does the acronym "AEAD" mean in the context of Cybersecurity?**
   a. Authenticated Encryption and Associated Data.
   b. Authenticated Encryption with Associated Data.
   c. Authenticated Encryption for Additional Data.
   d. Advanced Encryption and Decryption.

18. **What does the acronym "RABC" stand for in Cybersecurity?**
   a. Resource Allocation and Budgeting Committee.
   b. Risk Assessment and Business Continuity.
   c. Role-Based Access Control.
   d. Revenue Accounting and Billing Code.

19. **What does the acronym "TKIP" stand for in Cybersecurity?**
   a. Temporal Key Integrity Protocol.
   b. Tethering Kit for Image Processing.
   c. Translucent Key Index Provider.
   d. Transportation Key Infrastructure Program.

20. **What does the acronym "AICS" stand for in Cybersecurity?**
   a. Airborne Imaging and Communications System.
   b. Artificial Intelligence and Computer Science.
   c. Artificial Intelligence for Cyber Security.
   d. Army Institute of Computer Science.

21. **What does the acronym "KMI" stand for in Cybersecurity?**
   a. Key Management Infrastructure.
   b. Knowledge Media Institute.
   c. Key Manager Infrastructure.
   d. Key Maintenance Institute.

22. **What does the acronym "CISP" stand for in Cybersecurity?**
   a. Community Information and Support Program.
   b. Centre for International Security and Policy.
   c. Counterintelligence Support Plan.
   d. Computer Information Systems Program.

23. **What does the acronym "CISSM" stand for in Cybersecurity?**
   a. Component Industry System Security Manager.
   b. Complete Information System Security Manager.
   c. Component Information System Service Manager.
   d. Component Information System Security Manager.

24. **What does the acronym "PKI" stand for in Cybersecurity?**
    a. Public Key Infrastructure.
    b. Payment Key Information.
    c. Private Key Infrastructure.
    d. Public and Private Key Information.

25. **What does the acronym "ISAKMP" stand for in Cybersecurity?**
    a. Information Security Association and Key Management Protocol.
    b. Internet Security Association and Key Maintenance Program.
    c. Internet Security Association and Key Management Protocol.
    d. Information Security Assessment and Key Management Protocol.

26. **What does the acronym "PPTP" stand for in Cybersecurity?**
    a. Place-to-Place Tunnelling Protocol.
    b. Point-to-Place Tunnelling Protocol.
    c. Place-to-Point Tunnelling Protocol.
    d. Point-to-Point Tunnelling Protocol.

27. **What does the acronym "APWG" stand for in Cybersecurity?**
    a. Anti-Physical Security Working Group.
    b. American Public Works Group.
    c. Android Working Group.
    d. Anti-Phishing Working Group.

28. **What does the acronym "PWC" stand for in Cybersecurity?**
    a. Proactive Worm Containment.
    b. Professional Writing and Communication.
    c. Power and Worm Corporation.
    d. Proactive Wireless Committee.

29. **What does the acronym "CERT" stand for in Cybersecurity?**
    a. Centre for Education and Research in Computer and Information Security.
    b. Collaborative Electronic Research and Training.
    c. Computer Emergency Response Team.
    d. Computer Engineers Readiness Team.

30. **What does the acronym "DAC" stand for in Cybersecurity?**
    a. Direct Access Control.
    b. Development Access Control.
    c. Data Allow Control.
    d. Discretionary Access Control.

31. **What does the acronym "ACFT" stand for in Cybersecurity?**
    a. Association of Certified Fraud Examiners.
    b. Advanced Conventional Fuel Technologies.
    c. Advanced Computer Forensic Techniques.
    d. Advanced Core Flight Technology

32. What does the acronym "APKI" stand for in Cybersecurity?
   a. Architecture for Private Key Infrastructure.
   b. Architecture for Personal Key Infrastructure.
   c. Architecture for Pure Key Infrastructure.
   d. Architecture for Public Key Infrastructure.

33. What does the acronym "EAL" stand for in Cybersecurity?
   a. Evaluation Assurance Level.
   b. Environmental Analysis Level.
   c. Engineering Animation Library.
   d. Evaluation Acceptance Level.

34. What does the acronym "MITM" stand for in Cybersecurity?
   a. Machine-In-The-Middle.
   b. Man-In-The-Mobile.
   c. Man-in-the-Middle.
   d. Man-In-The-Marker.

35. What does the acronym "AOPB" stand for in Cybersecurity?
   a. Advanced Office Protocol Breaker.
   b. Advanced Office Password Breaker.
   c. Advanced Options for Password Breaker.
   d. Advanced Option of Protocol Breaker.

36. What does the acronym "DMCA" stand for in Cybersecurity?
   a. Data Millennium Copyright Act.
   b. Digital Millennium Contract Act.
   c. Digital Millennium Copyright Act.
   d. Data Millennium Control Act.

37. What does the acronym "ANTS" mean in the context of Cybersecurity?
   a. Airborne Network Test System.
   b. Agile Network Transformation Solutions.
   c. A New Trojan Scanner.
   d. Asymmetric Numeral Systems.

38. What does the acronym "BSA" stand for in Cybersecurity?
   a. Ballot-Stuffing Attack.
   b. Ballot-Staffing Attack.
   c. Ballot-Surprise Attack.
   d. Ballot-Super Attack.

39. What does the acronym "2FA" stand for in Cybersecurity?
   a. Two-Face Authorization.
   b. Two-Face Authentication.
   c. Two Factor Authentications.
   d. Two-Face Availability.

40. What does the acronym "CISSP" stand for in Cybersecurity?

a. Certified Information Security Systems Professional.

b. Certified Information Systems Specialization Professional.

c. Certified Information Systems Security Professional.

d. Certified Information Systems Service Professional.

41. What does the acronym "OSA" stand for in Cybersecurity?

a. Open System Attack.

b. Opportunistic Service Attack.

c. Open Source Attack.

d. Online Solutions Attack.

42. What does the acronym "ASIMS" stand for in Cybersecurity?

a. Automated Security Information Measuring System.

b. Automated Security Incident Monitoring System.

c. Automated Security Information and Metre System.

d. Automated Security Incident Measuring System.

43. What does the acronym "COBIT" mean in the context of Cybersecurity?

a. Control Objectives for Information and Related Techniques.

b. Corporate Objectives for Business and Information Technology.

c. Control Objectives for Information and Related Technology.

d. Control Oriented Business and Information Technology.

44. What does the acronym "NGFW" stand for in Cybersecurity?

a. Next-General Firewall.

b. New-Generation Firewall.

c. Next-Generation Firewall.

d. New-General Firewall.

45. What does the acronym "NIDS" stand for in the context of Cybersecurity?

a. Network-based Intrusion Detection System.

b. Number-based Intrusion Detection System.

c. Network-based Information Detection System.

d. Number-based Information Detection System.

46. What does the acronym "OOA" stand for in Cybersecurity?

a. Object-Oriented Attack.

b. Order-Off Attack.

c. On-Off Attack.

d. Operational Objectives Attack.

47. What does the acronym "OSINT" stand for in Cybersecurity?

a. Operating System Intelligence.

b. Off-Site Intelligence.

c. Open Source Intelligence.

d. Open System Intelligence.

48. What does the acronym "CRL" stand for in Cybersecurity?
a. Criminal Records List.
b. Cyber Records List.
c. Certificate Revocation List.
d. Criminal Release List.

49. What does the acronym "FERPA" stand for in Cybersecurity?
a. Family Education Rights and Privacy Act.
b. Family Entertainment Rights and Privacy Act.
c. Family Education Rights and Public Act.
d. Family Entertainment Rights and Public Act.

50. What does the acronym "GIAC" stand for in Cybersecurity?
a. Global Information Assurance Certification.
b. Global Information Acceptance Certification.
c. Global Information Allowance Certification.
d. Global Information Authentication Certification.

51. What does the acronym "GMA" stand for in Cybersecurity?
a. Grand-Mouthing Attack.
b. Graphics-Mode Attack.
c. Generic-Mouthing Attack.
d. Good-Mouthing Attack.

52. What does the acronym "HIPS" stand for in Cybersecurity?
a. Host-based Intrusion Penetration System.
b. Host-based Intruder Proactive System.
c. Host-based Intrusion Prevention System.
d. Host-based Intervention Pervasive System.

53. What does the acronym "IRRA" stand for in Cybersecurity?
a. Independent Renewable Resources Authority.
b. Incident Research and Risk Assessment.
c. International Response Risk Assessment.
d. Incident Response Risk Assessment.

54. What does the acronym "CSEA" stand for in Cybersecurity?
a. Communications Security Establishment Act.
b. Common Service Entrance Examination.
c. Cyber Security Enhancement Act.
d. Customer Service Excellence Award.

55. What does the acronym "CHAP" stand for in Cybersecurity?
a. Challenge-Handshake Authentication Protocol.
b. Challenge-Handshake Authentication Practice.
c. Challenge-Handshake Authorization Protocol.
d. Challenge-Handshake Authentication Procedure.

56. What does the acronym "CIRT" stand for in Cybersecurity?
a. Clinical Investigation and Research Team.
b. Centre for Innovative Research and Technology.
c. Computer Incident Response Team.
d. Child Investigation Response Team.

57. What does the acronym "CISO" stand for in Cybersecurity?
a. Chief Information Service Officer.
b. Charted Information Service Officer.
c. Chief Information Security Officer.
d. Charted Innovative Security Officer.

58. What does the acronym "CSEC" stand for in Cybersecurity?
a. Cyber Security and Enterprise Command.
b. Cyber Security and Education Committee.
c. Cyber System and Enterprise Consortium.
d. Cyber Security Education Consortium.

59. What does the acronym "AVERT" stand for in Cybersecurity?
a. A Victim-Empowered Response Team.
b. Autonomous Vehicle Emergency Response Team.
c. Anti-Virus Emergency Response Team.
d. Anticipatory Versus Reactive Encoding of Threats.

60. What does the acronym "BLP" stand for in Cybersecurity?
a. Bell–LaPadula Model.
b. Bayesian Linear Model.
c. Biased-LaPadula Modelling.
d. Break Log Model.

61. What does the acronym "BAM" stand for in Cybersecurity?
a. Business Activity Monitoring.
b. Bad-Month Attack.
c. Bad-Monitoring Attack.
d. Bad-Mouthing Attack.

62. What does the acronym "CAMSS" stand for in Cybersecurity?
a. Cloud Analytics Mobile Social Security.
b. Computer-Aided Manufacturing Software System.
c. Customer Acquisition, Monetization, Retention, Social Media, and Search.
d. Cloud Anomaly Movement Social Security.

63. What does the acronym "CSIR" stand for in Cybersecurity?
a. Council of Scientific and Industrial Research.
b. Computer Security Incident Response.
c. Centre for Strategic and International Studies.
d. Customer Service Incident Report.

64. **What does the acronym "CVE" stand for in Cybersecurity?**
    a. Common Vulnerabilities and Exposures.
    b. Centre for Vocational Education.
    c. Combat Vehicle Engineer.
    d. Cross-Validated Experiment.

65. **What does the acronym "TGT" stand for in Cybersecurity?**
    a. Trustworthy Computing Group.
    b. Total Group Technology.
    c. Ticket Granting Ticket.
    d. Target Gang Identification.

66. **What does the acronym "UTM" stand for in Cybersecurity?**
    a. Universal Transverse Mercator.
    b. Unified Threat Management.
    c. Unified Threat Management.
    d. Unmanned Traffic Management.

67. **What does the acronym "VAS" stand for in Cybersecurity?**
    a. Value-Added Service.
    b. Visual Analog Scale.
    c. Voice Application Server.
    d. Vulnerability Assessment System.

68. **What does the acronym "WPA2" stand for in Cybersecurity?**
    a. Wi-Fi Private Access 2.
    b. Wi-Fi Protected Access 2.
    c. Wi-Fi Public Access 2.
    d. Wi-Fi Public-Private Access 2.

69. **What does the acronym "DIDS" stand for in Cybersecurity?**
    a. Dynamic Image Display System.
    b. Digital Image Design and Synthesis.
    c. Developmental Immaturity of the Destination System.
    d. Distributed Intrusions Detection System.

70. **What does the acronym "APT" stand for in Cybersecurity?**
    a. Association for Preservation Technology.
    b. Advanced Persistent Threat.
    c. Automatic Programmed Tools.
    d. Adaptive Performance Test.

Answer Key

1. (c) TRNGs are commonly used in Cybersecurity applications, such as cryptographic key generation, to ensure system security. TRNGs work by taking a source of entropy, such as thermal noise, atmospheric noise, or radioactive decay, and converting it into a stream of random bits. These random bits can then generate keys and other highly secure cryptographic materials resistant to attacks.

2. (a) CARO is an international group of leading anti-virus researchers who share information and coordinate efforts to combat computer viruses and other malware. CARO was founded in 1990 and comprises researchers from anti-virus companies, government agencies, and academic institutions worldwide.

3. (c) OWASP is a non-profit organization dedicated to improving the security of software and web applications. The organization provides resources, tools, and guidelines to help developers and security professionals build secure applications and improve the overall security of the web. OWASP is perhaps best known for its OWASP Top 10 list, ranking the most critical security risks to web applications. The Top 10 list is updated every few years to reflect the current threat landscape and provide developers guidance on mitigating these risks. OWASP also provides various other resources, including training materials, research papers, and community forums, to help developers and security professionals stay up-to-date on the latest threats and best practices in application security.

4. (b) A DHA is an email-based attack in which an attacker attempts to obtain a list of valid email addresses by querying a target email server for addresses that match a specific format or pattern. In a DHA, the attacker typically sends many requests to the email server using a variety of possible email address formats. The attacker may also use a dictionary or list of commonly used email addresses and domain names to create the email addresses for the attack. The goal of a DHA is to obtain a list of valid email addresses that can be used for further attacks, such as spamming or targeted phishing campaigns. Email administrators can implement security measures such as rate limiting, sender verification protocols, and content filtering to prevent a DHA. Additionally, it is essential for users to use strong and unique passwords and to be cautious when sharing personal information online.

5. (d) S/MIME is a protocol for securing email messages using public key cryptography. S/MIME allows email senders and recipients to digitally sign and encrypt email messages, providing Authentication, integrity, and confidentiality. S/MIME is widely used in business and government settings where email security and privacy are critical. S/MIME is supported by most email clients and servers, including Microsoft Outlook, Apple Mail, and Gmail, and is interoperable with other email security protocols such as PGP (Pretty Good Privacy) and DKIM (Domain Keys Identified Mail).

6. (c) SSL is a protocol for establishing secure communications over the Internet. SSL provides a secure channel between two devices, such as a web server and a web browser, by encrypting the transmitted data between them. SSL secures online transactions and sensitive data, such as credit card numbers and personal information. SSL has been replaced by TLS (Transport Layer Security), a newer and more secure protocol for establishing secure communications over the Internet. However, SSL and TLS are often used interchangeably for the same protocol.

7. (a) CGI is a protocol for running programs on a web server in response to user requests. CGI allows web servers to generate dynamic content, such as database-driven web pages, in response to user input. CGI is widely used in web development but can also be a security risk if not correctly configured. Poorly designed CGI scripts can allow attackers to execute arbitrary code on a web server or to gain unauthorized access to sensitive data. To mitigate the risks associated with CGI, web administrators should ensure that CGI scripts are secure, up-to-date, and properly configured. Best practices for securing CGI scripts include input validation, output filtering, and proper permissions management. Additionally, web administrators should regularly monitor their servers for unusual activity and implement security measures such as firewalls and intrusion detection systems.

8. (c) The GII is a term that refers to the global network of information and communication technologies (ICTs) that enable the exchange of information and data across the world. The GII includes a variety of ICTs, such as the Internet, telecommunications networks, and satellite communications systems. The GII is critical in modern society, enabling businesses, governments, and individuals to communicate and exchange information globally. However, the GII also presents significant Cybersecurity challenges, as it provides opportunities for cyber attackers to exploit vulnerabilities in ICTs and steal sensitive data or disrupt critical infrastructure. To mitigate these risks, organizations must implement strong Cybersecurity measures, such as firewalls, encryption, and intrusion detection systems, to protect their networks and data from cyber threats. Additionally, governments and international organizations must work together to develop global Cybersecurity standards and protocols to ensure the security and resilience of the GII.

9. (b) Economic Denial of Sustainability (EDoS) is a cyber-attack targeting block chain-based systems by exploiting their underlying economic models. EDoS attacks attempt to disrupt the economics of a block chain network by exploiting the cost structure of its transactions, thereby making it unsustainable for users to continue to use the network. EDoS attacks typically involve spamming the network with many transactions intentionally designed to be economically inefficient, such as transactions with very low fees or large amounts of data attached. These transactions can cause congestion on the network, leading to longer transaction processing times, higher fees, and reduced overall network performance. The goal of an EDoS attack is to make the cost of using the network prohibitively expensive for legitimate users, which can lead to a loss of confidence in the network and a reduction in its overall usage. To mitigate the risk of EDoS attacks, block chain networks can implement various measures, such as transaction fee structures, rate limiting, and congestion control algorithms, to discourage and prevent malicious actors from disrupting the network's economics. In an external denial-of-service (EDoS) attack, the attacker uses a network of compromised devices (called a botnet) to flood the target system with traffic, overwhelming its capacity to handle legitimate requests and causing it to crash or become unavailable.

10. (a) An Automated Key Management Centre (AKMC) is a centralized system for managing cryptographic keys. It automates the process of generating, distributing, and revoking cryptographic keys, which are used to encrypt and decrypt sensitive data. The AKMC is responsible for managing the entire lifecycle of the keys, from their creation to their eventual retirement. This includes storing the keys securely, controlling access to them, and ensuring that they are used in compliance with security policies and regulations. Using an AKMC can help organizations improve the security and efficiency of their cryptographic key management processes, reduce the risk of key theft or loss, and ensure compliance with regulatory requirements.

11. (d) CAPTCHA is a challenge-response test used in computing to determine whether or not the user is human. CAPTCHAs are designed to be easy for humans to solve but difficult for computer programs. They typically display a distorted image of a word or phrase and require the user to type the correct characters into a text box. The purpose of CAPTCHAs is to prevent automated bots from performing specific actions on websites, such as creating accounts, sending spam messages, or conducting fraudulent activities. By requiring users to solve a CAPTCHA, websites can ensure that the user is a human, not a computer program. CAPTCHAs have become a common feature on many websites, but they have also been criticized for being difficult for some users, such as those with visual impairments, and for being vulnerable to automated attacks that can bypass the test.

12. (b) The Treaty Information Management System (TIMS) is a software system the United Nations uses to manage information related to international treaties and agreements. The United Nations Office of Legal Affairs (OLA) developed the system, and various UN bodies and member states use it. TIMS provides a centralized platform for storing and sharing information related to treaties, such as the text of the treaties,

signatories, reservations, declarations, and other related information. The system also provides tools for managing workflows related to the treaty-making process, such as notifications, reminders, and status updates. Using TIMS helps to improve the efficiency and transparency of the treaty-making process, as it allows multiple parties to access and share information in real-time. The system also helps ensure the accuracy and completeness of treaty-related information, as all updates are tracked and recorded.

13. (d) Attackers manipulate their reputation by falsely increasing it.

14. (a) L2TP is a tunnelling protocol that supports virtual private networks (VPNs). It was developed as a collaboration between Microsoft and Cisco Systems in the late 1990s as an improvement over the earlier PPTP (Point-to-Point Tunnelling Protocol). L2TP works by encapsulating data packets from one network protocol (such as IP) within another protocol (such as PPP), creating a tunnel between two endpoints. This tunnel can then transmit data securely between the endpoints over an untrusted network, such as the Internet. L2TP does not provide encryption or Authentication but can be combined with protocols such as IPsec to provide a secure VPN connection. L2TP has become a popular VPN choice due to its compatibility with various platforms and devices, including Windows, Mac, Linux, and mobile devices. It is also supported by network hardware devices, such as routers and switches, making it a versatile and flexible solution for creating secure connections between remote networks or devices.

15. (c) A "Fake Human" is an online persona created by an attacker to appear legitimate to gain a target's trust and manipulate them into divulging sensitive information or performing actions that could compromise their security. Fake Humans can take various forms, such as fake social media profiles, chatbots, or automated emails. These personas aim to establish a relationship with the target and gradually build trust over time, making it more likely that the target will fall for the attacker's requests or phishing attempts. To protect against Fake Human attacks, being cautious when engaging with unknown individuals or entities online is essential. Users should be sceptical of unsolicited messages or requests for sensitive information and verify the legitimacy of any individual or organization before providing personal or financial information or clicking on links. It is also recommended to use anti-phishing tools and to keep security software up to date to prevent phishing attacks.

16. (d) DRM is a set of technologies, techniques, and standards used to control the use and distribution of digital content, such as music, movies, software, and e-books. DRM aims to prevent unauthorized copying, distribution, or modification of digital content and ensure that content owners can monetize their intellectual property. DRM typically encrypts digital content and requires users to obtain a license or key to access or use the content. The license may specify the conditions under which the content can be used, such as the number of devices on which it can be installed or the length of time it can be used. DRM may also include measures to prevent users from circumventing the encryption or tampering with the content. While DRM can help protect the intellectual property rights of content owners, it has also been criticized for limiting the ability of users to access and use digital content. For example, DRM may restrict the ability to transfer content between devices, limit the ability to make backups or create copies for personal use, or prevent users from using content in ways considered fair use under copyright law.

17. (b) AEAD is an encryption algorithm providing confidentiality and authenticity for a message or data. In other words, AEAD ensures that the data is kept secret from unauthorized parties while verifying its integrity and authenticity. AEAD is typically used when confidentiality and authenticity are essential, such as secure messaging, online payments, or cloud storage. It is beneficial in cases where data is transmitted over an insecure network, as it protects the data against eavesdropping, tampering, or replay attacks. To achieve authenticated encryption with associated data, AEAD algorithms typically use a combination of encryption and message authentication codes (MACs). The encryption ensures confidentiality by

scrambling the plaintext into cipher text, while the MAC ensures authenticity by generating a tag that is appended to the cipher text and used to verify the integrity and authenticity of the data. Some examples of AEAD algorithms include GCM (Galois Counter Mode), CCM (Counter with CBC-MAC), and EAX (Encrypt-then-Authenticate-then-Translate). AEAD algorithms are widely used in modern cryptographic protocols, such as TLS (Transport Layer Security) and SSH (Secure Shell).

18. (c) RBAC is a type of access control mechanism that restricts system access based on the roles of individual users within an organization. RBAC assigns users to roles and then grants permissions or access rights to the roles rather than to individual users. RBAC allows organizations to manage access control more centrally and efficiently. Instead of managing access per user, RBAC allows administrators to manage access rights based on job functions or responsibilities. This reduces the complexity of managing access control, particularly in larger organizations with many users and resources. In an RBAC system, users are assigned to one or more roles, and each role is granted a set of permissions or access rights relevant to that role. For example, an IT administrator might be assigned to the "System Administrator" role, which grants permissions to manage user accounts, install software, and configure system settings. A help desk technician might be assigned to the "Help Desk" role, which grants permission to reset passwords and provide essential support. RBAC can be implemented in various ways, from simple to complex. Simple RBAC systems might have only a few roles and permissions, while more complex systems might have hundreds or thousands of roles and permissions, with complex rules for determining access rights. Overall, RBAC is a valuable tool for managing access control in organizations of all sizes, as it helps ensure that users have access to the resources they need to do their jobs while preventing unauthorized access or data breaches.

19. (a) TKIP is a security protocol developed as part of the Wi-Fi Protected Access (WPA) standard for wireless networks. TKIP is designed to provide more secure wireless communications by improving wireless devices' encryption and authentication mechanisms. TKIP works by dynamically changing the encryption keys used by wireless devices, which helps prevent unauthorized access to the network. It also includes mechanisms for verifying the integrity of the data transmitted over the network, which helps prevent tampering and data loss. One of the critical features of TKIP is its use of a "Message Integrity Check" (MIC) to verify the integrity of each wireless packet. The MIC is computed using a secret key shared between the wireless device and the access point to verify that the packet has not been modified or tampered with during transmission. TKIP also includes mechanisms for preventing replay attacks, in which an attacker captures and replays wireless packets to gain unauthorized access to the network. To prevent replay attacks, TKIP includes a "Sequence Counter" that ensures that each wireless packet is unique and has not been previously transmitted. While TKIP improved over the previous Wired Equivalent Privacy (WEP) protocol, it has since been replaced by the more secure Advanced Encryption Standard (AES) encryption protocol in modern Wi-Fi networks. However, TKIP is still supported by some legacy devices and networks that cannot use AES encryption.

20. (c) AI has become an increasingly important tool in cyber security, as it can automate many tasks in detecting, preventing, and responding to cyber-attacks. AI technologies, such as machine learning and natural language processing, can analyse large volumes of data and identify patterns or anomalies that might indicate a cyber-attack is underway.

21. (a) KMI refers to the processes, policies, and systems used to manage cryptographic keys throughout their lifecycle. Cryptographic keys secure data and communications in various contexts, such as secure messaging, online transactions, and digital signatures. KMI includes several key components, including key generation: This involves creating new cryptographic keys that will be used to encrypt and decrypt data. Keys may be generated using various methods, such as random number generators or hardware

security modules. Key distribution: This involves securely transferring keys to the parties using them for encryption and decryption. Key distribution may be handled manually or automated using key management software. Key storage involves securely storing cryptographic keys to prevent unauthorized access or theft. Key storage may be handled using hardware security modules or specialized key management software. Key usage: This involves using cryptographic keys to encrypt and decrypt data. Keys may be used for a single transaction, session, or extended period. Key revocation involves invalidating cryptographic keys that are no longer needed or have been compromised. The revocation may be handled manually or automated using key management software.

22. (c) A CISP is a plan developed by a government agency or military organization to support counterintelligence activities. Counterintelligence involves detecting and preventing espionage, sabotage, and other activities by foreign intelligence services or adversaries. A CISP typically outlines the roles and responsibilities of different agencies and personnel involved in counterintelligence and the resources and capabilities that will be used to support these activities. It may include information on training programs, information-sharing protocols, and other measures to enhance counterintelligence efforts. Developing and implementing a CISP is a critical component of national security, as it helps to ensure that sensitive information and operations are protected from foreign intelligence services and other adversaries. Effective counterintelligence requires a comprehensive approach that involves the cooperation and coordination of multiple agencies and personnel across different levels of government.

23. (d) A CISSM is a person within an organization responsible for managing the security of that organization's information systems and networks. The CISSM is typically a senior-level position that requires significant knowledge and experience in information security. The specific responsibilities of a CISSM may vary depending on the organization and the industry in which it operates. However, some everyday duties and responsibilities may include Developing and implementing security policies, procedures, and standards for the organization's information systems and networks and conducting risk assessments and vulnerability assessments to identify potential security threats and weaknesses in the organization's information systems and networks and developing and implementing security awareness training programs for employees to educate them about the importance of information security and their role in maintaining it and monitoring the organization's information systems and networks for unauthorized access, breaches, and other security incidents and investigating and responding to security incidents, including coordinating with law enforcement and other external organizations as needed. Maintaining up-to-date knowledge of emerging threats and vulnerabilities in the field of information security and taking proactive measures to address these threats.

24. (a) PKI is a system that uses public key cryptography and digital certificates to provide secure communication over the Internet or other networks. The PKI system is based on asymmetric encryption, where each user has a pair of public and private keys. The public key can be shared with anyone and is used to encrypt data or messages intended for the user. On the other hand, the private key is kept secret and is used to decrypt the encrypted data or messages. The PKI system also uses digital certificates from trusted third-party organizations known as certificate authorities (CA). These digital certificates contain the public key of the user, as well as other information about the user, such as their name and email address. When a user wants to communicate securely with another user, their PKI system first verifies the digital certificate of the other user to ensure that it is legitimate and issued by a trusted CA. If the digital certificate is valid, the PKI system uses the other user's public key to encrypt the data or message. PKI is used for various applications, including secure email communication, digital signatures, and online transactions. It provides a robust and secure way to protect communication over the Internet or other networks from eavesdropping, tampering, and other security threats.

25. (c) ISAKMP is a protocol for establishing security associations and managing cryptographic keys in IPsec (Internet Protocol Security) and VPNs (Virtual Private Networks). It defines the procedures and messages used to negotiate and establish security associations between two IPsec peers and manage the encryption and authentication keys. ISAKMP provides a framework for authenticating and securing the communication between IPsec peers, including negotiation of encryption algorithms, authentication methods, and security policies. It also defines the rules for exchanging keys and security information between peers. ISAKMP is an essential component of IPsec VPNs because it enables secure and automated key management to ensure the confidentiality, integrity, and authenticity of VPN traffic. It provides a standardized way for IPsec peers to establish and maintain a secure communication channel, even during eavesdropping, tampering, and other attacks. ISAKMP is used in many VPN products and solutions, including commercial and open-source VPN software, hardware VPN appliances, and cloud-based VPN services. It is typically implemented as part of the IPsec protocol suite and is used with other security protocols, such as IKE (Internet Key Exchange), to establish secure VPN connections between IPsec peers.

26. (d) PPTP is a protocol for creating VPNs (Virtual Private Networks) over the Internet or other networks. It enables remote users to securely access corporate networks and other resources over a public network, such as the Internet. PPTP creates a virtual private network by encapsulating the data packets from one network protocol inside another. It uses the GRE (Generic Routing Encapsulation) protocol to encapsulate the data packets and establish a secure tunnel between the client and the VPN server. PPTP supports various authentication and encryption methods, including MS-CHAP (Microsoft Challenge-Handshake Authentication Protocol), MS-CHAP v2, EAP (Extensible Authentication Protocol), MPPE (Microsoft Point-to-Point Encryption), and RSA (Rivest-Shamir-Adleman) encryption. PPTP is widely used in VPN products and solutions, including commercial and open-source VPN software, hardware VPN appliances, and cloud-based VPN services. However, it has been found to have some security weaknesses, and as a result, it has been replaced by more secure VPN protocols, such as L2TP (Layer 2 Tunnelling Protocol) and OpenVPN.

27. (d) The Anti-Phishing Working Group (APWG) is an international non-profit organization focused on preventing phishing, email spoofing, and other forms of online fraud. The APWG brings together Cybersecurity experts, law enforcement agencies, and industry stakeholders to develop and promote best practices for combating online fraud. The organization was founded in 2003 and operated as a global coalition with members from more than 2,000 companies and agencies in over 100 countries. The APWG aims to promote online fraud awareness and provide resources to help individuals and organizations protect themselves from phishing attacks. One of the key initiatives of the APWG is to maintain a global phishing reporting and response network. This network collects and analyses data on phishing attacks worldwide and uses this information to develop strategies for combating online fraud. The APWG also provides educational resources to help individuals and organizations recognize and respond to phishing attacks and works with law enforcement agencies to investigate and prosecute cybercriminals. Overall, the APWG plays an essential role in promoting Cybersecurity and combating online fraud by bringing together experts from different fields to share knowledge and collaborate on best practices.

28. (a) Proactive Worm Containment (PWC) is a technique used in computer network security to prevent the spread of computer worms. Computer worms are malicious software that self-replicate and spread across computer networks, causing damage to systems and compromising sensitive data. PWC involves using software tools and network protocols to detect and contain the spread of worms before they can cause damage. When a worm is detected, PWC systems isolate infected devices and block network access, preventing the worm from spreading further. PWC systems can also deploy patches and updates to

vulnerable devices, reducing the risk of future infections. PWC systems can be used with other network security measures, such as firewalls, intrusion detection systems, and anti-virus software. Organizations can create a comprehensive defence against cyber threats by combining multiple security measures. Overall, PWC is essential for preventing the spread of computer worms and protecting computer networks from cyber-attacks. By proactively detecting and containing worms, organizations can minimize the risk of data breaches and other security incidents.

29. (c) A CERT is a group of Cybersecurity experts responsible for responding to and managing computer security incidents within an organization or community. CERTs are typically formed by government agencies, universities, research institutions, or private companies to provide a coordinated response to Cybersecurity threats. CERTs are responsible for a wide range of activities, including monitoring network activity and detecting security incidents, Investigating security incidents and determining their scope and impact, Containing and mitigating the effects of security incidents, Developing and implementing incident response plans, Providing guidance and support to affected users and departments, Sharing information and collaborating with other CERTs and security organizations, Conducting research and developing new tools and techniques for incident response and Cybersecurity.

30. (d) DAC is an access control system that allows users to set permissions and control access to resources based on their discretion or judgment. In a DAC system, each user or owner of a resource can grant or deny access to that resource to other users or groups. Under a DAC system, access to resources is based on the identity of the user or group requesting access, as well as the permissions granted by the resource owner. This means that different users or groups may have different access levels to the same resource, depending on the permissions the owner sets. DAC systems are commonly used in small to medium-sized organizations, as they are relatively simple to implement and manage. However, they can be challenging to scale to larger organizations or complex systems, as they may become difficult to manage as the number of users and resources increases. One of the main drawbacks of DAC systems is that they rely on the discretion and judgment of individual users, which can lead to inconsistencies or errors in access control. In addition, DAC systems may be vulnerable to security threats such as social engineering or insider attacks, as users may be tricked or coerced into granting access to unauthorized individuals.

31. (c) Advanced Computer Forensic Techniques (ACFT) refers to the methods and tools used to investigate and analyse computer systems and digital evidence. ACFT typically involves using specialized software, hardware, and techniques to extract, analyse, and interpret digital data from computers, networks, and other digital devices. ACFT may include a wide range of techniques, depending on the nature of the investigation and the type of digital evidence being analysed. Some common examples of ACFT include Data recovery, Using specialized software and hardware to recover deleted or corrupted data from hard drives, flash drives, or other storage devices. Memory analysis: Analysing the contents of a computer's memory to identify running processes, open files, and other system information. Network analysis: Capturing and analysing network traffic to identify connections, data transfers, and other network activity. Steganography analysis: Detecting and analysing hidden messages or data embedded within images, audio files, or other digital media. Mobile device analysis: Extracting and analysing data from smartphones, tablets, and other mobile devices.

32. (d) PKI is a set of protocols, technologies, and standards for managing, issuing, distributing, and revoking digital certificates and public keys. PKI is based on digital certificates and electronic documents that bind a public key to an identity. The main components of a PKI include a Certificate Authority (CA), a Registration Authority (RA), a Certificate Repository, and a Certification Revocation List (CRL). The CA is responsible for issuing and managing digital certificates, while the RA is responsible for verifying the identity of certificate applicants. The Certificate Repository is used to store and distribute certificates, and

the CRL is used to revoke no longer valid certificates. PKI is widely used to secure online transactions, such as online banking, e-commerce, and secure email. It provides a secure and reliable way to authenticate the identity of parties involved in communication and ensure the confidentiality and integrity of the transmitted data.

33. (a) Evaluation Assurance Level (EAL) is a rating system used to evaluate and certify the security of IT products and systems. It is part of the Common Criteria for Information Technology Security Evaluation (CC), an international standard for evaluating the security of IT products and systems. The EAL rating system ranges from EAL 1 to EAL 7, with EAL 1 being the lowest level of assurance and EAL 7 being the highest. Each level specifies a set of security requirements the product or system must meet to achieve that level of assurance. At EAL 1, the security requirements are essential, and the evaluation process is relatively simple. At EAL 7, the security requirements are the most stringent, and the evaluation process is the most rigorous. The higher the EAL level, the more confidence organizations can have in the security of the product or system. EAL is used by government agencies, military organizations, and private companies to assess the security of IT products and systems. It provides a standardized method for evaluating the security of different products and systems, making it easier to compare and choose products that meet specific security requirements.

34. (c) Man-in-the-middle (MitM) is a cyber-attack where an attacker intercepts communications between two parties to eavesdrop, modify, or manipulate the messages being sent. The attacker positions themselves between the two parties, intercepts the communications, and can then read or modify the sent data. For example, in a MitM attack on an online banking session, the attacker could intercept the login credentials entered by the user and use them to log into the user's account. The attacker could then steal sensitive information or perform unauthorized transactions. MitM attacks can be carried out using various techniques, including ARP spoofing, DNS spoofing, and SSL stripping. These attacks can be challenging to detect because the attacker can monitor the communication without the two parties realizing their messages have been intercepted. To prevent MitM attacks, it is essential to use encryption protocols such as SSL/TLS to protect communication channels. It is also essential to verify the identity of the parties involved in the communication to ensure that they are who they claim to be. Additionally, users should be cautious when using public Wi-Fi or unsecured networks, as these are often used as entry points for MitM attacks.

35. (b) Advanced Office Password Breaker (AOPB) is a software tool to recover passwords for Microsoft Office documents. It can recover passwords for documents created in Microsoft Word, Excel, PowerPoint, and other Office applications. AOPB uses advanced encryption cracking algorithms to recover passwords from encrypted Office documents. The software can crack passwords for documents encrypted with Office 97-2003 file formats and documents encrypted with the newer Office 2007-2016 file formats. Forensic investigators and law enforcement agencies typically use AOPB to recover password-protected documents during investigations. However, it can also be used by individuals who have forgotten their Office documents' passwords. It is important to note that password recovery tools such as AOPB to gain unauthorized access to password-protected documents can be illegal and generally considered unethical. Using such tools only for legitimate purposes and with appropriate authorization is essential.

36. (c) The Digital Millennium Copyright Act (DMCA) is a United States copyright law that criminalizes the production and dissemination of technology, devices, or services intended to circumvent measures (such as digital rights management or DRM) that control access to copyrighted works. The DMCA also criminalizes circumventing such measures, even if there is no infringement of the underlying copyright. The DMCA was passed in 1998 in response to concerns that the rise of digital media and the Internet

would lead to widespread piracy and copyright infringement. It provides a framework for online service providers (such as websites or social media platforms) to limit their liability for copyright infringement committed by their users by providing a process for copyright holders to request the removal of infringing content. Under the DMCA, online service providers must have a designated agent to receive and respond to copyright infringement notices from copyright holders. They must also provide a process for users to dispute the removal of content and may be required to remove it to maintain their safe harbour protection from liability. The DMCA has been controversial and criticized, with some arguing that it places undue restrictions on using copyrighted material and limits free speech. However, it remains an essential piece of legislation in the United States copyright landscape.

37. (c) AnTS (A New Trojan Scanner) is a free and open-source tool developed by security researcher Andreas Marx. It is designed to detect and remove Trojans and other types of malware from Windows-based systems. AnTS uses heuristics-based detection techniques to identify malicious files and can scan the memory and file system. AnTS has been praised for its simplicity and effectiveness, and many security professionals and enthusiasts have used it to detect and remove malware from infected systems. However, as with any security tool, it is not 100% fool proof, and it is always recommended to use multiple layers of security, such as anti-virus software and firewalls, to protect your system from threats.

38. (a) A ballot-stuffing attack is a type of cyber-attack used to manipulate the results of an online poll, survey, or election. In this type of attack, the attacker casts multiple votes or responses, either manually or through automated means, to skew the results in favour of a particular candidate or outcome. Ballot-stuffing attacks can be carried out in various ways, such as creating multiple fake user accounts, using proxy servers or IP address spoofing to hide the attacker's identity, or exploiting polling or survey software vulnerabilities. The attack aims to manipulate the poll or survey results, making it difficult to obtain accurate information or make informed decisions based on the results. To prevent ballot-stuffing attacks, secure and reliable polling or survey software must implement strong authentication and verification measures to ensure that only legitimate votes or responses are counted. Additionally, regular monitoring and auditing of the results can help to identify and address any suspicious activity.

39. (c) Two-factor authentication (2FA) is a security measure that requires a user to provide two forms of identification before accessing a system or account. The two factors typically include something the user knows (like a password or PIN) and something the user has (like a physical token or a mobile device). 2FA provides an additional layer of security beyond just a password, as it requires an attacker to have both the user's password and the second form of Authentication to gain access to the system or account. This makes it much more difficult for unauthorized users to access sensitive information or perform fraudulent transactions.

40. (c) Certified Information Systems Security Professional (CISSP) is a globally recognized certification in information security. The International Information System Security Certification Consortium (ISC)² offers it and demonstrates an individual's expertise in designing, implementing, and managing various security programs to protect organizations from potential cyber threats. The CISSP certification requires a rigorous exam covering eight security knowledge domains, including security and risk management, asset security, security engineering, communications and network security, identity and access management, security assessment and testing, security operations, and software development security.

41. (b) Opportunistic or untargeted attacks may have no warning signs, as they are often executed spontaneously. Having no specific target, opportunistic attackers leverage the situation and take what they can get.

42. (d) "Automated Security Incident Measuring System (ASIMS)" is a term the United States Air Force uses to refer to their incident management and reporting system. It is an enterprise-level application that allows for real-time reporting, management, and analysis of Cybersecurity incidents across the Air Force enterprise. ASIMS improves situational awareness, streamlines response times, and enables effective communication and coordination during Cybersecurity incidents.

43. (c) COBIT is a framework for information technology management and governance developed by the Information Systems Audit and Control Association (ISACA) and the IT Governance Institute (ITGI). It provides a set of best practices and guidelines for managing and governing IT processes and systems in organizations.

44. (c) A next-generation firewall (NGFW) is a network security device that combines traditional firewall capabilities, such as packet filtering and network address translation (NAT), with advanced security features, such as intrusion prevention, deep packet inspection, and application awareness. NGFWs are designed to provide more advanced protection against modern threats such as advanced persistent threats (APTs), zero-day exploits, and other advanced malware. They typically also offer features such as user and application-based controls, identity and access management (IAM), and SSL/TLS decryption and inspection.

45. (a) A Network-based Intrusion Detection System (NIDS) is an intrusion detection system that monitors network traffic for suspicious activity and alerts administrators when such activity is detected. NIDS works by analysing network traffic and comparing it to a set of pre-defined rules or signatures to identify patterns of behaviour that may indicate an attack. This type of system operates at the network layer of the OSI model and can detect a wide range of attacks, including malware infections, network scans, and denial-of-service (DoS) attacks. NIDS can be combined with other security measures to provide a layered approach to network security.

46. (c) An on-off attack is a denial-of-service attack where the attacker repeatedly turns off the target system or service and then turns it back on, causing disruption and potential damage to the system. This type of attack can be challenging to detect and mitigate because the attacker can make it appear that the disruptions are due to legitimate failures or outages rather than an intentional attack. On-off attacks are typically carried out using botnets or other automated tools that can rapidly cycle through the attack sequence.

47. (c) Open Source Intelligence (OSINT) refers to collecting and analysing information available to the general public. This includes information from newspapers, social media, public records, and other publicly available data. OSINT is commonly used in various fields, including law enforcement, military intelligence, corporate intelligence, and Cybersecurity. The goal of OSINT is to gather relevant and actionable intelligence that can be used to inform decision-making processes. The use of OSINT has become increasingly important in recent years as the amount of online information continues to grow rapidly.

48. (c) A Certificate Revocation List (CRL) is a list of digital certificates revoked by the Certificate Authority (CA) before expiration. It is a security measure used in public key infrastructure (PKI) to check whether a particular digital certificate is still valid or has been revoked for various reasons such as compromised private key, change of affiliation, or expiration. The CRL is regularly updated and distributed to certificate users to ensure they have the latest information about the status of their digital certificates.

49. (a) The Family Educational Rights and Privacy Act (FERPA) protects student education records privacy. It applies to all schools receiving funds under a U.S. Department of Education program. FERPA gives parents certain rights concerning their children's education records, including the right to review and request changes to the records and control the disclosure of personally identifiable information from the records. It also sets requirements for how schools must protect the privacy of education records, including limiting who has access to them and under what circumstances they may be disclosed.

50. (a) Global Information Assurance Certification (GIAC) is a professional information security certification entity that offers a variety of vendor-neutral credentials across different domains of information security. GIAC certifications are designed to validate the knowledge and skills of information security professionals and demonstrate their proficiency in various areas of information security, including incident response, penetration testing, digital forensics, network defence, and software security. The GIAC certification program is recognized globally and is often used as a benchmark for the competence of Cybersecurity professionals in the industry.

51. (d) A good-mouthing attack is a type of social engineering attack in which an attacker tries to make themselves or their actions appear positive or helpful to gain the trust of their target. The goal of a good-mouthing attack is to manipulate the victim into disclosing sensitive information, giving access to restricted areas, or performing actions that are not authorized. This attack can be made in person, over the phone, or via email or instant messaging. Good-mouthing attacks can be challenging to detect because the attacker is often skilled at appearing friendly and helpful, making it essential for individuals and organizations to be cautious and vigilant when sharing information or granting access to others.

52. (c) A host-based intrusion prevention system (HIPS) is a type of security software installed on individual computers or servers that protects the host by monitoring its behaviour and preventing potentially malicious activity. HIPS is designed to protect the host system from malware, viruses, spyware, and other types of attacks by analysing system calls and other operating system activities. When HIPS detects suspicious or unauthorized behaviour, it prevents the activity from continuing. This can include blocking network connections, terminating processes, and alerting the user or administrator. Unlike a network-based intrusion prevention system (NIPS), which monitors network traffic, a HIPS focuses on protecting the host system.

53. (d) Incident Response Risk Assessment (IRRA) evaluates and assesses the risks of an incident response plan. It involves identifying the potential risks and threats to an organization's assets, evaluating the likelihood and impact of those risks, and developing strategies to mitigate or manage those risks. IRRA aims to ensure that the incident response plan is effective and can protect an organization's assets from various threats, including cyber-attacks, natural disasters, and other emergencies. An effective IRRA process involves regular testing and updating the incident response plan to ensure it remains relevant and practical.

54. (c) The Cyber Security Enhancement Act is a legislative bill proposed in the United States Congress to improve Cybersecurity measures and promote information sharing between government agencies and private sector organizations. The bill aims to provide additional resources and funding for Cybersecurity research, education, and training programs and establish new standards and best practices for Cybersecurity risk management. It also includes provisions for enhancing law enforcement capabilities in investigating and prosecuting cybercrimes. The bill has been introduced in various forms since 2003, with the most recent version being introduced in 2019.

55. (a) The Challenge-Handshake Authentication Protocol (CHAP) is an authentication protocol to authenticate remote users and devices to a network. It is commonly used in Point-to-Point Protocol (PPP) connections, such as those used for dial-up and virtual private network (VPN) connections. CHAP uses a three-way handshake process to authenticate the remote user or device, in which the server sends a challenge to the client, the client responds with a hashed value of the challenge using a secret key, and the server compares the hashed value with its calculation. If the values match, the client is authenticated and granted access to the network. CHAP provides more robust security than the older Password Authentication Protocol (PAP), as it uses a one-way hash function to protect the password and can be configured to periodically re-authenticate the client during the connection.

56. (c) A Computer Incident Response Team (CIRT) is responsible for detecting, analysing, and responding to computer security incidents. CIRTs are typically composed of members from different areas of an organization, such as IT, security, and legal, and work together to investigate and mitigate security incidents, such as malware infections, network breaches, and data theft. The goal of a CIRT is to minimize the impact of security incidents on the organization by quickly identifying and resolving security issues and implementing measures to prevent similar incidents in the future.

57. (c) Chief Information Security Officer (CISO) is a senior-level executive responsible for managing the information security program within an organization. The CISO is responsible for developing and implementing policies, procedures, and controls to ensure the organization's information assets' confidentiality, integrity, and availability. The CISO also manages and oversees the organization's response to security incidents and compliance with applicable laws and regulations and ensures that security risks are appropriately managed and mitigated. The CISO may report to the Chief Information Officer (CIO), Chief Operating Officer (COO), or directly to the Chief Executive Officer (CEO), depending on the organizational structure.

58. (d) The Cyber Security Education Consortium (CSEC) is a group of colleges and universities in the United States that have joined to improve Cybersecurity education and workforce development. CSEC was established in 2015 to address the growing shortage of skilled Cybersecurity professionals by developing and sharing best practices, resources, and curricula. The consortium members collaborate to develop innovative Cybersecurity education programs, conduct research, and provide training and support for students, faculty, and industry professionals.

59. (d) The Anti-Virus Emergency Response Team (AVERT) is a group of experts responsible for providing technical support and assistance to customers affected by computer viruses and malware. AVERT is a part of McAfee, a leading computer security company providing anti-virus software solutions to consumers and businesses. The team works to provide virus detection and removal tools, as well as information and advice to help users prevent future virus infections. AVERT also works closely with other security organizations to share information about emerging threats and to develop strategies for dealing with them.

60. (a) The Bell-LaPadula computer security model describes how information can be protected using mandatory access control (MAC) policies. It was first introduced by David Elliott Bell and Leonard J. LaPadula in 1973 and is widely used in government and military contexts. The Bell-LaPadula model is based on two fundamental principles: the Simple Security Property (SSP) and the *-property. The SSP states that a subject at a particular security level should not be able to read an object at a higher security level (no read-up). The *-property states that a subject at a particular security level cannot write to an object at a lower security level (no write-down). The model defines different security levels for subjects and objects, typically using a hierarchical classification scheme. Access to objects is controlled by a

security policy, which enforces the SSP and *-property. The model is often used to protect classified or sensitive information in military or government contexts. The Bell-LaPadula model has been extended and modified and remains integral to computer security theory and practice.

61. (d) A bad-mouthing attack is a type of attack in which an attacker attempts to damage the reputation of a person or an organization by spreading false or negative information about them. This can be done through various means, such as social media, online forums, or spreading rumours. A bad-mouthing attack aims to tarnish the victim's image and cause harm to their personal or professional life. It can be a form of cyber bullying or cyber defamation and may have legal consequences.

62. (a) Cloud Analytics Mobile Social Security (CAMSS) is a term that describes integrating cloud computing, mobile technology, social media, and big data analytics into an organization's security strategy. It is a holistic approach to security that recognizes the importance of these technologies in today's interconnected world and seeks to leverage them for better threat detection, incident response, and risk management. Cloud computing allows organizations to store and process large amounts of data in the cloud, reducing the need for on-premises infrastructure and increasing scalability. Mobile technology allows employees to access data and applications from anywhere, while social media provides a platform for communication and collaboration. Big data analytics can help organizations make sense of the vast amounts of data they collect, identify patterns and anomalies, and detect potential threats. By combining these technologies, organizations can gain a more comprehensive view of their security posture, quickly detect threats, and respond more effectively to security incidents. CAMSS also requires a strong focus on risk management, as organizations must balance the benefits of these technologies against the potential risks and vulnerabilities they introduce.

63. (b) Computer Security Incident Response refers to managing and responding to security incidents or events that could threaten the confidentiality, integrity, or availability of an organization's information or information systems. This process involves detecting, analysing, containing, eradicating, and recovering from security incidents and implementing measures to prevent similar incidents. Computer Security Incident Response typically involves a dedicated team overseeing and coordinating the response to security incidents.

64. (a) Common Vulnerabilities and Exposures (CVE) is a dictionary of publicly known Cybersecurity vulnerabilities and exposures that provides a standardized naming convention for identifying and sharing information about these vulnerabilities. Each CVE entry includes a unique identifier, a brief description of the vulnerability, and any relevant references or resources. CVE is maintained by the MITRE Corporation and is used by a wide range of organizations and security researchers to facilitate the sharing of vulnerability information and coordination of vulnerability management efforts.

65. (c) A ticket Granting Ticket (TGT) is a ticket generated by the Kerberos authentication server in response to a user's authentication request. The user then uses the TGT to request additional tickets, such as service tickets, from the Kerberos Ticket Granting Server (TGS). The TGT is encrypted with the user's password and is valid for a certain period, after which it must be renewed. The TGT is a critical component of the Kerberos authentication protocol and is key in providing secure authentication and access control in a distributed computing environment.

66. (c) Unified Threat Management (UTM) is a Cybersecurity approach consolidating multiple security functions into a single device or software platform. UTM typically includes firewalls, intrusion detection and prevention, anti-virus and antimalware, content filtering, and virtual private networking (VPN). By combining these different security functions into a single solution, UTM provides a more streamlined

approach to security management, with simplified administration and better visibility into network activity. UTM is often used by small and medium-sized businesses that lack the resources to manage multiple security tools separately.

67. (d) A Vulnerability Assessment System (VAS) is a software tool designed to identify, evaluate, and prioritize security vulnerabilities in computer systems, networks, or applications. VAS tools scan systems and networks for known security weaknesses, misconfigurations, and other issues that attackers could exploit to gain unauthorized access or steal sensitive data. The results of a VAS scan are typically presented in a report that includes recommendations for mitigating the identified vulnerabilities and improving the organization's overall security posture. VAS is an essential component of a comprehensive vulnerability management program, which helps organizations stay ahead of potential security threats and protect their assets from cyber-attacks.

68. (b) Wi-Fi Protected Access 2 (WPA2) is a security protocol to protect wireless computer networks. It is the successor to WPA, designed to replace the older and less secure Wired Equivalent Privacy (WEP) protocol. WPA2 uses the Advanced Encryption Standard (AES) algorithm for encryption and offers more robust security features than WPA. It provides Authentication and encryption of wireless network traffic, ensuring that unauthorized users cannot access the network and that data transmitted over the network is secure.

69. (d) Distributed Intrusion Detection System (DIDS) is a security solution that combines multiple intrusion detection systems in a distributed manner to increase the chances of detecting and responding to network attacks. DIDS architecture allows the deployment of multiple intrusion detection sensors across different network segments, and each sensor analyses the traffic for any signs of intrusions or malicious activity. The information collected from all the sensors is then consolidated and analysed centrally to identify network traffic patterns and trends that may indicate an attack. Using multiple sensors, DIDS can provide a more comprehensive network view and help detect attacks that a single intrusion detection system may miss. Additionally, DIDS can distribute a load of intrusion detection across multiple systems, reducing the risk of a single point of failure.

70. (b) Advanced Persistent Threat (APT) refers to a targeted attack designed to gain unauthorized access to a network or system over an extended period. APT attacks are typically carried out by skilled and well-funded attackers who use various techniques to infiltrate the targeted system or network, often using social engineering tactics to trick users into giving away sensitive information. Once inside the system, APT attackers typically work to stay hidden and maintain access for as long as possible, allowing those to collect valuable data and carry out further attacks over an extended period. APT attacks are considered particularly dangerous because they can be challenging to detect and cause significant damage if left unchecked.

The page was left intentionally blank.

Chapter 4
Vulnerability, Risk, Threat and Attack

This chapter includes questions from the following topics:
- Vulnerability and its types
- Types of risks
- Threats and their types
- Types of attacks
- Attack surfaces

1. **What are the two factors determining vulnerabilities based on the Vulnerability Assessment Methodology?**
   a. Identify Indicators and Exposure.
   b. Sensitivity and Adaptive Capacity.
   c. Exposure and Sensitivity.
   d. Potential Impacts and Adaptive Capacity.

2. **What type of attack can actively alter data or communications?**
   a. Active and Passive Attacks.
   b. Neither Active nor Passive attacks.
   c. Active attacks.
   d. Passive attacks.

3. **What is the definition of a Zero-day exploit?**
   a. A Trojan horse that conceals itself behind another program.
   b. An attack exploits a vulnerability that has not been previously discovered before it is executed.
   c. A program that a security analyst has not previously utilized.
   d. Anti-virus software that takes advantage of unknown malware.

4. **What is the term used to refer to gathering or using data from a system without affecting the system's resources?**
   a. Active attack.
   b. Passive attack.
   c. Insider attack.
   d. External attack.

5. **What is the term used to refer to the possibility of an employee inadvertently revealing confidential data?**
   a. Exposure
   b. Vulnerability
   c. Threat
   d. Risk

6. **What types of attacks are the most challenging to identify and prevent?**
   a. Insider attacks.
   b. External attacks.
   c. Unforeseen attacks.

    d.   Predictable attacks.

7. **What is the term used for a flaw in a system? When a malicious actor exploits this flaw, it becomes a/an ____, which is a/an ____.**
   a. Threat actor, vulnerability, exposure.
   b. Vulnerability, threat, exploits.
   c. Risk, exploit, threat.
   d. The threat, exposure, risk.

8. **Sam and Cathy exchange messages over the Internet, but Daniel intercepts and reads them. What type of attack is being described in this scenario?**
   a. Active attack.
   b. Denial of Service attack.
   c. Passive attack.
   d. Masquerade

9. **What is the name given to an illicit user who gains entry into a system by using a legitimate user's account?**
   a. Misfeasor
   b. Covert user
   c. Masquerader
   d. Security analyst

10. **Which of the following statements about vulnerabilities is accurate? (Select all that apply)**
    a. An exploit is a method of exploiting software vulnerabilities.
    b. Vulnerability is a defect in application code that can be exploited.
    c. An exploit is a strategy that capitalizes on flaws and vulnerabilities.
    d. The vulnerability pertains to the likelihood of loss in an attack.

11. **What is the purpose of Trojan horse programs?**
    a. To gradually infect and take over an operating system until it crashes.
    b. To exploit a system's vulnerabilities openly until the user detects them.
    c. Pretending to be benign software while exploiting a system's vulnerabilities.
    d. To conduct a sequence of brute-force attacks internally and externally on other servers.

12. **What term collectively refers to Trojan horses, spyware, and worms?**
    a. Spyware
    b. Botnets
    c. Virus
    d. Malware

13. **Which of the following is a general term for malicious software that pretends to be harmless so that a user willingly allows it to be downloaded onto the computer?**
    a. Spyware
    b. Virus
    c. Trojan horse
    d. Botnets

14. **"A situation in which one is exposed to danger." Which of the following is the definition of a critical Cybersecurity term?**
    a. Exploit
    b. Vulnerability
    c. Risk
    d. Threat

15. **What is the term used to describe a "defined method of breaching the security of an IT system via vulnerability" in the context of Cybersecurity?**
    a. Vulnerability
    b. Threat
    c. Risk
    d. Exploit

16. **Which statement regarding attack surfaces is correct?**
    a. It is a security mechanism.
    b. It is an exploitable vulnerability.
    c. It is an expected attack.
    d. It is a potential attack.

17. **Which one of the following is not a commonly encountered type of vulnerability?**
    a. Improper file and directory permissions.
    b. Phishing.
    c. Misconfigurations.
    d. Race conditions.

18. **Which element of a holistic approach to Cybersecurity involves assessing, creating teams, setting benchmarks, identifying and simulating threats, specifying use cases, defining risks, and establishing monitoring and control criteria?**
    a. Technical controls.
    b. Administrative controls.
    c. Security program.
    d. Asset management.

19. **What are the examples of cyber threats and vulnerabilities a system can face? (Select all that apply)**
    a. Tailgating
    b. Exploits
    c. Attacks
    d. Defence

20. **Which three security challenges are exacerbated by their rapid growth in numbers? (Select all that apply)**
    a. Time available
    b. Required knowledge
    c. Threats
    d. Alerts
    e. Number of available analysts

21. **What is the best definition of the term "threat vector"?**
    a. A means or method utilized by an attacker to exploit a network.
    b. Malware that displays unwanted advertisements.
    c. Flaws in software that attackers can exploit.
    d. The malware encrypts a victim's data and demands payment for its release.

22. **Among the following threat sources, which is most likely to possess advanced skills and knowledge?**
    a. Organized crime.
    b. Hacktivist.
    c. Advanced Persistent Threat.
    d. Script kiddies.

23. **Which of the following sources accounts for the majority of cyber-attacks?**
    a. Factors internal to the organization, such as current and former employees.
    b. Malicious events, such as a foreign government-sponsored attack.
    c. External threats include cybercriminals, malware, and viruses.
    d. Hurricanes, lightning, and tornadoes are all natural occurrences.

24. **What security controls are considered the most effective protection against zero-day attacks?**
    a. Conducting vulnerability scans.
    b. Using signature-based anti-virus software.
    c. Deploying intrusion prevention systems.
    d. Implementing application control.

25. **What are the most common methods of introducing vulnerabilities into a system? (Select all that apply)**
    a. The use of malware, like Trojan horses, can introduce significant vulnerabilities into a system.
    b. Much vulnerability is inherent in the operating system of a system and cannot be fixed through patching, but it can be monitored.
    c. Several operating systems have known and unknown security flaws, including insecure default settings.
    d. A substantial portion of vulnerabilities results from the misconfiguration of system administrators.

26. **What is the definition of a key Cybersecurity term that refers to "a flaw, loophole, oversight, or error that can be exploited to violate the system's security policy?"**
    a. Risk
    b. Vulnerability
    c. Exploit
    d. Threat

27. **What critical Cybersecurity term is defined as "an event, either caused by nature or humans, which can harm an organization"?**
    a. Threat
    b. Vulnerability
    c. Exploit
    d. Risk

28. **In what way are vulnerability and exploit related to each other?**
    a. The vulnerability exploits the user to execute arbitrary code or gain access.
    b. An exploit technique exploits a vulnerability to execute arbitrary code or gain access.
    c. An exploit creates a hole in a system that allows for unauthorized access.
    d. Vulnerability and exploitation have nothing to do with one another.

29. **Which of the following statements accurately describes vulnerability?**
    a. It is a form of hacking.
    b. It helps to protect our information technology systems.
    c. It is a flaw that attackers can exploit.
    d. None of the above.

30. **What is the term used to describe the estimated potential harm that could be caused by a threat exploiting a vulnerability?**
    a. Adversary
    b. Attack
    c. Countermeasure
    d. Risk

31. **Could you provide an example of revealing sensitive information to a competitor?**
    a. Disclosing software vulnerability.
    b. Revealing data vulnerability.
    c. Disclosing hardware vulnerability.
    d. Revealing network vulnerability.

32. **Recognize the various threats to a computer system.**
    a) Creation b) Fabrication c) Interruption d) Interception e) Modification
    a. a, b, c, and d only.
    b. b, c, d, and e only.
    c. a, b, c, and e only.
    d. a, b, c, d, and e.

33. **As the security administrator for your company, you must be aware of and plan for all forms of attack that could occur. Which form of attack targets the victim with many computers?**
    a. DoS
    b. DDoS
    c. Worm
    d. UDP attack

34. **An alert notifies you that a server in your network is executing a program that circumvents permission. What kind of attack did you have?**
    a. DoS
    b. DDoS
    c. Backdoor
    d. Social engineering.

35. **According to an organization's administrator, the most recent threat is attempting to meddle in a communications session by placing a computer between two connecting systems. This is an example of which of the following types of attack?**

a. Man-in-the-middle attack.
b. Backdoor attack.
c. Worm.
d. TCP/IP hijacking.

36. **You have noticed that an expired certificate is being exploited to get login credentials repeatedly. What kind of attack do you think this is most likely to be?**
    a. Man-in-the-middle attack.
    b. Backdoor Attack.
    c. Replay Attack.
    d. TCP/IP Hijacking.

37. **Which exploit prevents authorized users from accessing network resources?**
    a. DoS
    b. Worm
    c. Logic Bomb.
    d. Social Engineering.

38. **What term is used when an item used to validate a user's session, such as a cookie, is stolen and utilized by another to establish a session with a host that believes it is still talking with the first party?**
    a. Patch infiltration.
    b. XML injection.
    c. Session hijacking.
    d. DTB exploitation.

39. **Mr Raja believes he has discovered malware on the servers, which is a form of a man-in-the-middle attack in which a Trojan horse manipulates browser calls while still displaying the user's intended transaction. What kind of attack may he have come across?**
    a. Man-in-the-browser.
    b. Man-in-the-castle.
    c. Man-in-the-code
    d. Man-in-the-business

40. **An attacker has placed an opaque layer on your web page over the Request a Catalog button. This layer deceives visitors into filling out a form on another website and giving their personal information to someone other than you, while their objective was to provide it to you. What is the name of this attack?**
    a. Click jacking.
    b. Man-in-the-middle.
    c. XSRF.
    d. Zero-day.

41. **Which of the following is used to provide information to the DNS server about a name server that it believes is valid but is not?**
    a. DNS tagging.
    b. DNS kiting.
    c. DNS poisoning.
    d. DNS foxing.

42. It has come to your attention that a would-be attacker in Indiana has been purchasing domains based on common misspellings of your company's name to establish websites that look exactly like yours and preying on anyone who stumbles upon these pages by accident. What is the name of this attack?
    a. Watering hole.
    b. Poisoned well.
    c. Faulty tower.
    d. Typo-Squatting.

43. As the security administrator for your organization, you must be aware of all types of attacks that can occur and plan for them. Which type of attack uses more than one computer to attack the victim?
    a. DoS
    b. DDoS
    c. Worm
    d. UDP attack

44. An alert signals that a server in your network has a program running on it that bypasses authorization. Which type of attack has occurred?
    a. DoS
    b. DDoS
    c. Backdoor.
    d. Social engineering.

45. When an attacker manipulates the database code to exploit its weakness, what is it known?
    a. SQL tearing.
    b. SQL manipulation.
    c. SQL cracking.
    d. SQL injection.

46. Which of the following involves unauthorized commands from a trusted user to the website?
    a. ZDT
    b. HSM
    c. TT3
    d. XSRF

47. When a flaw is found in a web browser or other software, and attackers begin exploiting it before the developer can respond, what type of attack is it known as?
    a. Polymorphic
    b. Zero-day
    c. Xmas
    d. Malicious insider

48. What is a risk? (Select all that apply)
    a. The likelihood of a threat occurring.
    b. The impact of a threat if it occurs.
    c. A weakness in a system that can be exploited.
    d. An intentional attempt to harm a system.

49. What is a threat?
   a. The impact of vulnerability if it is exploited.
   b. The likelihood of a vulnerability being discovered.
   c. The likelihood of a risk occurring.
   d. An event or action that could potentially harm a system.

50. What is an attack?
   a. The impact of vulnerability if it is exploited.
   b. The likelihood of a vulnerability being discovered.
   c. An intentional attempt to harm a system.
   d. The likelihood of a threat occurring.

51. What is a zero-day vulnerability?
   a. A vulnerability that an attacker discovers before the developer has a chance to patch it.
   b. A vulnerability that is easy to exploit.
   c. A vulnerability that is already known and has been patched.
   d. A vulnerability that is caused by a user error.

52. What is social engineering?
   a. The use of technical means to exploit vulnerability.
   b. The use of social tactics to deceive someone into revealing sensitive information.
   c. The use of brute force to gain unauthorized access to a system.
   d. The use of a zero-day vulnerability to gain unauthorized access to a system

53. What is a phishing attack?
   a. An attack that uses physical force to gain access to a system.
   b. An attack that exploits a vulnerability in a web browser.
   c. An attack that uses social engineering to deceive someone into revealing sensitive information.
   d. An attack that uses a zero-day vulnerability to gain unauthorized access to a system.

54. What is a denial-of-service (DoS) attack?
   a. An attack that uses social engineering to deceive someone into revealing sensitive information.
   b. An attack floods a system with traffic to make it unavailable.
   c. An attack that exploits a vulnerability in a web browser.
   d. An attack that uses a zero-day vulnerability to gain unauthorized access to a system.

55. What is Ransomware?
   a. Malware that steals sensitive information from a system.
   b. Malware locks a user out of their system until a ransom is paid.
   c. Malware that deletes files from a system.
   d. Malware that modifies files on a system.

56. What is a brute-force attack?
   a. An attack that uses social engineering to deceive someone into revealing sensitive information.
   b. An attack that exploits a vulnerability in a web browser.
   c. An attack that uses a zero-day vulnerability to gain unauthorized access to a system.
   d. It is an attack that tries every possible password until the correct one is found.

Answer Key

1. (c) The Vulnerability Assessment Methodology is a systematic approach used to identify and evaluate vulnerabilities in a system or organization. It involves assessing the system's exposure to potential threats and its sensitivity to those threats. Exposure refers to the system's susceptibility to threats or hazards that could cause harm. For example, a system that is accessible from the Internet is more exposed than a system that is only accessible internally. Sensitivity refers to the impact that a threat or hazard would have on the system. For example, a system that stores sensitive data is more sensitive than one that stores publicly available information. By evaluating exposure and sensitivity, the Vulnerability Assessment Methodology helps identify areas of weakness in a system or organization and prioritize remediation efforts to minimize the potential impact of an attack or incident.

2. (c) Active attacks involve somehow altering or manipulating data or communications. Examples of active attacks include Man-in-the-middle (MITM) attacks, where the attacker intercepts and alters the communication between two parties. Denial-of-service (DoS) attacks: the attacker floods a system or network with traffic to make it unavailable to legitimate users—malware attacks: where the attacker infects a system with malicious software that can alter or steal data.

3. (b) A zero-day exploit is a cyber-attack targeting previously unknown software vulnerabilities. This vulnerability could be in an operating system, application software, or any other type of software. The term "zero-day" refers to the fact that the vulnerability is not yet known to the software developer or security community, meaning there is zero time to prepare or patch it before it is exploited. Zero-day exploits can be perilous because attackers can use them to gain unauthorized access to systems or steal sensitive information without being detected by traditional security measures. Attackers may use zero-day exploits to deliver malware, steal data, or access sensitive systems and networks. Once a zero-day exploit is discovered, software vendors may release a patch or update to address the vulnerability and prevent future attacks. However, until a patch is available, organizations may need to implement other security measures to protect themselves from potential zero-day attacks.

4. (b) A passive attack is a cyber-attack where the attacker monitors or eavesdrops on data or communications without altering them or affecting the system's resources. The goal of a passive attack is to collect sensitive information, such as passwords or credit card numbers, without being detected.

5. (d) Risk refers to the possibility of loss or harm resulting from a particular action or event. In Cybersecurity, the risk is the likelihood that a threat will exploit the vulnerability in a system, resulting in a negative impact.

6. (c) Unforeseen attacks, also known as zero-day attacks, are the most challenging to identify and prevent. These attacks exploit vulnerabilities unknown to the security community or software vendor, making it difficult to defend against them.

7. (b) A vulnerability is a flaw or weakness in a system's security that a malicious actor can exploit. When a malicious actor successfully exploits the vulnerability, it becomes a threat, an event, or an action that can cause harm to a system or organization. An exploit is a method or technique used to exploit vulnerability and carry out a threat. Exploits can be in the form of malicious software, such as viruses or Trojans, or can be carried out through social engineering, such as phishing attacks.

8. (c) A passive attack is a cyber-attack in which an attacker eavesdrops on or monitors network communications to gather information. In this scenario, Daniel intercepts and reads messages between Sam and Cathy, an example of a passive attack.

9. (c) A Masquerader is an unauthorized user who gains access to a computer system by posing as a legitimate user. This type of attack is also known as impersonation or identity theft. Masqueraders often use stolen login credentials or exploit vulnerabilities in the system to gain access to sensitive data or resources. Once inside the system, they may attempt to cover their tracks and maintain access for an extended period.

10. (a,b) An exploit is a method of exploiting software vulnerabilities. This statement is accurate because an exploit is an attack that takes advantage of a vulnerability in a software system. Vulnerability is a defect in application code that can be exploited. This statement is also accurate because vulnerability is a flaw or weakness in a software system that attackers can exploit.

11. (c) Trojan horse programs are malware disguised as legitimate software to trick users into installing and running it. Once installed, the Trojan horse can carry out a variety of malicious actions, including stealing sensitive data, taking control of the user's computer, and creating backdoors for other attackers to exploit. Unlike viruses or worms, Trojan horses do not replicate themselves or infect other systems. Instead, they rely on social engineering tactics to convince users to download and run them.

12. (d) Malware is software designed to damage, disrupt, or take control of a computer system or network. It includes a variety of malicious programs, including viruses, worms, Trojan horses, spyware, adware, and Ransomware.

13. (c) Trojan horses are malware that disguises them as legitimate software to trick users into installing and running them. Once installed, they can carry out a variety of malicious actions, such as stealing data or taking control of the user's computer.

14. (c) In Cybersecurity, "risk" refers to the likelihood or probability of harm or damage occurring due to a potential threat exploiting vulnerability in a system or network. Risks can include data breaches, cyber-attacks, and other security incidents that could compromise data or systems' confidentiality, integrity, or availability. Risk management is an essential aspect of Cybersecurity, as it involves identifying, assessing, and mitigating potential risks through measures such as implementing security controls and procedures, training staff, and regularly monitoring and updating systems to stay ahead of evolving threats.

15. (d) In the context of Cybersecurity, an "exploit" is a defined method of breaching the security of an IT system by taking advantage of vulnerability in the system or network. Cybercriminals often create and use exploitation to gain unauthorized access to systems or data or to cause damage or disruption to a targeted system or network. Exploits can take many forms, such as malicious code or scripts, social engineering tactics, or attacks that exploit specific software or hardware weaknesses.

16. (d) An "attack surface" refers to the potential vulnerabilities or points of entry that an attacker could exploit to gain unauthorized access to a system or network. It includes any system element that could be targeted or exploited, such as network ports, user accounts, applications, and hardware devices.

17. (b) Phishing is not a type of vulnerability but a social engineering technique used to trick users into revealing sensitive information or taking harmful actions. Phishing attacks typically involve emails or messages that appear legitimate and trustworthy but contain malicious links or attachments that can infect a user's computer with malware, steal login credentials, or harvest other sensitive data.

18. (c) A security program is a comprehensive approach to managing Cybersecurity risk across an organization. It involves assessing the organization's assets, defining risks, establishing policies and procedures, creating teams, setting benchmarks, identifying and simulating threats, specifying use cases, and establishing monitoring and control criteria.

19. (b,c) Exploits: These are defined methods of breaching the security of an IT system by taking advantage of vulnerabilities in the system or network. Cybercriminals may use exploits to gain unauthorized access to systems or data or to cause damage or disruption to a targeted system or network. Attacks: Attacks can take many forms, such as malware, denial-of-service attacks, social engineering, and phishing attacks. They are intended to compromise data, systems, or networks' confidentiality, integrity, or availability.

20. (b,c,e) b. Required knowledge: As the number and complexity of Cybersecurity threats increase, the knowledge and skills required to detect, prevent, and respond to those threats also increase. Cybersecurity professionals must keep up-to-date with the latest threats and techniques to protect their organizations effectively. c. Threats: The number of cyber threats is becoming more sophisticated and diverse. Cybercriminals are constantly developing new tactics and techniques to breach defences and steal sensitive data or cause damage to systems and networks. e. The number of available analysts: As the volume and complexity of cyber threats increase, there is a growing demand for skilled Cybersecurity professionals to analyse and respond to those threats. However, there is a shortage of qualified Cybersecurity professionals, making it difficult for organizations to keep up with the pace of threats and defend against them effectively.

21. (a) A threat vector is a path by which a cyber-attacker can access a network or system to carry out an attack. It can be an email attachment, a malicious website, a phishing email, a social engineering scheme, a vulnerability in software or hardware, or any other method that can trick or force a victim to download malware or enter credentials. Understanding and mitigating threat vectors is an essential part of Cybersecurity defence.

22. (c) APT actors are typically well-funded and well-organized groups that use advanced tactics and techniques to compromise targeted organizations. They are usually nation-state sponsored, and their objectives are often long-term espionage, intellectual property theft, or sabotage. APT actors may use a combination of social engineering, spear phishing, and custom malware to penetrate targeted networks and remain undetected for extended periods. As a result, they have generally considered the most sophisticated and advanced threat source among the options given.

23. (c) External threats, such as cybercriminals, malware, and viruses, account for most cyber-attacks. These threats can come from various sources, including nation-state actors, criminal organizations, Hacktivists, and individuals seeking financial gain. While internal threats from current and former employees are a concern, they generally account for a smaller percentage of cyber-attacks. Natural disasters such as hurricanes, lightning, and tornadoes are unrelated to cyber-attacks and are not a source of Cybersecurity threats.

24. (d) Zero-day attacks exploit previously unknown vulnerabilities; therefore, traditional signature-based anti-virus software and intrusion prevention systems may not be effective. Conducting vulnerability scans can help identify known vulnerabilities that can be patched or mitigated, but it may not protect against zero-day attacks. The most effective protection against zero-day attacks is to implement application control. Application control restricts the applications that can run on a system, preventing the execution of unapproved applications that could be used to exploit zero-day vulnerabilities. This can limit the attack surface and reduce the likelihood of a successful zero-day attack.

25. (a,d) The two most common methods of introducing vulnerabilities into a system are: a. The use of malware, like Trojan horses, can introduce significant vulnerabilities into a system. d. A substantial portion of vulnerabilities results from the misconfiguration of system administrators.

26. (b) The definition of the key Cybersecurity term that refers to "a flaw, loophole, oversight, or error that can be exploited to violate the system's security policy" is vulnerability.

27. (d) A risk in Cybersecurity refers to the likelihood or probability of a Cybersecurity incident occurring and its potential impact on an organization's assets, operations, and reputation. Risks can result from various factors, including software, systems, or network vulnerabilities, threats from cybercriminals or other malicious actors, and inadequate or ineffective Cybersecurity controls and procedures. Assessing and managing risks is a critical component of a comprehensive Cybersecurity program.

28. (b) An exploit technique exploits a vulnerability to execute arbitrary code or gain access. Vulnerability refers to a weakness in a system that an attacker could exploit, while an exploit is a technique or tool that takes advantage of that weakness to execute malicious code or gain unauthorized access to the system. In other words, an exploit exploits a vulnerability to achieve its malicious objectives.

29. (c) Vulnerability refers to a weakness or flaw in a system or application that attackers can exploit to gain unauthorized access, steal data, or cause harm to the system. Vulnerabilities can exist in software, hardware, or network configurations and can result from human errors, misconfigurations, or programming errors. Identifying and addressing vulnerabilities is critical to Cybersecurity, as attackers often search for and exploit these weaknesses to carry out their malicious activities. Properly managing vulnerabilities can help reduce the risk of successful cyber-attacks and protect sensitive information.

30. (d) The term used to describe the estimated potential harm that could be caused by a threat exploiting vulnerability is "risk." Risk is a combination of the likelihood of a threat exploiting the vulnerability and the impact that such an exploit could have on an organization. It is essential to assess and manage information systems and network risks to protect against potential threats and minimize the impact of successful attacks.

31. (b) An example of revealing sensitive information to a competitor could be disclosing the details of a company's new product design or business strategy during a meeting or negotiation, giving the competitor an advantage in the market. Another example could be a disgruntled employee sharing confidential customer data or trade secrets with a competitor.

32. (d) The various threats to a computer system can be broadly classified into five categories: a) Creation: Unauthorized creation or execution of any malicious code or program that harms the system. For example, malware, viruses, etc. b) Fabrication: The creation of false information or data compromises the system's integrity. For example, false data entry, bogus messages, etc. c) Interruption: Disruption or denial of access to the services or resources of the system. For example, a DDoS attack. d) Interception: Unauthorized access to the system or data during transmission, compromising the system's confidentiality. For example, Man-in-the-Middle (MitM) attacks. e) Modification: Unauthorized changes to the system or data, compromising the system's integrity. For example, changing data in transit, modifying code, etc.

33. (b) DDoS (Distributed Denial of Service) attack targets the victim with many computers, overwhelming the targeted system with a flood of internet traffic, making it difficult or impossible for legitimate users to access the system or service.

34. (c) A backdoor is an attack that bypasses security mechanisms to gain unauthorized access to a system or network. In this case, the program circumvents permission, indicating that it will likely create a backdoor into the server.

35. (a) A man-in-the-middle attack is a cyber-attack in which an attacker intercepts communication between two parties and can eavesdrop on or manipulate the communication. In this scenario, the attacker places a computer between two connecting systems to intercept the communication, making it an example of a man-in-the-middle attack. The attacker can then read, modify, or inject messages into the communication, potentially stealing sensitive information or altering it to their advantage.

36. (c) It is most likely a replay attack in this scenario. A replay attack is when an attacker captures a legitimate data transmission and replays it repeatedly, hoping to gain unauthorized access. In this case, the expired certificate is being exploited to gain login credentials repeatedly, indicating that the attacker is replaying a previously captured transmission to trick the system into granting access.

37. (a) DoS (Denial of Service) is an exploit that prevents authorized users from accessing network resources. This attack is accomplished by overwhelming the target system or network with traffic and denying access to legitimate users. A DoS attack can be carried out using various methods, including flooding the target with traffic, exploiting software vulnerabilities, and launching DDoS (Distributed Denial of Service) attacks using botnets.

38. (c) Session hijacking is an attack technique where an attacker intercepts a valid session ID to hijack a user's session with a website or server. This can occur when an attacker steals a user's session ID through packet sniffing or cross-site scripting (XSS) attacks. Once the attacker has obtained the session ID, they can access the user's account or perform actions on their behalf without knowing their login credentials. The stolen session ID essentially acts as a temporary password that grants the attacker access to the user's account until the session expires or the user logs out.

39. (a) Mr Raja may have come across a man-in-the-browser attack. This attack involves malware installed on the user's computer that intercepts and modifies real-time web page requests and responses. The malware can modify web content, steal sensitive information such as login credentials or credit card details, and manipulate user transactions while still displaying the user's intended actions. The attack is called "man-in-the-browser" because the attacker essentially sits between the user's browser and the web server, intercepting and manipulating data in transit.

40. (a) Click jacking is an attack where an attacker places a transparent or opaque layer over a legitimate website, making it appear that the user is interacting with the intended website. In reality, clicking on buttons or links leads to malicious websites or performing unintended actions. In this case, the attacker has placed an opaque layer over the Request a Catalog button, deceiving visitors into filling out a form on another website and giving their personal information to someone other than the intended recipient. This is an example of a clickjacking attack.

41. (c) The term used to provide information to the DNS server about a name server that it believes is valid but is not is DNS poisoning. DNS poisoning occurs when a server is given false information that redirects a domain name to a different IP address. This can be done by an attacker who sends false DNS queries and responses to the DNS server, causing it to cache false information. Users are redirected to the attacker's malicious site when they attempt to access the legitimate domain name.

42. (d) The name of this attack is Typo-squatting.

43. (b) DDoS (Distributed Denial of Service) attacks use multiple computers or devices to overwhelm a victim's system or network with traffic, making it unavailable to legitimate users.

44. (c) The type of attack is a backdoor attack, which refers to bypassing standard authentication or encryption in a computer system or network by installing a backdoor, a secret entry point into a system. The program running on the server could be the backdoor installed to allow unauthorized access to the system.

45. (d) SQL injection is an attack where an attacker manipulates the database code by inserting malicious SQL statements into an entry field or input data in a web application, exploiting vulnerabilities in the application's software to gain unauthorized access to the database contents. This attack can result in the disclosure of sensitive data, modification or deletion of data, or even complete system compromise.

46. (d) XSRF (Cross-Site Request Forgery) involves unauthorized commands from a trusted user to the website. ZDT (Zero Day Threat), HSM (Hardware Security Module), and TT3 are unrelated to this concept.

47. (b) The type of attack that is known when a hole is found in a web browser or other software, and attackers begin exploiting it before the developer can respond is a zero-day attack. Therefore, option B is correct. Option A refers to malware that changes its code to evade detection. Option C refers to a type of port scanning technique. Option D refers to an attack by an authorized user who abuses their access to harm the system.

48. (a,b) A risk is a potential event or action that could harm an organization's objectives. It would involve both the likelihood of a threat occurring and its impact if it did occur. Therefore, options A and B are both correct. Options C and D refer to specific types of risks (vulnerabilities and threats, respectively) but do not encompass the full definition of risk.

49. (d) A threat is an event or action that has the potential to cause harm to a system or organization. Therefore, option D is correct. Options A and B refer to specific aspects of vulnerabilities and are not the definition of a threat. Option C is incorrect because it refers to the likelihood of a risk occurring rather than a specific event or action.

50. (c) An attack is an intentional attempt to exploit a system or organization's vulnerability or weakness to cause harm, steal information, or disrupt normal operations. Therefore, option C is correct. Options A and B refer to specific aspects of vulnerabilities and are not the definition of an attack. Option D refers to the likelihood of a threat occurring, which is not the same as an attack.

51. (a) A zero-day vulnerability is a software vulnerability that is not yet known to the software vendor or the public and has not been patched. Attackers often discover and exploit this type of vulnerability before the software vendor can release a patch, giving the attacker a "zero-day" window of opportunity to exploit the vulnerability. Therefore, option A is correct. Option B is incorrect because the ease of exploitation is not a defining characteristic of zero-day vulnerabilities. Option C is incorrect because a patched vulnerability is not a zero-day vulnerability. Option D is incorrect because user errors are not vulnerabilities in software.

52. (b) Social engineering uses psychological manipulation or social tactics to trick or deceive people into giving up sensitive information or performing actions that can lead to unauthorized access to systems or data. Therefore, option B is correct. Option A refers to the technical exploitation of vulnerabilities, not

social engineering. Option C refers to a different type of attack, brute force attacks. Option D refers to a specific type of vulnerability exploitation, not social engineering.

53. (c) A phishing attack is a type of social engineering attack that involves sending fraudulent emails or messages that appear to be from a legitimate source to trick the recipient into revealing sensitive information or performing an action that can lead to unauthorized access to systems or data. Therefore, option C is correct. Option A refers to physical attacks, which are not phishing. Option B refers to a different type of attack, web browser exploitation. Option D refers to a specific type of vulnerability exploitation, not phishing.

54. (b) A denial-of-service (DoS) attack is an attack that floods a system or network with traffic, requests, or commands to overwhelm the system's resources and make it unavailable to legitimate users. Therefore, option B is correct. Option A refers to social engineering attacks, not DoS attacks. Option C refers to a different type of attack, web browser exploitation. Option D refers to a specific type of vulnerability exploitation, not a DoS attack.

55. (b) Ransomware is a type of malware that encrypts the files on a system, making them inaccessible to the user and demands a ransom payment in exchange for the decryption key needed to restore the files. Therefore, option B is correct. Option A refers to a different type of malware, data-stealing malware. Option C refers to a different type of malware, destructive malware. Option D refers to a different type of malware, file infecting malware.

56. (d) A brute-force attack is an attack that tries every possible combination of characters (usually starting with passwords) until the correct one is found or until the attacker gives up. Therefore, option D is correct. Option A refers to social engineering attacks, not brute-force attacks. Option B refers to a different type of attack, web browser exploitation. Option C refers to a specific type of vulnerability exploitation, not a brute-force attack.

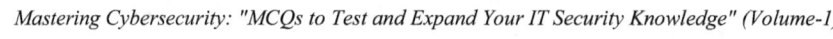

The page was left intentionally blank.

Chapter 5
Cryptographic Tools

This chapter includes questions from the following topics:
- Symmetric Encryption
- Asymmetric Encryption
- Digital Signature
- Digital Certificate
- Steganography
- Modes of Operation
- Certificate Authority
- Key Management
- Elliptical Curve Cryptography
- Public Key Infrastructure (PKI)

1. **Which of the following options does not describe the role of encryption?**
   a. Ensuring user authentication.
   b. Preventing data corruption.
   c. Ensuring data integrity.
   d. Protecting data from unauthorized access during transmission.

2. **Which of the following options provides authentication, non-repudiation, and integrity?**
   a. Symmetric-key encryption.
   b. Public-key encryption.
   c. Digital signatures.
   d. Hashing

3. **In the key recovery process, which key must be recoverable?**
   a. Escrow key.
   b. Secret key.
   c. Previous key.
   d. Rollover key.

4. **Which of the following are the public keys of asymmetric key pairs used to encrypt keys using a public key algorithm?**
   a. Private signature key.
   b. Public signature verification key.
   c. Private key transport key
   d. Public key transport key.

5. **During a security review, Raja discovered a system that used the RC4 cipher with a 40-bit key to secure communications between systems using the Remote Desktop Protocol. Which findings should Raja include in his report on the risk associated with this service?**
   a. RC4 is an insecure cipher that should be avoided at all costs.
   b. The system employs a secure cipher with a sufficiently long key length.
   c. The length of the key is insufficient and should be increased to 1,024 bits.

d.   There is insufficient information to draw any conclusions.

6. **Which key is usually used by a Certificate Authority (CA) to sign the digital certificate of a client?**
    a.   The public key of the client.
    b.   The private key of the client.
    c.   The public key of the CA.
    d.   The private key of the CA.

7. **Which protocol requires a website (when accessed through it) to encrypt the session using a digital certificate?**
    a.   TCP
    b.   SHTTP
    c.   HTTPS
    d.   XHTTP

8. **What is the effect of encrypting your data?**
    a.   It is transformed into an unreadable format.
    b.   It is transformed into a readable format.
    c.   It is sent to a recipient.
    d.   It is duplicated on the local machine.

9. **Which technique does DES use to operate?**
    a.   Only permutations on 128-bit blocks.
    b.   Permutation and substitution on 64-bit plain text blocks.
    c.   Exclusive-OR operation between 64-bit blocks and key bits.
    d.   Four rounds of substitution on 64-bit blocks using 56-bit keys.

10. **What are the benefits of digital signatures?**
    a.   Authentication.
    b.   Non-repudiation.
    c.   Integrity protection.
    d.   All of the above.

11. **Which standard defines Digital Certificates?**
    a.   X.508
    b.   X.509
    c.   X.507
    d.   X.506

12. **If you want to add a crypto-processor chip to improve security with PKI systems, which of the following should you choose?**
    a.   OCSP (Online Certificate Status Protocol).
    b.   HSM (Hardware Security Modules).
    c.   MTU (Maximum Transmission Module).
    d.   PIV (Personal Identity Verification).

13. **Raja wants to encrypt his laptop hard drive but is worried about performance and wants a built-in hardware-based cryptographic processor. To meet this requirement, what must Raja ensure his laptop has?**
    a. AES (Advanced Encryption Standard).
    b. FDE (Full-Disk Encryption).
    c. PAM (Privileged Access Management).
    d. TPM (Trusted Platform Module).

14. **Which of the following is a legitimate Key Management System?**
    a. Third-Party Key Management System.
    b. Dynamic Key Management System.
    c. Integrated Key Management System.
    d. All of the above.

15. **What method does PKI employ to allow prompt verification of a certificate's validity?**
    a. OCSP (Online Certificate Status Protocol).
    b. CRL (Certificate Revocation List).
    c. MD5 (Message Direct 5).
    d. SSHA (Secure Shell).

16. **What is the primary objective of steganography?**
    a. Verifying data.
    b. Concealing data.
    c. Accessing remote computers.
    d. Carving graphic files.

17. **Which method is employed to create a range of elliptic curve cryptographic techniques?**
    a. Elliptic curve arithmetic.
    b. Binary curve.
    c. Prime curve.
    d. Cubic equation.

18. **What is the most effective approach to prevent the "Using hardcoded/easily known keys" while encrypting data at rest?**
    a. Use a new, random initialization vector every time.
    b. Store keys in secure storage areas.
    c. Phase them out.
    d. Choose cryptographically random keys and do not reuse keys for different installations.

19. **What results from adding three points on an elliptic curve that lie on a straight line?**
    a. 0
    b. 1
    c. 3
    d. 6

20. **What is the name of the single element denoted by "O" in the definition of an elliptic curve?**
    a. Prime point.
    b. Zero point.
    c. Abelian point.

    d.   Elliptic point.

21. **In cryptography, the variables and coefficients are usually elements of which of the following?**
    a.   An infinite group.
    b.   An infinite algebraic structure.
    c.   Infinite bit size.
    d.   A finite algebraic structure.

22. **Which algorithm creates a temporary secure session for exchanging key information?**
    a.   KDC (Key Distribution Centre)
    b.   KEA (Key Exchange Agreement)
    c.   SSL (Secure Socket Layer)
    d.   RSA (Rivest –Shamir- Adleman)

23. **For RSA, where modulus n=pq (p and q are distinct primes) and d is the secret exponent, what maximum value can the plaintext P have?**
    a.   p
    b.   q
    c.   n
    d.   r

24. **Which of the following represents a cryptographic key generated for each execution of a key establishment process?**
    a.   Private Key transport key.
    b.   Public signature verification key.
    c.   Public authentication key.
    d.   Private ephemeral key agreement key.

25. **Which of the following represents a cryptographic key intended to be used for a long time?**
    a.   Private static key agreement key.
    b.   Private Key transport key.
    c.   Public authentication key.
    d.   Public signature verification key.

26. **Which of the following is a correct type of ephemeral key?**
    a.   Asymmetric ephemeral random number generation keys.
    b.   Public ephemeral verification key.
    c.   Symmetric ephemeral random number generation keys.
    d.   Public ephemeral key agreement key.

27. **Which technology enables secure and private data exchange or transfer over an unsecured public network?**
    a.   Public Key Infrastructure.
    b.   Virtual Key Infrastructure.
    c.   Private Key Infrastructure.
    d.   All of the above

28. **Which of the following is a symmetric algorithm used in cryptography?**
    a.   MD4

    b.   El Gamal

    c.   IDEA

    d.   RSA

29. **Which two factors contribute to the strength of cryptography? (Select all that apply)**
    a. The use of ciphers that have undergone public scrutiny.
    b. The use of ciphers that are based on complex mathematical algorithms.
    c. The use of ciphers that have been kept very secret.
    d. The use of asymmetric ciphers.

30. **What keys are used to encrypt other keys using symmetric key algorithms?**
    a. Symmetric key wrapping keys.
    b. Asymmetric random number generation keys.
    c. Symmetric random number generation keys.
    d. Public signature verification keys.

31. **How many keys are required for two parties to communicate using symmetric cryptography?**
    a. One
    b. Two
    c. Three
    d. Four

32. **What do Alice and Bob need to use for symmetric key cryptography to work between them?**
    a. Different encryption/decryption algorithms and duplicate keys.
    b. The same encryption/decryption algorithms but different keys.
    c. Different encryption/decryption algorithms and different keys.
    d. The same encryption/decryption algorithms and the duplicate keys.

33. **VRR Academy has hired a software development company to create a bulk file upload tool for their website. During the requirements planning meeting, the developers asked about the required encryption type. After some discussion, Mr Raja decided that the file upload tool should use an algorithm to encrypt 8 bits of data simultaneously before transmitting the files from the web developer's workstation to the web server. Which of the following should be selected to meet this security requirement?**
    a. Stream cipher
    b. Block cipher
    c. CRC
    d. Hashing algorithm

34. **Mr Raja works for a start-up that develops secure smartphone banking apps. The company needs to choose an asymmetric encryption algorithm to encrypt the data used by the app. Due to the high-security requirements of banking data, the company needs to ensure that the encryption used is robust while minimizing the processing power required, as it will run on a mobile device with limited computing power. Which algorithm should Mr Raja choose to provide the same level of high encryption strength with a lower overall key length?**
    a. Diffie-Hellman
    b. RSA
    c. ECC
    d. Twofish

35. **Frank and John have started a secret club and want to ensure their messages are unbreakable when sent to each other. Which encryption key would provide the most robust and secure encryption?**
    a. DES with a 56-bit key.
    b. AES with a 256-bit key.
    c. ECC with a 256-bit key.
    d. Randomized one-time-use pad.

36. **Advanced Encryption Standard (AES) has three different configurations concerning the number of rounds and _____.**
    a. Data size
    b. Round size
    c. Key size
    d. Encryption size

37. **An attacker can break the ElGamal encryption algorithm by being able to do what?**
    a. Solve the discrete logarithm problem.
    b. Generate large prime numbers.
    c. Perform fast exponentiation.
    d. Execute a chosen cipher text attack.

38. **In public key encryption, if A wants to send an encrypted message, he should do what?**
    a. Encrypt using his private key.
    b. Encrypt the message with B's private key.
    c. Encrypt the message using B's public key.
    d. Encrypt the message using his public key.

39. **In a public key encryption system, if A encrypts a message using his private key and sends it to B, then what?**
    a. If B knows it is from A, he can decrypt it using A's public key.
    b. It cannot be decrypted even if B knows who sent the message.
    c. It cannot be decrypted since no one knows A's private key.
    d. A should send his public key with the message to enable decryption by B.

40. **"Messages can be sent more securely using DES." Find the option that best achieves this goal.**
    a. Encrypting plain text by a different randomly selected key for each transmission.
    b. Encrypting plain text by a different random key for each message transmission and sending the key to the receiver using a public key system.
    c. Using an algorithm to implement DES instead of using hardware.
    d. Designing DES with high security and not publicizing the algorithm used by it.

41. **When DES and a public key algorithm are combined, it is primarily to achieve what?**
    a. To speed up encrypted message transmission.
    b. To ensure higher security, use a different key for each transmission.
    c. To provide better security than the individual systems.
    d. To meet the requirements of e-commerce.

42. **What is meant by the encryption of plain text?**
    a. Converting it into code to preserve its confidentiality.

    b.   Reducing its size.

    c.   Converting it into another language.

    d.   Generating a hash value.

43. **Why is encryption necessary? (Select all that apply)**
    a. To safeguard business data from interception when transmitted over the internet.
    b. To optimize bandwidth utilization available in PSTN.
    c. To protect sensitive data stored in a company's database from unauthorized access.
    d. To keep the confidentiality of the information stored in databases in case an unauthorized person accesses it.

44. **Choose the correct statement concerning Symmetric Key encryption.**
    a. The use of symmetric private and public keys.
    b. The use of only public keys for encryption.
    c. The use of only a symmetric key for encryption.
    d. The use of a single key for both encryption and decryption.

45. **Which of the following are valid types of cryptographic keys? (Select all that apply)**
    a. Public authentication key.
    b. Public signature verification key.
    c. Private signature key.
    d. All of the above.

46. **Which statement about Public Key Encryption is correct?**
    a. Anyone can encrypt with the public key, and only one person can decrypt with the private key.
    b. Anyone can encrypt with the public key and decrypt with the private key.
    c. Anyone can encrypt with the private key, and only one person can decrypt with the public key.
    d. Only one person can encrypt with the public key, and anyone can decrypt with the private key.

47. **Which AES encryption mode is considered less secure?**
    a. OCB (Offset Codebook Mode)
    b. ECB (Electronic Codebook Mode)
    c. CTR (Counter Mode)
    d. CBC (Cipher Block Chaining)

48. **What is the term used for attempting to crack an encryption key by trying every possible combination of characters?**
    a. A brute force attack.
    b. A known cipher text attack.
    c. A social engineering attack.
    d. It is a rainbow table attack.

49. **How many unique encryption keys are required for two people to communicate using symmetric key encryption?**
    a. 0
    b. 1
    c. 2
    d. 4

50. **What impact will quantum computing have on the effectiveness of cryptography?**
    a. Both symmetric and public key encryption will be worthless, and the only hope for cryptography will be to develop new quantum encryption technology.
    b. Symmetric-key encryption will be weakened, and public key encryption will be broken.
    c. Symmetric and public key encryption will work fine if quantum keys are used.
    d. Symmetric-key encryption will be weakened, but public key encryption will not be affected.

51. **Which of the following is not a flaw in encryption?**
    a. Implementing reliable and proven cryptography.
    b. Using hardcoded/predictable weak keys.
    c. Relying on algorithms being secret.
    d. Missing encryption of data and communications.

52. **When is it appropriate to encrypt data?**
    a. While at rest only.
    b. While in transit and while in use only.
    c. While at rest or in transit only.
    d. While at rest, in transit, and use.

53. **Which statement about encryption is correct concerning data in use?**
    a. Data should always be encrypted since modern CPUs can operate directly on encrypted data.
    b. Data in active memory registers are not at risk of being stolen.
    c. It is vulnerable to theft and should be decrypted only for the briefest possible time while it is being operated on.
    d. Short of orchestrating a memory dump from a system crash, there is no practical way for malware to access the data being processed, so dump logs are your only genuine concern.

54. **What is an advantage symmetric key encryption has over asymmetric key encryption?**
    a. Symmetric key encryption is faster than asymmetric key encryption.
    b. Symmetric key encryption is harder to break than asymmetric key encryption.
    c. Symmetric keys can be exchanged more securely than asymmetric keys.
    d. Symmetric key encryption provides better security against man-in-the-middle attacks than is possible with asymmetric key encryption.

55. **Which of the following is a set of voluntary standards governing encryption?**
    a. PKI (Public Key Infrastructure).
    b. PKCS (Public Key Cryptography Standards).
    c. ISA (Interconnection Security Agreement).
    d. SSL (Secure Socket Layer).

56. **Which of the following practices helps assure the best results when implementing encryption?**
    a. Develop a unique cryptographic algorithm for your organization and keep them secret.
    b. Choose a reliable and proven published algorithm.
    c. Change the cryptographic algorithm used monthly.
    d. Hard-code encryption keys into your applications to ensure consistent use.

57. **Which of these is not crucial to learning from cryptography's best practices?**
    a. Do rely on your encryption algorithms.
    b. Do use hard-to-guess keys and store them correctly.

   c.   Do encrypt all sensitive data at rest, in use, and transit.

   d.   Do rely on proven algorithms.

58. Identify the correct statements about digital signatures. (Select all that apply)
   a.   It uses symmetric essential encryption.
   b.   Ensures authentication, non-repudiation, and integrity.
   c.   Uses hashing.
   d.   Uses public-key encryption.

59. Public key encryption ensures which of the following?
   a.   Confidentiality only.
   b.   Confidentiality and Availability.
   c.   Confidentiality and Integrity.
   d.   Confidentiality, Integrity, and Authenticity.

60. Identify the length of the sub-key used in each round of DES.
   a.   56
   b.   48
   c.   32
   d.   64

61. Analyse the figure below to determine Bob's identity in this scheme.

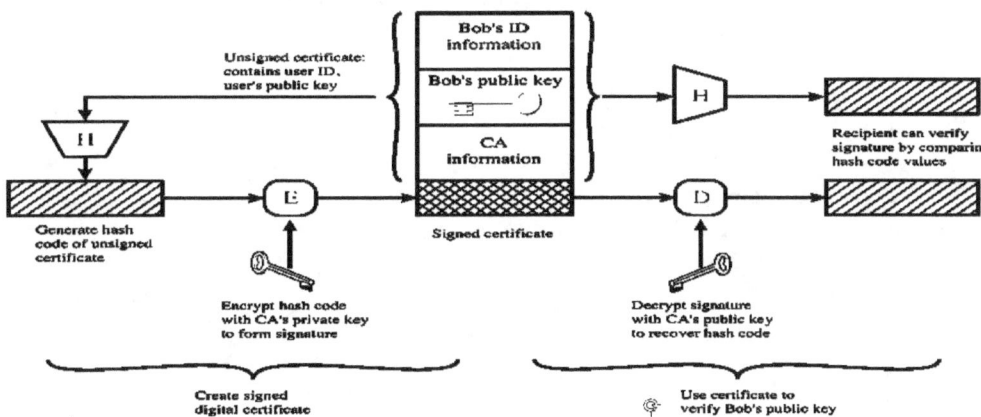

   a.   Bob certifies the public key, and the recipient confirms the signature using Bob's public key.
   b.   Bob is a machine, a server, or an individual from whom we extract the public key for verification purposes. Before employing Bob's public key, the receiver checks the CA's signature using its public key.
   c.   Bob is the entity that created the signature using the private key of the certification authority.
   d.   Bob is the entity that verifies the signature of the certifying authority.

62. Analyse the diagram below and determine the type of block encryption depicted.

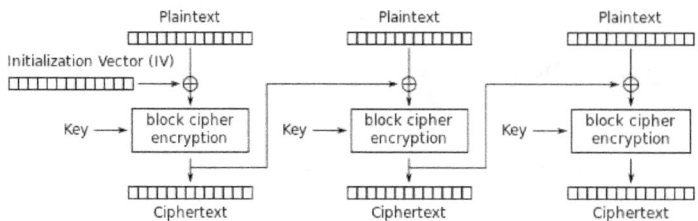

a. ECB (Electronic Codebook Mode)
b. CBC (Cipher Block Chaining)
c. CFB (Cipher Feedback Mode)
d. OFB (Output Feedback Mode)

63. Which of the following is a benefit of digital signatures?

a. Authentication
b. Non-repudiation
c. Integrity
d. All of the above.

64. Symmetric key encryption ensures which of the following?

a. Confidentiality and Availability.
b. Confidentiality and Integrity.
c. Confidentiality only.
d. Confidentiality, Integrity, and Availability.

65. What aspect of cryptography ensures the integrity of an email message during transmission?

a. Confidentiality.
b. Authentication.
c. Non-repudiation.
d. Integrity.

66. How would you define a digital signature?

a. A small string of characters identifying the sender of an email.
b. A unique identifier of a message sender.
c. The authentication of an electronic record by uniquely tying it to a key only the sender knows.
d. An encrypted signature of a sender.

67. In what situations is a digital signature required? (Select all that apply)

a. To tie an electronic message to the sender's identity.
b. For non-repudiation of communication by a sender.
c. To prove that the sender sent a message in a court of law.
d. In all email transactions.

68. Which of the following applies to the Triple DES?

a. 168-bit keys on 64-bit blocks of plaintext.
b. Works on 64-bit blocks of plaintext and 56-bit keys by applying the DES algorithm for three rounds.
c. Works with 144-bit blocks of plaintext and applies the DES algorithm once.
d. It uses 128-bit blocks of plaintext and 112-bit keys and applies the DES algorithm thrice.

69. **Which of the following is true about Triple DES?**
    a. It is a symmetric key encryption method.
    b. It guarantees excellent security.
    c. It is implementable as a hardware VLSI chip.
    d. It is a public key encryption method with three keys.

70. **What is the maximum key length of the Advanced Encryption Algorithm (AES)?**
    a. 6
    b. 156
    c. 256
    d. Variable-Length Key.

71. **What is the significant disadvantage of Symmetric Key Cryptography?**
    a. Non-repudiation.
    b. Key distribution.
    c. Scalability.
    d. Security

72. **Which of the following algorithms are typical components of a digital signature scheme?**
    a. Key generation, signing, and signature verifying algorithm.
    b. Signature verifying algorithm.
    c. Key generation algorithm.
    d. Signing algorithm

73. **What is the responsibility of a certification authority (CA) for digital signatures?**
    a. Authenticate the hash function used.
    b. Authenticate the private keys of subscribers.
    c. Authenticate the public keys of subscribers.
    d. Authenticate the key used in DES.

74. **Why is the certification of digital signatures by an independent authority necessary?**
    a. It is safe.
    b. It gives confidence to a business.
    c. The authority checks and assures customers that the public key indeed belongs to the business that claims ownership.
    d. The private key claimed by a sender may not belong to them.

75. **Which of the following is not a component of an X.509 certificate issued to a user?**
    a. Certificate's validity dates.
    b. User's private key.
    c. Certificate's serial number.
    d. User's public key.

76. **What encryption process involves using one message to hide another?**
    a. Steganography.
    b. Hashing.
    c. MDA.
    d. Crypto-intelligence.

77. **Analyse the picture below and choose the correct statement. (Select all that apply)**

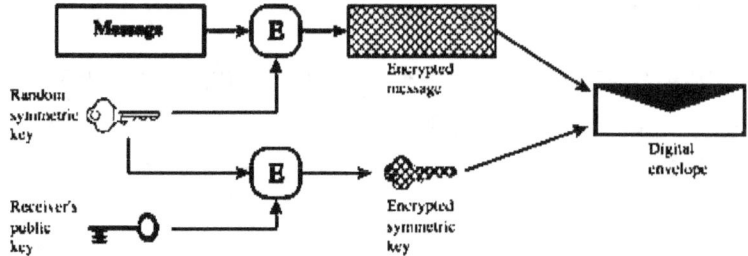

   a. The message is encrypted using a secret key that should be pre-shared before encryption.
   b. The message is encrypted using the receiver's public key.
   c. The message is signed by the receiver's public key for message origin authentication.
   d. The digital envelope is used for confidentiality protection.

78. **When a user digitally signs a document, the asymmetric algorithm encrypts what?**
   a. Certificates
   b. Secret passkeys
   c. Hash results
   d. File contents

79. **Which of the following uses asymmetric cryptography?**
   a. VoIP (Voice Over IP)
   b. SSL (Secure Socket Layer)
   c. Both VoIP and SSL
   d. None of these

80. **Analyse the picture below and choose the correct statement.**

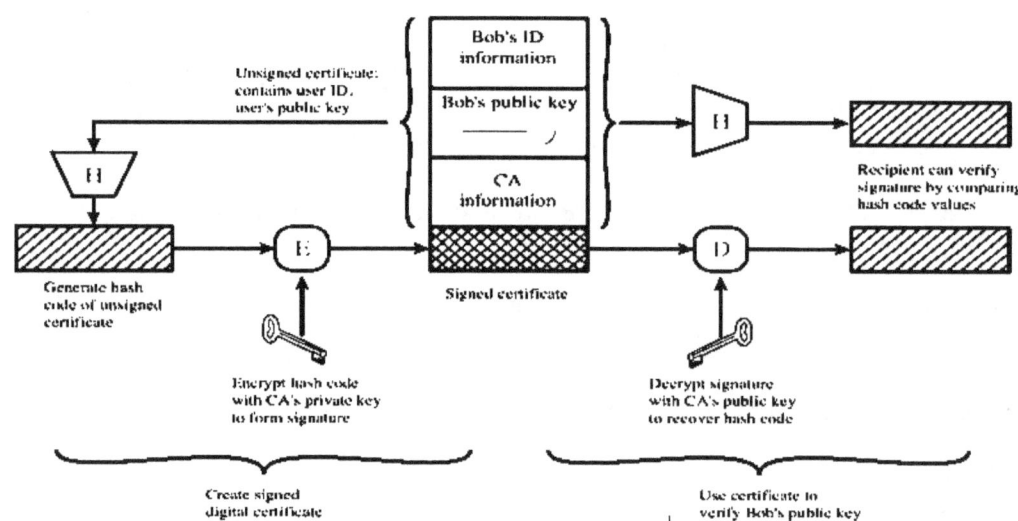

a. A certification authority has generated the signature.
b. Bob is the entity that verifies the signature of the certification authority.
c. The receiver, Alice, is responsible for generating this signature.
d. The sender, Bob, has generated this signature and will verify it using his symmetric secret key.

81. **Which encryption method uses a 160-bit key?**
    a. El-Gamal
    b. SHA-1
    c. MD-4
    d. MD-5

82. **What is the definition of cipher-block chaining (CBC)?**
    a. Data is logically 'ANDed' with the previous block.
    b. Data is logically 'XORed' with the previous block.
    c. Data is logically 'ORed' with the previous block.
    d. Data is logically 'NOTed' with the previous block.

83. **Which of the following is not considered an encryption standard?**
    a. AES
    b. TES
    c. Triple DES
    d. DES

84. **Which technology provides end-to-end security to protect information transmitted over the internet?**
    a. TDEA and AES
    b. DES and RC2
    c. HTTP and HTTPS
    d. TLS and SSL

85. **How many keys are required for "n" users to communicate with each other through a public key cryptographic system?**
    a. 2n
    b. n(n-1)/2
    c. n ^ 2
    d. n

86. **Which protocol is used to securely log in to another computer over a network and transfer files between computers?**
    a. SSL
    b. SHA
    c. SSH
    d. RSA

87. **Which protocol is used for secure authentication between a client and a server?**
    a. SSL
    b. SHA
    c. RSA
    d. SSH

88. **If Mr Raja wants to sign a message digitally for his colleague, Mr Sam, which key should he use to create the digital signature?**
    a. Raja's public key.
    b. Sam's public key
    c. Sam's private key.
    d. Raja's private key.

89. **How can an individual's key pair be verified?**
    a. MD5 hashing.
    b. Public-key certificate.
    c. Private-key certificate.
    d. Digital signature.

90. **Which of the following is not a stream cipher?**
    a. RC5
    b. TBONE
    c. RC4
    d. Twofish

91. **Identify the asymmetric encryption algorithm from the list below**
    a. SHA
    b. RSA
    c. AES
    d. DES

92. **How is the strength of an encryption algorithm determined?**
    a. By using message digests.
    b. By keeping the algorithm secret.
    c. By using a digital signature.
    d. By using the key.

93. **What is a nonce?**
    a. A random or pseudorandom number.
    b. A checksum and a check digit.
    c. A timestamp and a sequence number.
    d. The public key and the private key.

94. **Mr Raja recently received a digitally signed message from Mr Sam. Which encryption key should Mr Raja use to verify the digital signature?**
    a. Raja's public key.
    b. Sam's private key.
    c. Raja's private key.
    d. Sam's public key.

95. **Cryptography provides all the following services except what? (Select all that apply)**
    a. Authentication
    b. Confidentiality
    c. Integrity

    d.   Availability

96. **Identify the correct difference between public key cryptography and public key infrastructure (PKI).**
    a. Public key cryptography is the use of an asymmetric algorithm, while public key infrastructure is the use of a symmetric algorithm.
    b. Public key cryptography is another name for asymmetric cryptography, while public key infrastructure consists of public key cryptographic mechanisms.
    c. Public key cryptography provides authentication and non-repudiation, while public key infrastructure provides confidentiality and integrity.
    d. Public key cryptography creates public/private key pairs, and public key infrastructure performs key exchange and agreement.

97. **How many numbers of keys are required for a set of n users to communicate with each other using the secret key?**
    a. n(n-1)
    b. 2n
    c. $((n(n-1))/2)$
    d. n/2

98. **Find the drawbacks of symmetric key systems.**
    a. Work much more slowly than asymmetric systems.
    b. The key must be delivered via a secure courier.
    c. Carry out mathematically intensive tasks.
    d. Computationally less intensive than asymmetric systems.

99. **Identify a suitable mechanism to ensure the messages are safe from unauthorized observation and ensure the identities of the sender and receiver during communications.**
    a. Symmetric encryption.
    b. Steganography
    c. Hashing
    d. Asymmetric encryption.

100. **What is the purpose of a digital certificate in public key infrastructure (PKI)?**
    a. To encrypt and decrypt messages.
    b. To establish a secure connection between two parties.
    c. To verify the identity of a user or system.
    d. To generate symmetric encryption keys.

101. **Which of the following is an advantage of using symmetric encryption over asymmetric encryption?**
    a. Symmetric encryption is faster than asymmetric encryption.
    b. Symmetric encryption provides better security than asymmetric encryption.
    c. Symmetric encryption requires only one key for both encryption and decryption.
    d. Symmetric encryption does not require a secure channel for key exchange.

102. **Which of the following is a characteristic of a strong password?**
    a. It is less than eight characters long.
    b. It is a common dictionary word.

    c.   It contains a combination of uppercase and lowercase letters, numbers, and symbols.

    d.   It is easy to remember.

103. What does the term "Collision attack" mean in cryptography?

    a.   Collision attacks attempt to obtain the public key.

    b.   Collision attacks attempt to break the hash into three parts to obtain the plaintext value.

    c.   Collision attacks attempt to break the hash into two parts, with the same bytes in each part, to obtain the private key.

    d.   Collision attacks attempt to find two inputs that produce the same hash.

Answer Key

1.   (a) Ensuring user authentication does not describe the role of encryption. Encryption protects data confidentiality and prevents unauthorized access to data during transmission or storage. User authentication, on the other hand, is used to verify a user's identity and ensure that only authorized users are allowed access to a system or application.

2.   (c) Digital signatures provide authentication, non-repudiation, and integrity guarantees. Digital signatures are created using a private key and can only be verified using the corresponding public key. They provide authentication by ensuring the message came from the person who claims to have sent it. They provide non-repudiation by ensuring the sender cannot deny sending the message. They guarantee integrity by ensuring that the message has not been altered in transit.

3.   (a) The escrow key must be recoverable in the key recovery process. An escrow key is a cryptographic key held by a third party, such as a government agency or a trusted authority. It is used to recover or reconstruct a user's private key if the user loses or forgets it. In other words, the escrow key allows authorized parties to access the encrypted data or communication when the user cannot. The other options listed (secret key, previous key, rollover key) do not typically play a role in the key recovery process.

4.   (d) A public key transport key is used to encrypt keys using a public key algorithm. In public key cryptography, a pair of keys - a public key and a private key - are used for encryption and decryption. The public key can be freely distributed, while the private key must be kept secret. In a public key transport system, a sender encrypts data using a randomly generated symmetric key and then encrypts the symmetric key using the recipient's public key. The recipient can then decrypt the symmetric key using their private key and use it to decrypt the message. The other options listed (private signature key, public signature verification key, private key transport key) are not typically used to encrypt keys using public key algorithms.

5.   (a) Raja should include in his report that RC4 is an insecure cipher that should be avoided at all costs. While RC4 was once widely used, it is vulnerable to attacks, and its use is no longer recommended. In addition, a 40-bit key is too short and can be easily brute-forced. Therefore, it is insufficient to secure communications, and the key length should be increased to a more secure level. Option b is incorrect, as the 40-bit key length cannot provide strong security. Option c is partially correct as the key length should be increased, but 1,024 bits is unnecessarily long for most use cases. Option d is incorrect as there is sufficient information to conclude the security risks associated with using RC4 with a 40-bit key.

6.   (d) The digital certificate of a client is signed by the private key of the Certificate Authority (CA) that issues the certificate. This process is known as certificate signing. The CA's private key is used to create a digital signature for the certificate, which can be verified using the CA's public key. This allows others to

verify the certificate's authenticity and the client's identity. The other options listed (public key of the client, private key of the client, public key of the CA) are not used by the CA to sign the client's digital certificate.

7. (c) The protocol that requires a website to encrypt the session using a digital certificate is HTTPS (Hypertext Transfer Protocol Secure). HTTPS is an extension of HTTP that uses encryption protocols such as SSL (Secure Sockets Layer) or TLS (Transport Layer Security) to secure communications between a client and a server. When a website is accessed through HTTPS, the server presents a digital certificate containing the server's public key to the client. The client can use this key to encrypt the session, ensuring that data transmitted between the client and server is secure and cannot be intercepted or modified by third parties. The other options listed (TCP, SHTTP, XHTTP) are not protocols that specifically require digital certificates for encryption.

8. (a) The effect of encrypting your data is that it is transformed into an unreadable format. Encryption converts data into a coded language that can only be decoded and read by authorized individuals with the key or password to access it. When data is encrypted, it is transformed into a format that appears as gibberish or random characters, making it unreadable to anyone who does not have the proper decryption key. The other options listed (b, c, d) do not accurately describe the effect of encrypting data.

9. (b) DES (Data Encryption Standard) uses permutation and substitution techniques on 64-bit plain text blocks to encrypt data. Permutation involves reordering the bits in the input data according to a specific algorithm, while substitution involves replacing bits or blocks of bits with other bits or blocks of bits according to a specific algorithm. The combination of permutation and substitution operations in DES creates a complex encryption algorithm that is difficult to break without the key. DES uses a 56-bit key to encrypt the data and operates on data in 64-bit blocks. The other options listed (b, c, d) are not accurate descriptions of the technique used by DES to operate.

10. (d) Digital signatures provide authentication, non-repudiation, and integrity protection. Authentication: A digital signature proves that a message or document was sent by the person or entity claiming to have sent it, as it is signed using the sender's private key. Non-repudiation: Once a digital signature is affixed to a message or document, the sender cannot deny signing it, providing non-repudiation and accountability. Integrity protection: A digital signature ensures that the contents of a message or document have not been altered or tampered with since the time of signing, as any changes to the content would invalidate the signature. Thus, digital signatures offer multiple benefits that can be used to secure and authenticate digital communications, and they are widely used in various industries, such as finance, healthcare, and legal services.

11. (b) The X.509 standard defines digital certificates. X.509 is a widely-used standard for defining digital certificates, which authenticate the identity of individuals, devices, and services in a networked environment. The X.509 standard defines the format and content of digital certificates and the procedures for issuing, revoking, and managing them. It is used in many applications, including secure web browsing, email, and virtual private networks (VPNs).

12. (b) If you want to add a crypto-processor chip to improve security with PKI systems, you should choose a Hardware Security Module (HSM). HSMs are tamper-resistant hardware devices that provide cryptographic services and key management functions, including the secure storage of private keys, encryption/decryption, and digital signature generation/verification. HSMs are designed to protect sensitive cryptographic material from unauthorized access and use and are commonly used in high-

security environments, such as financial institutions, government agencies, and cloud service providers. The other options listed are not directly related to using a crypto-processor chip for PKI security. OCSP (Online Certificate Status Protocol) is a protocol used for checking the validity of digital certificates. MTU (Maximum Transmission Unit) is the largest packet transmitted over a network without fragmentation. PIV (Personal Identity Verification) is a standard for smart cards for physical and logical access control.

13. (d) William must ensure that his laptop has a Trusted Platform Module (TPM) to have a built-in hardware-based cryptographic processor. The TPM is a secure crypto processor that generates and stores cryptographic keys for encryption and decryption operations. It is designed to perform cryptographic operations and provide hardware-based security functions, such as secure boot and disk encryption, which can help protect against attacks that exploit software vulnerabilities. FDE (Full Disk Encryption) is a technique to encrypt the entire hard drive, while AES (Advanced Encryption Standard) is an encryption algorithm. PAM (Pluggable Authentication Modules) is a mechanism used by Linux systems to provide authentication services.

14. (d) All options above (a, b, and c) are legitimate key management systems.

15. (a) PKI (Public Key Infrastructure) employs OCSP (Online Certificate Status Protocol) to allow prompt verification of a certificate's validity. OCSP is a protocol that enables the real-time checking of a digital certificate's status, whether it is still valid, revoked, or expired.

16. (b) The primary objective of steganography is to conceal data within another medium, such as hiding a message within an image or audio file, without being detected. Therefore, the answer is (b) Concealing data.

17. (a) Elliptic curve arithmetic is employed to create a range of elliptic curve cryptographic techniques.

18. (d) Choose cryptographically random keys and do not reuse keys for different installations. Using hardcoded or easily known keys is a vulnerability that can lead to compromised data encryption. Choosing vital, cryptographically random keys that cannot be easily guessed or brute-force is essential to prevent this. Additionally, keys should not be reused across different installations or environments, as this can make it easier for an attacker to compromise multiple systems once they have obtained one key. Storing keys in secure storage areas is also essential, but it is not the most effective approach to prevent the use of hardcoded or easily known keys. Using a new, random initialization vector every time can help prevent some attacks but is not directly related to preventing the use of hardcoded or easily known keys.

19. (a) Adding three points on an elliptic curve that lie on a straight line results in the point at infinity, denoted as 0. Therefore, the answer is (a) 0.

20. (b) The name of the single element denoted by O in the definition of an elliptic curve is "zero point."

21. (d) A finite algebraic structure.

22. (c) The SSL (Secure Sockets Layer) protocol creates a temporary secure session for exchanging key information.

23. (c) The maximum value of the plaintext P in RSA is N-1, where N is the modulus. So, the answer is (c) N.

24. (d) Private ephemeral key agreement key. This key is generated for each execution of a key establishment process, such as the Diffie-Hellman key exchange protocol. In this protocol, both parties generate their private ephemeral keys and use them to calculate a shared secret. This shared secret is the basis for a symmetric key used for encryption and decryption. The private ephemeral key agreement key protects the shared secret's confidentiality and ensures an attacker does not compromise it. Once the key establishment process is complete, the private ephemeral keys are discarded, making it more difficult for an attacker to recover the shared secret.

25. (a) The cryptographic key intended to be used for a long time is the Private static key agreement key.

26. (d) Public ephemeral key agreement key. Ephemeral keys are temporary ones generated for a specific communication session and discarded after use. Public ephemeral key agreement keys are generated by both parties during a key agreement protocol and are used to derive a shared secret key for encryption and decryption. Asymmetric ephemeral random number generation keys are not a suitable type of key, and symmetric ephemeral random number generation keys and ephemeral public verification keys do not exist.

27. (a) Public Key Infrastructure.

28. (c) The symmetric algorithm used in cryptography is c. IDEA (International Data Encryption Algorithm). MD4 is a hashing algorithm, El Gamal is an asymmetric algorithm, and RSA is an asymmetric one.

29. (a,b) The two factors contributing to the strength of cryptography are: a) The use of ciphers that have undergone public scrutiny, The cryptographic algorithm has been studied and tested by field experts, and its security has been analysed. This helps to identify any weaknesses or vulnerabilities in the algorithm and improve its security. b) Using ciphers based on complex mathematical algorithms: Cryptographic algorithms based on complex mathematical algorithms are generally considered more secure, as they are more challenging to crack. However, it is essential to note that complexity alone does not guarantee security, and public scrutiny is still necessary to identify any weaknesses.

30. (a) Symmetric key wrapping keys encrypt other keys using symmetric key algorithms.

31. (a) Only one key is required for two parties to communicate using symmetric cryptography. This key is shared between the two parties and is used to encrypt and decrypt the messages exchanged.

32. (d) Alice and Bob must use the same encryption/decryption algorithms and the duplicate keys for symmetric key cryptography to work between them.

33. (b) The encryption requirement specified in the question suggests that a block cipher would be better than a stream cipher. Block ciphers encrypt data in fixed-size blocks, whereas stream ciphers encrypt data one bit or byte at a time. A block cypher would be more efficient since the requirement specifies that 8 bits of data should be encrypted at a time. Therefore, the correct answer is (b) Block cipher.

34. (c) ECC (Elliptic Curve Cryptography) is an asymmetric encryption algorithm that can provide the same level of encryption strength as other algorithms like RSA but with a smaller key size, making it more suitable for mobile devices with limited computing power. ECC uses elliptic curves over finite fields to generate public and private key pairs for encryption and decryption. It is widely used in many applications, including secure smartphone banking apps.

35. (d) The most secure encryption key for Frank and John to use for their secret club would be a randomized one-time-use pad. One-time pads are theoretically unbreakable as long as the pad is truly random, at least as long as the plaintext message, and only used once. It provides perfect secrecy, meaning that the cipher text provides no information about the plaintext, and the key can never be broken by any cryptanalytic attack, assuming the key is random, kept secret, and only used once. DES with a 56-bit key is considered outdated and no longer secure, while AES with a 256-bit key and ECC with a 256-bit key are also secure but not as secure as a one-time pad.

36. (c) Key size.

37. (a) Solve the discrete logarithm problem.

38. (c) In public key encryption, if A wants to send an encrypted message, he should encrypt the message using B's public key.

39. (a) If A encrypts a message using his private key and sends it to B, B can decrypt it using A's public key if B knows that the message is from A. This process provides authenticity and non-repudiation, as only A could have encrypted the message using his private key, and anyone can verify the message's authenticity using A's public key.

40. (b) Encrypting plain text by a different random key for each message transmission and sending the key to the receiver using a public key system would achieve the goal of sending messages more securely using DES. This approach is known as hybrid encryption and combines the speed of symmetric encryption with the security of asymmetric encryption. The message can be transmitted more securely by encrypting the message with a unique symmetric key for each transmission and sending that key using a secure asymmetric encryption algorithm.

41. (c) When DES and a public key algorithm are combined, it is primarily to provide better security than the individual systems. DES is a symmetric encryption algorithm that uses the same key for encryption and decryption. On the other hand, public key cryptography uses a pair of keys: a public key for encryption and a private key for decryption. Combining these two types of encryption creates a hybrid system that leverages both methods' strengths. The public key algorithm can securely exchange a randomly generated symmetric key, which can then be used for fast encryption and decryption using DES. This approach offers the advantages of both systems, namely the speed of symmetric encryption and the security of public key encryption.

42. (a) The encryption of plain text refers to converting it into code to preserve its confidentiality. Encryption is a technique used to transform plain text into cipher text that is unreadable without the use of a key or password. The cipher text can then be transmitted or stored without fear of unauthorized access or disclosure. Encryption typically involves a mathematical algorithm that transforms the original text using a key or password. The resulting cipher text can only be decrypted and restored to its original form by someone with the correct key or password.

43. (a,c,d) Encryption is necessary for the following reasons: a) To safeguard business data from interception when transmitted over the internet: When data is transmitted over the internet, it is vulnerable to interception by hackers and other malicious actors. Encryption ensures that the data remains secure and confidential, even if intercepted. c) To protect sensitive data stored in a company's database from unauthorized access: Databases often contain sensitive information, such as financial records, personal information, and trade secrets. Encryption can be used to protect this information from unauthorized

access or disclosure. d) To keep the confidentiality of the information stored in databases if an unauthorized person accesses it: Even if an unauthorized person gains access to a database, encryption can prevent them from accessing or reading the data. The encrypted data cannot be read without the decryption key.

44. (d) By symmetric key encryption, we use a single key for encryption and decryption. In symmetric key encryption, the same key is used to encrypt and decrypt the data. This means that both the sender and the recipient of the data must have the same key in order to communicate securely. Symmetric key encryption is a fast and efficient way to secure data but has some limitations. The biggest challenge is securely sharing the key between the sender and the recipient. If the key falls into the wrong hands, the security of the data is compromised.

45. (d) All options given are correct. Cryptographic keys come in many different types, including: a) Public authentication key: This is a type of public key used to authenticate the identity of the sender of a message. b) Public signature verification key: This type of public key is used to verify the signature of a digitally signed message. c) Private signature key: This type of private key is used to sign a message with a digital signature. Other types of cryptographic keys include symmetric keys, used for symmetric key encryption, and key exchange keys, used to establish a shared secret key between two parties.

46. (a) Anyone can encrypt with the public key, and only one person can decrypt with the private key. Public Key encryption (also known as asymmetric encryption) uses a pair of keys - a public key and a private key. The public key is freely distributed and can be used by anyone to encrypt a message, while the private key is kept secret by the owner and is used to decrypt the message. When a message is encrypted with the public key, only the owner of the corresponding private key can decrypt it. This allows for secure communication between two parties without a shared secret key.

47. (b) ECB (Electronic Codebook) is considered less secure among the AES encryption modes. ECB is a block cipher mode that encrypts each block of plaintext independently. This means that if two plaintext blocks are identical, the resulting cipher text blocks will also be identical. Attackers can exploit this to perform various attacks, such as pattern recognition and dictionary attacks. In contrast, other AES encryption modes, such as CBC (Cipher Block Chaining) and CTR (Counter) mode, provide better security by introducing randomness and diffusion into the encryption process.

48. (a) The term used for attempting to crack an encryption key by trying every possible combination of characters is "a brute force attack." In a brute force attack, an attacker tries every possible combination of characters until the correct key is found. This method is time-consuming and resource-intensive but can be successful against weak encryption algorithms or short encryption keys. Robust encryption algorithms and longer encryption keys are used to mitigate the risk of a brute-force attack. Other security measures, such as limiting login attempts and using multi-factor authentication, can also help prevent successful brute-force attacks.

49. (b) For two people to communicate using symmetric encryption, only one unique encryption key is required. The same key is used for encryption and decryption in symmetric key encryption. Therefore, if two people want to communicate securely using symmetric key encryption, they only need one key they both know and use to encrypt and decrypt their messages. This key can be generated and shared securely using key exchange protocols such as Diffie-Hellman or RSA.

50. (b) Symmetric-key encryption will be weakened, and public key encryption will be broken. Quantum computing has the potential to break many of the commonly used cryptographic algorithms that rely on

the difficulty of specific mathematical problems, such as factoring large numbers and computing discrete logarithms. Public key encryption, in particular, is vulnerable to attacks by quantum computers using Shor's algorithm, which can efficiently factor in large numbers and break the security of commonly used public key encryption schemes such as RSA and Elliptic Curve Cryptography (ECC). Symmetric key encryption is also vulnerable to quantum attacks, but to a lesser extent. Grover's algorithm can speed up the search for a specific key in a symmetric encryption algorithm, reducing the effective key length by a factor of two. However, this requires a quantum computer with many qubits, so symmetric encryption may provide sufficient security against quantum attacks with current technology by increasing the key length. Overall, the impact of quantum computing on cryptography is a significant concern, and researchers are actively developing new quantum-resistant cryptographic algorithms to ensure secure communication in the post-quantum era.

51. (a) Implementing reliable and proven cryptography is not a flaw in encryption. Implementing reliable and proven cryptography is, in fact, one of the most critical components of a secure encryption system.

52. (d) While at rest, in transit, and in use. It is appropriate to encrypt data in all three states: at rest, in transit, and in use. Encrypting data at rest protects it from unauthorized access if stored on a physical device such as a hard drive, USB drive, or mobile device. Encrypting data in transit protects it while transmitted between devices or over a network, such as during online banking or e-commerce transactions. Moreover, encrypting data in use protects it while it is being processed or used by an application, such as when entering a password into a web form or accessing a sensitive file on a computer. Encrypting data in all three states is essential to protect the confidentiality and integrity of sensitive information and prevent unauthorized access and data breaches.

53. (c) It is vulnerable to theft and should be decrypted only for the briefest possible time while it is being operated on. Data in use refers to data that is actively being processed or used by an application, and it is particularly vulnerable to theft since it is in an unencrypted form while being used. Therefore, it is recommended to decrypt the data for the briefest possible time while it is being operated on and then re-encrypt it as soon as possible to minimize the risk of unauthorized access.

54. (a) Symmetric key encryption is faster than asymmetric key encryption. Symmetric and asymmetric key encryption are two standard encryption algorithms to secure data. Symmetric key encryption uses a single shared secret key to encrypt and decrypt data, while asymmetric key encryption uses a pair of keys, public and private keys, to encrypt and decrypt data. One advantage of symmetric key encryption over asymmetric key encryption is that it is faster. Symmetric key encryption algorithms are typically much faster than asymmetric key encryption algorithms, making them better suited for encrypting large amounts of data or for real-time communication applications where low latency is essential.

55. (b) PKCS stands for Public Key Cryptography Standards, a set of voluntary standards developed by RSA Laboratories that govern public-key cryptography, including encryption, digital signatures, and key management. PKCS provides a common framework for implementing secure communication and authentication protocols using public-key cryptography.

56. b. Choose a reliable and proven published algorithm. When implementing encryption, it is essential to use a reliable and proven published algorithm rather than developing a unique cryptographic algorithm for your organization and keeping it secret. Security experts around the world have developed and tested well-known algorithms, such as Advanced Encryption Standard (AES), Triple Data Encryption Standard

(3DES), and Rivest-Shamir-Adleman (RSA), which are widely used and have proven to be effective against attacks.

57. (a) Do rely on your encryption algorithms. This statement is not crucial to learning from cryptography's best practices because it is essential to rely on proven algorithms rather than developing your own. While it may seem tempting to develop a custom algorithm, it is difficult to ensure that it is secure and has not been compromised by attackers. It is better to use established and proven algorithms, which have been thoroughly reviewed and tested by experts in the field.

58. (b,c,d) The correct three statements about digital signatures are: b) Ensures authentication, non-repudiation, and integrity: Digital signatures provide a way to verify the authenticity of a digital document or message and ensure its integrity. The recipient of a digitally signed message can be confident that it has not been altered since it was signed and that the sender is who they claims to be. c) Uses hashing: Digital signatures use a hash function to create a unique fingerprint of the document or message that is being signed. This fingerprint is then encrypted with the sender's private key to create the digital signature. d) Uses public-key encryption: Digital signatures use public-key encryption to verify the signature's authenticity. The recipient of a digitally signed message uses the sender's public key to decrypt the signature and verify that it was created with the sender's private key.

59. (d) Public key encryption ensures confidentiality, integrity, and authenticity. Confidentiality: Public key encryption ensures that only the intended recipient can read the message by encrypting it with the recipient's public key. Integrity: Public key encryption ensures that the message has not been tampered with during transmission by using a message digest or hash function to generate a unique value for the message, which is then encrypted with the sender's private key. The recipient can use the sender's public key to decrypt the digest and compare it with a newly computed digest to verify the message's integrity. Authenticity: Public key encryption ensures that the claimed sender has sent the message using a digital signature created by encrypting the message digest with the sender's private key. The recipient can use the sender's public key to decrypt the signature and verify that it matches the message digest, ensuring its authenticity.

60. (a) In the Data Encryption Standard (DES), the sub-key length used in each round is 56 bits. The key length is 64 bits, but eight are used for parity checking and not used in encryption. The remaining 56 bits are divided into 16 sub-keys, each 48 bits long, and used in a specific round of the encryption process.

61. (b) Bob is a machine, a server, or an individual from whom we extract the public key for verification purposes. Before employing Bob's public key, the receiver checks the CA's signature using its public key.

62. (b) CBC (Cipher Block Chaining)

63. (d) All of the above. Digital signatures provide authentication, non-repudiation, and integrity.

64. (b) Symmetric key encryption ensures confidentiality and integrity.

65. (d) Cryptographic techniques such as message digests and digital signatures can ensure the integrity of an email message during transmission, making it resistant to modification or tampering.

66. (c) A digital signature is the authentication of an electronic record by uniquely tying it to a key only the sender knows.

67. (a,b,c) Digital signatures are not required in all email transactions, but they can be helpful in situations where the sender's authenticity needs to be verified, and there is a need for non-repudiation of the message.

68. (d) Uses 128-bit blocks of plaintext and 112-bit keys and applies the DES algorithm thrice.

69. (a) It is a symmetric key encryption method.

70. (c) The maximum key length of the Advanced Encryption Algorithm (AES) is 256.
71. (b) The significant disadvantage of Symmetric Key Cryptography is key distribution.

72. (a) Key generation, signing, and signature verifying algorithm.

73. (c) Authenticate the public keys of subscribers. The responsibility of a certification authority for digital signatures is to authenticate the public keys of subscribers.

74. (c) The certification of digital signatures by an independent authority is necessary to give confidence to the users that the public key indeed belongs to the entity that claims ownership. The Certification Authority (CA) checks and verifies the entity's identity and issues a digital certificate containing the public key and other information. The digital certificate is then used to verify the authenticity of the digital signature. This process ensures that the recipient can trust the digital signature and that the message has not been tampered with.

75. (b) User's private key is not a component of an X.509 certificate issued to a user. The components of an X.509 certificate typically include the user's identity information, their public key, the digital signature of the certificate issuer (Certification Authority), and other relevant information such as the certificate's validity dates and serial number.

76. (a) Steganography is concealing secret information within another non-secret file or message so that it is not apparent to anyone observing the communication. It involves hiding the existence of the message rather than the message itself. For example, steganography can involve hiding a message within an image, video, or audio file by modifying the pixels or bytes in a way that is not noticeable to the human eye or ear. Steganography aims to keep the communication secret while avoiding detection by third parties who may intercept the communication.

77. (a,d)

78. (c) When a user digitally signs a document, the asymmetric algorithm does not encrypt any part of the document. Instead, it generates a digital signature by using the sender's private key to encrypt a hash value of the document, which can then be verified by anyone with access to the sender's public key. So, the answer is c. Hash results.

79. (b) SSL (Secure Sockets Layer) uses asymmetric cryptography (also known as public-key cryptography) for key exchange and authentication purposes. VoIP (Voice over Internet Protocol) typically uses symmetric encryption to protect voice communication.

80. (b) Bob is the entity that verifies the signature of the certification authority.

81. (b) SHA-1 uses a 160-bit key.

82. (b) Cipher-block chaining (CBC) is a mode of operation for block ciphers. In CBC mode, each plaintext block is XORed with the previous cipher text block before being encrypted with the block cipher algorithm. The result is then used as the cipher text for the current block. This creates a chain of cipher text blocks that depend on all the plaintext blocks processed up to that point. The initialization vector (IV) is used to XOR the first plaintext block before encryption. This adds randomness and makes the encryption more secure.

83. (b) TES is not considered an encryption standard.

84. (d) TLS (Transport Layer Security) and SSL (Secure Sockets Layer) provide end-to-end security to protect information transmitted over the internet.

85. (b) $n(n-1)/2$. Each user has public and private keys in a public key cryptographic system. To enable communication between n users, users must have n-1 public keys to encrypt messages sent to other users. Therefore, the total number of keys required is $n(n-1)$. However, each user also has their private key, so the total number of keys required is $n(n-1)+n$, which simplifies to $n(n-1)/2$.

86. (c) The protocol used to securely log in to another computer over a network and transfer files between computers is SSH (Secure Shell).

87. (d) The protocol used for secure authentication between a client and a server is SSH (Secure Shell).

88. (d) Mr Raja should use his private key to create the digital signature for his colleague, Mr Sam.

89. (c) A public key certificate can verify an individual's key pair.

90. (d) Twofish is a block cipher, while RC5, RC4, and TBONE are all examples of stream ciphers.

91. (b) RSA is the asymmetric encryption algorithm. SHA, AES, and DES are all symmetric encryption algorithms.

92. (d) The strength of an encryption algorithm is determined by the complexity of the algorithm and the size of the key used. More robust algorithms typically have larger key sizes and are more difficult to crack.

93. (a) A nonce is a random or pseudorandom number used only once in a cryptographic communication. It is typically used to prevent replay attacks, in which an attacker intercepts and retransmits a message or generates unique session keys. Nonce is often combined with other data, such as timestamps or sequence numbers, to increase their randomness further and prevent collisions. Therefore, the correct option is b: a timestamp and a sequence number.

94. (d) Mr Raja should use Mr Sam's public key to verify the digital signature.

95. (a,b,c) Cryptography provides all of the following services except availability.

96. (b) Public key cryptography is another name for asymmetric cryptography, while public key infrastructure comprises public key cryptographic mechanisms. Public key cryptography, also known as asymmetric cryptography, refers to using a key pair for encryption and decryption, where one key is public and can be shared with anyone, and the other key is private and must be kept secret. Public key infrastructure (PKI)

refs to a set of public key cryptographic mechanisms and services that support the secure exchange of digital certificates, which are used to verify the identity of individuals, devices, and organizations in a networked environment.

97. (c) For a set of n users to communicate with each other using the secret key, the number of keys required is equal to the number of unique pairs of users, which is given by the formula (n(n-1))/2. This is because each user needs a separate key for each other user they communicate with, but a pair of users only needs one shared key for both of them to communicate securely.

98. (b) The drawback of symmetric key systems is that the key must be securely delivered to the intended recipient, which can be challenging if the communication channel is insecure.

99. (d) The suitable mechanism to ensure the messages are safe from unauthorized observation and ensure the identities of the sender and receiver during communications is asymmetric encryption.

100. (c) The purpose of a digital certificate in public key infrastructure (PKI) is to verify a user's or system's identity. A digital certificate is an electronic document that contains information about the identity of the certificate holder, such as their name, public key, and other identifying information. A trusted third party digitally signs the certificate, called a Certificate Authority (CA), to verify that the information in the certificate is accurate and that the certificate holder is who they claim to be. This allows other parties to trust the certificate holder and securely communicate with them using their public key.

101. (a) Symmetric encryption is faster than asymmetric encryption.

102. (c) It contains a combination of uppercase and lowercase letters, numbers, and symbols. A strong password is difficult for attackers to guess or crack. Including a combination of uppercase and lowercase letters, numbers, and symbols can increase the complexity and strength of a password. A password less than eight characters long and a common dictionary word is considered weak and can be easily guessed or cracked. A password that is easy to remember may also be easy for an attacker to guess or crack.

103. (d) The term "Collision attack" in cryptography refers to an attack that attempts to find two inputs that produce the same hash.

Chapter 6
Public-Key Cryptography and Message Authentication

This chapter includes questions from the following topics:
- Public Key Cryptography.
- Hash Algorithms.
- Secure Hash Function.
- HMAC, RSA.
- Diffie-Hellman.

1. **What is the purpose of a secure hash function?**
    a. To generate random numbers.
    b. To encrypt messages.
    c. To compress data.
    d. To create a fixed-size output for a given input.

2. **Which of the following is a widely-used secure hash function?**
    a. SHA-512.
    b. RC4 (Rivest Cipher 4).
    c. DES (Data Encryption Standard).
    d. AES (Advanced Encryption Standard).

3. **What is the output size of SHA-256?**
    a. 128 bits.
    b. 256 bits.
    c. 512 bits.
    d. 1024 bits.

4. **Which of the following is a property of a secure hash function?**
    a. Collision resistance.
    b. Key recovery.
    c. Block cipher mode.
    d. Stream cipher mode.

5. **Which is not a common use case for a secure hash function?**
    a. Digital signatures.
    b. Password storage.
    c. Encryption.
    d. Message authentication.

6. **Which type of attack targets the input of a secure hash function?**
    a. Collision attack.
    b. Birthday attack.
    c. Brute-force attack.
    d. Side-channel attack.

7. **Which type of attack targets the output of a secure hash function?**
    a.   Collision attack.
    b.   Pre-image attack.
    c.   Brute-force attack.
    d.   Birthday attack.

8. **Which of the following is a feature of SHA-3?**
    a.   It uses the same internal structure as SHA-2.
    b.   It is based on the MD5 hash function.
    c.   It has a variable output size.
    d.   It has a fixed output size of 512 bits.

9. **Which of the following is a property of a cryptographic hash function?**
    a.   It is reversible.
    b.   It has a variable output size.
    c.   It can be decrypted.
    d.   It is deterministic.

10. **Which of the following is a potential weakness of a secure hash function?**
    a.   It may produce the same output for different inputs.
    b.   It may require a large amount of memory to operate.
    c.   It may be vulnerable to brute-force attacks.
    d.   It may be unable to process certain types of data.

11. **What does HMAC stand for?**
    a.   Hashed Message Access Code.
    b.   Hash-based Message Authentication Code.
    c.   High-level Message Authentication Cipher.
    d.   Hybrid Message Authentication Code.

12. **What is the purpose of HMAC?**
    a.   To encrypt messages.
    b.   To generate random numbers.
    c.   To create a fixed-size output for a given input.
    d.   To authenticate messages.

13. **Which cryptographic primitive is used in HMAC?**
    a.   Hash function.
    b.   Encryption algorithm.
    c.   Key exchange protocol.
    d.   Digital signature scheme.

14. **Which of the following is widely used with the HMAC algorithm?**
    a.   RSA.
    b.   MD5.
    c.   Diffie-Hellman.
    d.   AES.

15. **Which of the following is not a requirement for a secure HMAC algorithm?**

    a.   Collision resistance of the hash function.
    b.   Strong cryptographic key.
    c.   Fixed input size.
    d.   The secret key is shared between the sender and receiver.

16. **Which type of attack is not a threat to HMAC security?**
    a.   Brute-force attack.
    b.   Side-channel attack.
    c.   Collision attack.
    d.   Birthday attack.

17. **Which of the following is a feature of HMAC-SHA-256?**
    a.   It has a variable output size.
    b.   It is based on the MD5 hash function.
    c.   It has a fixed output size of 512 bits.
    d.   It is widely used for digital signatures.

18. **Which of the following is a potential weakness of HMAC?**
    a.   It may be vulnerable to brute-force attacks on the key.
    b.   It may be unable to process certain types of data.
    c.   It may produce the same output for different inputs.
    d.   It may require a large amount of memory to operate.

19. **Who is credited with the invention of the RSA algorithm?**
    a.   Ron Rivest.
    b.   Adi Shamir.
    c.   Leonard Adleman.
    d.   All of the above.

20. **What is the purpose of the RSA algorithm?**
    a.   To generate random numbers.
    b.   To create digital signatures.
    c.   To encrypt and decrypt messages.
    d.   To perform secure key exchanges.

21. **Which of the following is not a requirement for the security of the RSA algorithm?**
    a.   The difficulty of factoring large composite numbers.
    b.   The size of the public key.
    c.   The randomness of the prime numbers used to generate the keys.
    d.   The use of a symmetric encryption algorithm.

22. **What formula is used to generate the public and private keys in RSA?**
    a. $n = pq$, $phi(n) = (p-1)(q-1)$, $ed = 1 \bmod phi(n)$.
    b. $n = p+q$, $phi(n) = (p-1)(q-1)$, $ed = 1 \bmod phi(n)$.
    c. $n = pq$, $phi(n) = (p-1)(q-1)$, $ed = 1 \bmod n$.
    d. $n = pq$, $phi(n) = (p+1)(q+1)$, $ed = 1 \bmod phi(n)$.

23. **Which of the following is a potential weakness of the RSA algorithm?**
    a.   Brute-force attacks on the private key.

    b.   Side-channel attacks on the implementation of the algorithm.

    c.   The use of small prime numbers in key generation.

    d.   All of the above.

24. What is the purpose of padding in RSA encryption?

    a.   To add extra security to the encryption process.

    b.   To prevent attackers from guessing the plaintext.

    c.   To ensure that the message is a multiple of the block size.

    d.   To ensure that the cipher text is the same length as the plaintext.

25. What is the purpose of the Chinese Remainder Theorem in RSA decryption?

    a.   To speed up the decryption process.

    b.   To add an extra layer of security to the decryption process.

    c.   To prevent attackers from guessing the private key.

    d.   None of the above.

26. Which of the following is a widely-used RSA key length?

    a.   256 bits.

    b.   512 bits.

    c.   1024 bits.

    d.   2048 bits.

27. Which of the following is not a common use case for the RSA algorithm?

    a.   Digital signatures.

    b.   Secure communications.

    c.   Password storage.

    d.   Key exchange.

28. What is the main advantage of the RSA algorithm over symmetric encryption algorithms?

    a.   It is faster.

    b.   It requires a shorter key length.

    c.   It is more secure.

    d.   It allows for secure key exchange without prior communication.

29. What is the main advantage of using asymmetric encryption over symmetric encryption?

    a.   Faster encryption and decryption.

    b.   Better key management.

    c.   Smaller key sizes.

    d.   Lower computational requirements.

30. In the Diffie-Hellman key exchange, which of the following is true?

    a.   The sender encrypts the message with the recipient's public key.

    b.   The sender encrypts the message with the recipient's private key.

    c.   The sender and recipient exchange public keys to establish a shared secret key.

    d.   The sender and recipient exchange private keys to establish a shared secret key.

31. Which of the following is not a property of a secure hash function?

    a.   Deterministic.

    b.   One-way.

    c.   Collision resistant.

    d.   Reversible.

32. Which of the following is not a common use of asymmetric encryption?

    a.   Digital signatures.

    b.   Key exchange.

    c.   Data encryption.

    d.   Password storage.

33. In which of the following scenarios would a digital signature be most helpful?

    a.   Authenticating a user's identity.

    b.   Encrypting sensitive data.

    c.   Verifying the integrity of a document.

    d.   Exchanging keys between two parties.

34. Which of the following is true about RSA encryption?

    a.   It is a symmetric encryption algorithm.

    b.   It is a stream cipher.

    c.   It uses a public key and a private key.

    d.   It is not widely used for encryption.

35. Which of the following is an example of an asymmetric encryption algorithm other than RSA?

    a.   AES (Advanced Encryption Standard).

    b.   DES (Data Encryption Standard).

    c.   Blowfish.

    d.   ECC (Elliptical Curve Cryptography).

36. Which of the following is true about the security of asymmetric encryption?

    a.   It is vulnerable to attacks if the private key is compromised.

    b.   It is vulnerable to attacks if the public key is compromised.

    c.   It is immune to attacks due to its mathematical complexity.

    d.   It is less secure than symmetric encryption.

37. Which of the following is true about the key sizes used in asymmetric encryption?

    a.   The public key is typically smaller than the private key.

    b.   The private key is typically smaller than the public key.

    c.   Both the public and private keys are typically the same size.

    d.   Key size does not affect the security of asymmetric encryption.

38. Which of the following is a disadvantage of using asymmetric encryption?

    a.   Slower encryption and decryption compared to symmetric encryption.

    b.   Poor key management.

    c.   Vulnerability to brute force attacks.

    d.   Inability to support digital signatures.

39. What is the technique used to ensure the integrity of a transmitted message?
  a. Digital Signature.
  b. Decryption Algorithm.
  c. Message Digest.
  d. Protocol.

Answer Key

1. (d) The purpose of a secure hash function is to generate a fixed-size output, often called a hash or message digest, for any given input data. It is designed to be a one-way function, meaning it is computationally infeasible to reverse the process and obtain the original input from the hash. The output is typically a fixed length, regardless of the input data size. Secure hash functions are commonly used in various applications, such as data integrity checks, digital signatures, password storage, and data verification. They are designed to have specific properties, including collision resistance, which means it is extremely unlikely for two different inputs to produce the same hash value, and pre-image resistance, which means it is computationally difficult to find an input that corresponds to a given hash value without trying all possible inputs. Hash functions are not primarily used for generating random numbers, encrypting messages, or compressing data, although they may have applications in those areas as part of a more extensive system.

2. (a) SHA-512. Among the options provided, SHA-512 (Secure Hash Algorithm 512-bit) is a widely-used secure hash function. It is an SHA-2 (Secure Hash Algorithm 2) family member, including other variants such as SHA-224, SHA-256, SHA-384, and SHA-512/224.

3. (b) The output size of SHA-256 (Secure Hash Algorithm 256-bit) is 256 bits. SHA-256 is a widely used cryptographic hash function and is a member of the SHA-2 family. It produces a fixed-size output of 256 bits for any given input data. The 256-bit output balances security and efficiency, making it suitable for various applications such as digital signatures, data integrity checks, and password hashing.

4. (a) Collision resistance. A property of a secure hash function is collision resistance. Collision resistance means that finding two different inputs that produce the same hash output is computationally infeasible. In other words, it is highly unlikely for two different messages to result in the same hash value. This property is crucial for ensuring the integrity and security of hash functions in various applications, such as digital signatures and data verification.

5. (c) Encryption is not a common use case for a secure hash function. While encryption and hash functions are both cryptographic techniques, they serve different purposes.

6. (a) A collision attack targets the input of a secure hash function. In a collision attack, the attacker tries to find two different inputs that produce the same hash value (collision). The objective is to undermine the collision resistance property of the hash function. By finding a collision, an attacker can potentially create a malicious input that produces the same hash value as a legitimate input, leading to security vulnerabilities in various applications that rely on the integrity of the hash function.

7. (b) A pre-image attack targets the output of a secure hash function. In a pre-image attack, the attacker tries to find an input that generates a specific hash output. The objective is to undermine the pre-image resistance property of the hash function. The attacker can recreate an input that produces a desired hash value by finding a pre-image. Pre-image resistance is a crucial property of secure hash functions to prevent the reverse calculation of inputs from their hash outputs.

8. (c) SHA-2 has fixed output sizes (e.g., 224, 256, 384, or 512 bits), while SHA-3 allows for a more flexible output size. It can generate hash values of different lengths based on the application's specific needs, providing greater versatility in output size.

9. (d) A property of a cryptographic hash function is that it is deterministic. Given the same input, a cryptographic hash function will always produce the same output. The output, often called the hash or message digest, is a fixed-size input data representation.

10. (a) It may produce the same output for different inputs. One potential weakness of a secure hash function is the possibility of producing the same output (collision) for different input data. While secure hash functions are designed to have collision resistance, it is theoretically possible for collisions to occur due to limitations in the hash function's design or algorithm.

11. (b) HMAC stands for Hash-based Message Authentication Code. It is a specific algorithm used for message authentication and integrity checking. HMAC combines a cryptographic hash function (such as SHA-256) with a secret key to produce a unique code that can verify the authenticity and integrity of a message.

12. (d) The purpose of HMAC (Hash-based Message Authentication Code) is to authenticate messages. HMAC is a specific algorithm that uses a cryptographic hash function (e.g., SHA-256) combined with a secret key to generate a unique code or tag for a message. This code serves as a message authentication code, allowing the recipient to verify the authenticity and integrity of the message.

13. (a) The cryptographic primitive used in HMAC (Hash-based Message Authentication Code) is a hash function. HMAC combines a hash function, such as SHA-256 or MD5, with a secret key to generate an authentication code for a message. The hash function takes the message and the secret key as inputs and produces a fixed-size hash value as the output.

14. (d) AES (Advanced Encryption Standard) is widely used in HMAC algorithms. Although HMAC is not an encryption algorithm, it is commonly used with encryption algorithms to provide message authentication and confidentiality.

15. (c) Fixed input size. In HMAC (Hash-based Message Authentication Code), the input size can vary and is not required to be fixed. The HMAC algorithm can handle messages of different lengths and adapt to the input provided.

16. (b) Side-channel attack.

17. (c) It has a fixed output size of 512 bits. HMAC-SHA-256 (Hash-based Message Authentication Code with the SHA-256 hash function) has a fixed output size of 512 bits. The underlying hash function used in HMAC, SHA-256, determines the output size. SHA-256 produces a 256-bit hash value, and HMAC-SHA-256 concatenates two such hash values to create a fixed output size of 512 bits.

18. (a) It may be vulnerable to brute-force attacks on the key. Among the options provided, a potential weakness of HMAC (Hash-based Message Authentication Code) is that it may be vulnerable to brute-force attacks on the key. A brute-force attack involves systematically trying all possible combinations of keys until the correct one is found. If the cryptographic key used in HMAC is weak or has a low entropy, it becomes more susceptible to brute-force attacks.

19. (d) All of the above.

20. (c) To encrypt and decrypt messages.

21. (d) The use of a symmetric encryption algorithm.

22. (a) The formula used to generate the public and private keys in RSA is n = pq, phi(n) = (p-1)(q-1), and ed = 1 mod phi(n).

23. (d) All options listed are potential weaknesses of the RSA algorithm.

24. (c) To ensure that the message is a multiple of the block size.

25. (a) To speed up the decryption process. The purpose of the Chinese Remainder Theorem (CRT) in RSA decryption is to speed up the decryption process, specifically when dealing with significant cipher texts. The CRT allows for more efficient computation of the decryption process by reducing the number of modular exponentiations required. In RSA decryption, the private key operation involves modular exponentiation, which can be computationally expensive, especially with large numbers. The CRT provides a method to break down the decryption operation into smaller modular exponentiations using the Chinese Remainder Theorem, enabling parallelization and reducing computational complexity.

26. (d) A widely-used RSA key length is 2048 bits. This key length offers a good balance between security and computational efficiency. As computing power increases, longer key lengths may become more common to maintain adequate security against potential attacks.

27. (c) Password storage. RSA is not commonly used for password storage. Instead, password storage often involves specialized password hashing algorithms such as bcrypt, scrypt, or Argon2. These algorithms are designed for securely hashing and storing passwords, considering factors like salting and key stretching to protect against password-related attacks, such as dictionary attacks and rainbow table attacks.

28. (d) The main advantage of the RSA algorithm over symmetric encryption algorithms is that it allows for secure key exchange without prior communication. In symmetric encryption, the sender and receiver must have the same secret key to encrypt and decrypt the data. The challenge lies in securely exchanging this key, especially if the parties have not previously communicated or shared a secret. With RSA, asymmetric encryption enables secure key exchange without prior communication. The receiver can generate a public-private key pair and share the public key openly. The sender can then encrypt the symmetric key (used for data encryption) with the receiver's public key and send the encrypted key. Only the receiver, with their corresponding private key, can decrypt the encrypted key and obtain the symmetric key for decryption. This approach provides a secure means of key exchange even in scenarios where prior communication or shared secrets are not available.

29. (b) The main advantage of using asymmetric encryption (such as RSA) over symmetric encryption is better key management. In symmetric encryption, both the sender and receiver share the same secret key, and if this key is compromised, the security of the communication is compromised. Managing and securely distributing symmetric keys to all relevant parties can be challenging, especially in large-scale scenarios. With asymmetric encryption, each entity (sender and receiver) has a unique key pair consisting of a public and private key. The public key can be freely shared with others, while the private key is kept secret. This enables more flexible key management as each entity only needs to safeguard its private key, and public keys can be openly distributed.

30. (c) The sender and recipient exchange public keys to establish a shared secret key.

31. (d) Reversibility is not a property of a secure hash function. Once data is hashed, it cannot be reversed or converted back to the original input. Hash functions are designed to be one-way, meaning retrieving the original input from the hash output should be difficult or impossible.

32. (d) Asymmetric encryption is not commonly used for password storage. Storing passwords using asymmetric encryption would be inefficient and impractical due to the computational overhead and key management complexities.

33. (c) Verifying the integrity of a document. A digital signature is most helpful in verifying the integrity of a document. It provides a means to ensure that a document has not been tampered with and that it originated from the claimed sender.

34. (c) It uses a public key and a private key.

35. (d) ECC (Elliptic Curve Cryptography) is an example of an asymmetric encryption algorithm. It is based on the mathematics of elliptic curves and provides strong security with shorter key lengths compared to other asymmetric algorithms like RSA. ECC is widely used in various applications, including secure communications, digital signatures, and key exchange protocols.

36. (a) It is vulnerable to attacks if the private key is compromised. The security of asymmetric encryption relies on keeping the private key confidential. If the private key is compromised or falls into the wrong hands, it can be used to decrypt messages and impersonate the key's owner. Therefore, it is crucial to protect the private key to maintain the security of asymmetric encryption.

37. (b) The private key is typically smaller than the public key. In asymmetric encryption algorithms such as RSA and ECC, the key pairs consist of public and private keys. The private key is typically more minor in size compared to the public key. This is because the private key only needs to contain the necessary information for decryption or signing operations, while the public key needs to include additional information to facilitate encryption or signature verification.

38. (a) Slower encryption and decryption compared to symmetric encryption. One disadvantage of using asymmetric encryption is that it tends to be slower in encryption and decryption than symmetric encryption algorithms. This is primarily because asymmetric encryption involves more complex mathematical operations and longer key lengths. Asymmetric encryption is generally used for key exchange, digital signatures, and scenarios where secure communication channels are established, while symmetric encryption is often used for bulk data encryption due to its faster processing speed.

39. (c) The technique used to ensure the integrity of a transmitted message is message digest. A message digest, also known as a hash value or checksum, is a fixed-size string of bits generated from a message or data file using a mathematical function called a hash function. The message digest is unique to the input data and can be used to verify the integrity of the data. Any change to the input data, no matter how small, will result in a different message digest. By comparing the received message digest with the original, the receiver can ensure that the message has not been altered in transit. Message digests are commonly used in secure communication protocols, digital signatures, and file verification mechanisms.

The page was left intentionally blank.

Chapter 7
Symmetric Encryption and Message Authentication

This chapter includes questions from the following topics:
- Symmetric Encryption.
- Block Cipher.
- Key Distribution.
- Data Encryption Standard (DES).
- Advanced Encryption Standard (AES).
- RC4 (Rivest Cipher 4).
- Cipher Mode of Operations.

1. **What is the main advantage of symmetric encryption over asymmetric encryption?**
   a. Symmetric encryption is faster.
   b. Symmetric encryption is more secure.
   c. Symmetric encryption is easier to use.
   d. Symmetric encryption does not require a shared secret key.

2. **Which of the following is a type of symmetric encryption algorithm?**
   a. RSA (Rivest-Shamir-Adleman).
   b. AES (Advanced Encryption Standard).
   c. Diffie-Hellman.
   d. DSA (Digital Signature Algorithm).

3. **Which of the following is a mode of operation for a block cipher?**
   a. RSA (Rivest-Shamir-Adleman).
   b. ECB (Electronic Codebook).
   c. DH (Diffie-Hellman Key Exchange).
   d. DSA (Digital Signature Algorithm).

4. **Which of the following is not a requirement for a secure block cipher?**
   a. The cipher must be resistant to brute-force attacks.
   b. The cipher must be resistant to differential and linear cryptanalysis.
   c. The cipher must be resistant to birthday attacks.
   d. The cipher must be resistant to side-channel attacks.

5. **Which of the following is a type of symmetric key distribution method?**
   a. RSA (Rivest-Shamir-Adleman).
   b. Diffie-Hellman.
   c. DSA (Digital Signature Algorithm).
   d. Key exchange protocols.

6. **Which of the following is a type of attack that can be used to break symmetric encryption?**
   a. Birthday attack.
   b. Meet-in-the-middle attack.
   c. Side-channel attack.
   d. Timing attack.

7. **Which of the following is a standard mode of operation for symmetric block ciphers?**
   a.   Electronic Code Book (ECB).
   b.   Counter (CTR)
   c.   Cipher Feedback (CFB).
   d.   Public Key Cryptography Standards (PKCS).

8. **Which of the following is a type of symmetric encryption key?**
   a.   Private Key.
   b.   Public Key.
   c.   Shared Key.
   d.   Signature Key.

9. **Which of the following is not a type of symmetric encryption algorithm?**
   a.   DES
   b.   AES
   c.   RSA
   d.   Blowfish

10. **Which of the following is an example of a stream cipher?**
    a.   DES
    b.   AES
    c.   RC4
    d.   Blowfish

11. **What is the block size of the Data Encryption Standard (DES)?**
    a.   32 bits.
    b.   48 bits.
    c.   64 bits.
    d.   128 bits.

12. **What is the key size of DES?**
    a.   32 bits.
    b.   48 bits.
    c.   56 bits.
    d.   128 bits.

13. **Which of the following modes of operation can be used with DES?**
    a.   Electronic Code Book (ECB).
    b.   Cipher Block Chaining (CBC).
    c.   Cipher Feedback (CFB).
    d.   All of the above.

14. **Which of the following is a weakness of DES?**
    a.   It has a small key size.
    b.   It is vulnerable to differential cryptanalysis.
    c.   It is vulnerable to brute-force attacks.
    d.   All of the above.

15. **What is the role of the Initial Permutation (IP) in DES?**

a. It permutes the plaintext before encryption.
b. It permutes the key before encryption.
c. It permutes the cipher text after encryption.
d. It generates the sub-keys used in encryption.

16. **Which of the following is the correct order of the steps in a round of DES encryption?**
    a. Expansion, XOR, S-box substitution, permutation.
    b. Permutation, S-box substitution, XOR, expansion.
    c. XOR, S-box substitution, expansion, permutation.
    d. S-box substitution, expansion, permutation, XOR.

17. **Which of the following is used in DES to generate the sub-keys for each round?**
    a. A linear feedback shift register.
    b. A round function.
    c. A key schedule algorithm.
    d. A substitution box.

18. **Which of the following is a variant of DES that uses a longer key?**
    a. Triple DES (3DES).
    b. Advanced Encryption Standard (AES).
    c. Blowfish.
    d. RSA.

19. **Which of the following is a type of attack that can be used to break DES?**
    a. Brute-force attack.
    b. Differential cryptanalysis.
    c. Birthday attack.
    d. Timing attack.

20. **Which of the following is not a mode of operation for DES?**
    a. Electronic Code Book (ECB).
    b. Cipher Block Chaining (CBC).
    c. Cipher Feedback (CFB).
    d. Hashed Message Authentication Code (HMAC).

21. **What is the block size of the AES algorithm?**
    a. 64 bits.
    b. 128 bits.
    c. 256 bits.
    d. 512 bits.

22. **How many rounds are used in AES-128?**
    a. 10
    b. 12
    c. 14
    d. 16

23. **Which of the following key sizes is not supported by AES?**
    a. 128 bits.

b. 192 bits.
c. 256 bits.
d. 512 bits.

24. **Which of the following modes of operation does not require an initialization vector (IV) in AES?**
    a. ECB (Electronic Codebook).
    b. CBC (Cipher Block Chaining).
    c. OFB (Output Feedback).
    d. CFB (Cipher Feedback).

25. **Which of the following attacks is AES vulnerable to?**
    a. Brute-force attack.
    b. Differential cryptanalysis.
    c. Linear cryptanalysis.
    d. All of the above.

26. **What is the maximum key size supported by AES-256?**
    a. 128 bits.
    b. 192 bits.
    c. 256 bits.
    d. 512 bits.

27. **What is the main advantage of using AES over DES?**
    a. Larger key sizes.
    b. Faster encryption speed.
    c. More efficient use of memory.
    d. Better resistance to attacks.

28. **Which of the following is not a step in the AES algorithm?**
    a. Key expansion.
    b. Substitution.
    c. Permutation.
    d. Encryption.

29. **What is the minimum key size supported by AES?**
    a. 64 bits.
    b. 128 bits.
    c. 192 bits.
    d. 256 bits.

30. **Which organization specified the AES standard?**
    a. International Organization for Standardization (ISO).
    b. National Institute of Standards and Technology (NIST).
    c. Institute of Electrical and Electronics Engineers (IEEE).
    d. Internet Engineering Task Force (IETF).

31. **What is the range of key size of RC4?**
    a. 1 bit up to 2048 bits.
    b. 1 bit up to 1024 bits.
    c. 1 bit up to 128 bits.
    d. 1 bit up to 192 bits.

32. **Which of the following is true for stream ciphers?**
    a. They encrypt data in blocks.
    b. They generate a key stream combined with plaintext to generate the cipher text.
    c. They use symmetric encryption.
    d. They are less secure than block ciphers.

33. **Which of the following is a weakness of RC4?**
    a. The key size is too small.
    b. It is vulnerable to side-channel attacks.
    c. The algorithm is too slow.
    d. It is vulnerable to a known plaintext attack.

34. **Which of the following is not an advantage of stream ciphers?**
    a. They are fast.
    b. They require less memory than block ciphers.
    c. They are resistant to known plaintext attacks.
    d. They are easy to implement.

35. **What is the block size of RC4?**
    a. 40 bits.
    b. 56 bits.
    c. 64 bits.
    d. It is a stream cipher and does not have a block size.

36. **Which of the following is not a common use of stream ciphers?**
    a. Wireless communication.
    b. Virtual private networks.
    c. Disk encryption.
    d. SSL/TLS.

37. **Which of the following is true for stream ciphers compared to block ciphers?**
    a. Stream ciphers are less secure than block ciphers.
    b. Stream ciphers are more secure than block ciphers.
    c. Stream ciphers are faster than block ciphers.
    d. Stream ciphers are slower than block ciphers.

38. **Which of the following is a key stream generator used with stream ciphers?**
    a. RC2
    b. RC4
    c. DES
    d. AES

39. **Which of the following is a disadvantage of stream ciphers?**

    a.   They are vulnerable to side-channel attacks.
    b.   They require more memory than block ciphers.
    c.   They are slower than block ciphers.
    d.   They are less secure than block ciphers.

40. Which of the following is a use case for stream ciphers?
    a.   Storing sensitive data in a database.
    b.   Secure communication between web servers and browsers.
    c.   Encrypting entire hard drives.
    d.   Encryption of real-time video and audio streams.

41. Which cypher-block mode of operation is known for its ability to provide confidentiality and integrity?
    a.   ECB
    b.   CFB
    c.   GCM
    d.   OFB

42. Which of the following block cipher modes is most susceptible to a data integrity attack?
    a.   ECB
    b.   CBC
    c.   CTR
    d.   OFB

43. Which cypher-block mode of operation is known for its parallelizability?
    a.   ECB
    b.   CBC
    c.   CTR
    d.   OFB

44. Which block cipher mode of operation is most commonly used for disk encryption?
    a.   ECB
    b.   CBC
    c.   CTR
    d.   XTS

45. Which block cipher mode of operation requires the use of an initialization vector (IV)?
    a.   ECB
   b.   CBC
    c.   CTR
    d.   OFB

46. Which cypher-block mode of operation uses feedback to ensure the key stream is generated randomly?
    a.   ECB
    b.   CFB
    c.   GCM
    d.   OFB

47. Which block cipher mode of operation is susceptible to a replay attack?
    a. ECB
    b. CFB
    c. GCM
    d. CTR

48. Which block cipher mode of operation is known for its ability to provide confidentiality and parallel processing?
    a. ECB
    b. CFB
    c. CTR
    d. OFB

49. Which block cipher mode of operation uses a counter value for each block?
    a. ECB
    b. CBC
    c. CTR
    d. OFB

50. Where is the most common location for symmetric encryption devices?
    a. Network gateways.
    b. End-user devices.
    c. Cloud servers.
    d. Mainframe computers.

51. What is the main advantage of using symmetric encryption devices on end-user devices?
    a. Low cost.
    b. High performance.
    c. Easy management.
    d. Strong security.

52. Which of the following drawbacks to using symmetric encryption devices on network gateways?
    a. High cost.
    b. Low performance.
    c. Limited scalability.
    d. Difficult maintenance.

53. In what type of device is it common to find hardware-accelerated symmetric encryption capabilities?
    a. Servers
    b. Routers
    c. Smartphones
    d. Tablets

54. Which location for symmetric encryption devices is preferred in a distributed environment?
    a. Network gateways.
    b. End-user devices.
    c. Cloud servers.
    d. Mainframe computers.

55. **In a cloud environment, where should symmetric encryption devices be located?**
    a. In the cloud provider's infrastructure.
    b. On the customer's premises.
    c. In a hybrid configuration.
    d. It depends on the use case.

56. **Which of the following is a benefit of using symmetric encryption devices located in a mainframe environment?**
    a. High performance.
    b. Low cost.
    c. Ease of maintenance.
    d. High scalability.

57. **What type of device is typically used to provide hardware-based symmetric encryption capabilities for storage devices?**
    a. Network-attached storage (NAS) devices.
    b. Storage area network (SAN) devices.
    c. Tape drives.
    d. Solid-state drives (SSDs).

58. **Which of the following is a limitation of using symmetric encryption devices located on smartphones?**
    a. Low performance.
    b. Limited key size.
    c. Limited storage capacity.
    d. High cost.

59. **Which location for symmetric encryption devices is preferred for large-scale data centres?**
    a. Network gateways.
    b. End-user devices.
    c. Cloud servers.
    d. Mainframe computers.

60. **Which of the following is a common approach for key distribution in symmetric key encryption?**
    a. Using public-key encryption.
    b. Exchanging keys in person.
    c. Using digital signatures.
    d. Guessing the key.

61. **Which of the following is not a requirement for secure key distribution?**
    a. Confidentiality.
    b. Authentication.
    c. Integrity.
    d. Availability.

62. **Which protocols are commonly used for secure key distribution over an insecure network? (Select all that apply)**
    a. SSL (Secure Socket Layer).
    b. SSH (Secure Shell).

    c.   IPsec

    d.   Kerberos.

63. Which of the following is an example of a key distribution centre?

    a.   Certificate authority.

    b.   Firewall.

    c.   VPN.

    d.   Kerberos server.

64. Which of the following is not a disadvantage of key distribution using symmetric key encryption?

    a.   Key distribution is difficult to scale to large networks.

    b.   There is a risk of key compromise during transmission.

    c.   Each pair of users' needs a unique key.

    d.   Symmetric key encryption is computationally expensive.

65. Which of the following is a technique used to distribute keys hierarchically?

    a.   Diffie-Hellman key exchange.

    b.   Key wrapping.

    c.   Key derivation.

    d.   Key escrow.

66. Which of the following is an advantage of key distribution using public-key encryption?

    a.   The need for secure key distribution is eliminated.

    b.   It is faster than symmetric key encryption.

    c.   It is easier to implement in hardware.

    d.   It is less vulnerable to brute force attacks.

67. Which of the following is a disadvantage of key distribution using public-key encryption?

    a.   It requires a large amount of computation.

    b.   It is vulnerable to man-in-the-middle attacks.

    c.   It is not suitable for real-time applications.

    d.   It is not easy to implement in software.

68. Which of the following is a technique used to distribute keys securely over an unsecured channel?

    a.   Perfect forward secrecy.

    b.   Key exchange protocol.

    c.   Public-key cryptography.

    d.   Quantum cryptography.

69. Which technique is used to derive multiple keys from a shared secret key?

    a.   Key derivation function.

    b.   Key wrapping.

    c.   Key escrow.

    d.   Key splitting.

Answer Key

1. (a) Symmetric encryption is faster. The main advantage of symmetric encryption over asymmetric encryption is that it is faster. In symmetric encryption, the same key is used for encryption and decryption, which means the encryption and decryption processes are computationally efficient. On the other hand, asymmetric encryption, also known as public-key encryption, involves using a pair of keys: a public key for encryption and a private key for decryption. Asymmetric encryption algorithms are generally slower than symmetric encryption algorithms due to the mathematical operations' complexity.

2. (b) AES (Advanced Encryption Standard). Among the options provided, AES (Advanced Encryption Standard) is a symmetric encryption algorithm. AES is widely used and a robust encryption algorithm for securing sensitive data. It uses a symmetric key for both encryption and decryption processes. RSA is an example of an asymmetric encryption algorithm for tasks such as key exchange and digital signatures. Diffie-Hellman is a key exchange algorithm, and DSA (Digital Signature Algorithm) is used for creating digital signatures.

3. (b) ECB (Electronic Codebook). Among the options provided, ECB (Electronic Codebook) is a mode of operation for a block cipher. ECB is the simplest operation mode, where each plaintext block is encrypted independently using the same encryption key. However, ECB has some security limitations, as identical plaintext blocks will result in identical cipher text blocks, which can reveal patterns and information about the plaintext.

4. (c) The cipher must be resistant to birthday attacks. Among the options provided, the requirement for a secure block cipher is not specifically to be resistant to birthday attacks. Birthday attacks are a specific type of cryptographic attack that exploits the birthday paradox to find collisions in hash functions. Block ciphers are not typically evaluated or designed to resist birthday attacks.

5. (b) Diffie-Hellman. Diffie-Hellman is a type of symmetric key distribution method among the options provided. Diffie-Hellman is a key exchange protocol that allows two parties to establish a shared secret key over an insecure communication channel. It is based on mathematical principles and enables secure key exchange without pre-shared keys.

6. (b) Meet-in-the-middle attack. Among the options provided, a meet-in-the-middle attack is a type of attack that can be used to break symmetric encryption. In a meet-in-the-middle attack, the attacker tries to find a match between the encryption of plaintext using one key and the decryption of a cipher text using another key. The attacker can search for matches and determine the correct keys by storing intermediate results. This attack is feasible when the encryption algorithm and key size allow for a reasonable number of operations.

7. (b) Counter (CTR). Among the options provided, Counter (CTR) is a standard mode of operation for symmetric block ciphers. CTR mode uses a counter to generate a stream of unique values, which are then encrypted using the block cipher and XORed with the plaintext to produce the cipher text. CTR mode allows for parallel encryption and decryption and is commonly used in applications such as disk encryption and VPNs.

8. (c) Shared Key. Among the options provided, a shared key is a type of symmetric encryption key. The same key is used for encryption and decryption processes in symmetric encryption. This key, also known as a shared or secret key, is kept confidential and securely shared between the parties involved in the communication. It is used to encrypt the plaintext into cipher text and then decrypt the cipher text back into plaintext.

9. (c) RSA. Among the options provided, RSA is not a symmetric encryption algorithm. RSA is an asymmetric encryption algorithm that uses public and private keys for encryption and decryption. It is widely used for key exchange, digital signatures, and secure communication tasks.

10. (c) Among the options provided, RC4 is an example of a stream cipher. RC4 is a widely used symmetric stream cipher that generates a key stream based on a secret key. The key stream is combined with the plaintext using the XOR operation to produce the cipher text. RC4 is known for its simplicity and efficiency, although it has been found to have security vulnerabilities and is no longer recommended for use in new systems.

11. (c) The Data Encryption Standard (DES) block size is 64 bits. DES operates on blocks of 64 bits at a time and uses a 56-bit key for encryption and decryption. Each 64-bit plaintext block is divided into two 32-bit halves during the encryption process. DES has been widely used in the past but is now considered insecure for many applications due to its small key size and vulnerability to brute-force attacks.

12. (c) The key size of the Data Encryption Standard (DES) is 56 bits. DES uses a 56-bit key for encryption and decryption. However, due to the inclusion of parity bits, the effective key size is considered to be 56 bits rather than the full 64 bits. DES's small key size is one reason why it is no longer considered secure for many applications, as it is vulnerable to brute-force attacks with modern computing resources.

13. (d) All listed operation modes can be used with DES. DES is a block cipher, and various modes of operation can be employed to provide different properties and characteristics for encryption. These modes include Electronic Code Book (ECB), Cipher Block Chaining (CBC), and Cipher Feedback (CFB), among others.

14. (d) All of the listed options are weaknesses of DES. DES has a small key size (56 bits), now considered insufficient for robust security. It is vulnerable to differential cryptanalysis, an attack that exploits patterns in the plaintext and cipher text pairs. DES is also vulnerable to brute-force attacks, where an attacker tries all possible keys to decrypt the cipher text.

15. (a) It permutes the plaintext before encryption. The role of the Initial Permutation (IP) in DES is to permute the plaintext before encryption. It reorders the bits of the input plaintext according to a specific permutation rule. This permutation aims to introduce diffusion and spread the input bits across multiple rounds of encryption, ensuring that any small changes in the input plaintext result in significant changes in the output cipher text.

16. (c) XOR, S-box substitution, expansion, permutation. The correct order of steps in a round of DES encryption is: 1) XOR: The round key is XORed with a portion of the input data. 2) S-box substitution: The XOR result is passed through the S-boxes, which perform non-linear substitutions on specific bit patterns. 3) Expansion: The S-box output is expanded to match the next round's key size. 4) Permutation: A fixed permutation (P-box) is applied to the output of the expansion step. This order of steps is repeated for multiple rounds in DES encryption.

17. (c) A key schedule algorithm. In DES, the sub-keys for each round are generated using a key schedule algorithm. The key schedule algorithm takes the initial 56-bit key and generates a set of 16 sub-keys, each 48 bits in length, which are used in the respective rounds of encryption and decryption. The key schedule algorithm produces the sub-keys with various permutations, shifts, and transformations.

18. (a) Triple DES (3DES) is a variant of DES that uses a longer key. It applies the DES algorithm multiple times to provide enhanced security. In 3DES, the key length can be either 112 bits or 168 bits, depending on the specific variant used. By using multiple rounds of encryption with different keys, 3DES increases the effective key size and provides a higher security level than regular DES.

19. (a) Among the options provided, a brute-force attack is a type of attack that can be used to break DES. A brute-force attack involves trying all possible keys until the correct one is found. Due to DES's relatively small key size (56 bits), a brute-force attack is feasible using modern computational power and resources. Brute-force attacks on DES involve systematically trying all possible key combinations, which can be time-consuming but ultimately effective in breaking the encryption.

20. (d) Among the options provided, the Hashed Message Authentication Code (HMAC) is not a mode of operation for DES. HMAC is a specific construction for message authentication codes that combines a cryptographic hash function with a secret key. It is commonly used for verifying the integrity and authenticity of a message.

21. (b) The block size of the AES (Advanced Encryption Standard) algorithm is 128 bits. AES operates on blocks of 128 bits at a time, regardless of the chosen key size. AES supports key sizes of 128, 192, and 256 bits, but the block size remains constant at 128 bits for all key sizes.

22. (a) In AES-128, 10 rounds are used. Each round consists of various operations, including substitution, permutation, and data mixing. The key size determines the number of rounds, and for AES-128, ten rounds are applied to complete the encryption or decryption process.

23. (d) AES does not support the key size of 512 bits. AES supports key sizes of 128, 192, and 256 bits. These key sizes are defined explicitly for AES and provide different levels of security. The AES algorithm operates with fixed block sizes of 128 bits, but the key size determines the number of rounds used during encryption and decryption.

24. (a) ECB (Electronic Codebook). Among the options provided, the ECB (Electronic Codebook) mode does not require an initialization vector (IV) in AES. In ECB mode, each plaintext block is encrypted independently using the same encryption key. Since there is no dependence or chaining between blocks, an IV is unnecessary in this mode.

25. (d) AES (Advanced Encryption Standard) is not inherently vulnerable to any of the mentioned attacks. It has been extensively studied and is considered secure against various cryptographic attacks when implemented correctly with sufficient key size and proper usage.

26. (c) The maximum key size supported by AES-256 is 256 bits. AES (Advanced Encryption Standard) supports key sizes of 128, 192, and 256 bits. AES-256, specifically, uses a 256-bit key for encryption and decryption. The larger key size provides an increased level of security compared to AES-128 and AES-192.

27. (d) The main advantage of using AES (Advanced Encryption Standard) over DES (Data Encryption Standard) is its better resistance to attacks. AES was designed to address the vulnerabilities and weaknesses present in DES. It employs a larger block size (128 bits) and supports key sizes of 128, 192, and 256 bits, offering a much stronger cryptographic foundation compared to DES.

28. (d) Encryption is not a specific step in the AES (Advanced Encryption Standard) algorithm. Instead, it is the outcome or purpose of applying the AES algorithm. The AES algorithm is responsible for transforming the plaintext into cipher text, but the individual steps of the algorithm do not directly correspond to "encryption" as a distinct step.

29. (b) The minimum key size AES (Advanced Encryption Standard) supports 128 bits. AES is designed to operate with key sizes of 128, 192, and 256 bits. While AES-128 is the minimum supported key size, it still provides a high level of security when implemented correctly. AES-192 and AES-256 offer even larger key sizes for those seeking increased security or compliance with specific standards.

30. (b) The AES (Advanced Encryption Standard) standard was specified by the NIST, a U.S. federal agency responsible for developing and promoting standards in various fields, including cryptography. In 2001, NIST selected the Rijndael algorithm as the AES encryption standard after an open competition involving numerous encryption algorithms. AES has since become a widely adopted global encryption standard for secure communication and data protection.

31. (a) The key size of RC4 is typically variable. It can range from 1 bit up to 2048 bits. However, the most common and widely used key size for RC4 is 128 bits. This key size provides a higher security level than smaller key sizes. It is worth noting that RC4 has been found to have security vulnerabilities, and its usage is generally discouraged in modern cryptographic applications.

32. (b) Among the options provided, option b is true for stream ciphers. Stream ciphers generate a key stream, a sequence of random or pseudo-random bits, and combine it with the plaintext using a bitwise XOR operation to produce the cipher text. The key stream is generated based on a key and, in some cases, an initialization vector (IV).

33. (b) Among the options provided, a weakness of RC4 is that it is vulnerable to side-channel attacks. Side-channel attacks exploit information leaked through physical implementation characteristics of the cryptographic algorithm, such as power consumption, timing, electromagnetic emissions, or even sound. These attacks can reveal secret information, including the key used in RC4.

34. (c) Among the options provided, the statement that stream ciphers are resistant to known plaintext attacks is not an advantage of stream ciphers. Known plaintext attacks are a type of cryptographic attack where an adversary has access to both the cipher text and the corresponding plaintext for certain parts of the data. Stream ciphers, like block ciphers, can be vulnerable to known plaintext attacks if the encryption algorithm or its implementation is weak.

35. (d) RC4 is a stream cipher with no fixed block size. Stream ciphers encrypt data on a bit-by-bit or byte-by-byte basis without dividing the data into fixed blocks. The key stream generated by RC4 is combined with the plaintext or cipher text using a bitwise XOR operation, allowing for continuous encryption or decryption of data streams. Therefore, RC4 does not have a specific block size as block ciphers do.

36. (c) Among the options, disk encryption is not commonly used for stream ciphers. Stream ciphers are generally not used for disk encryption because disk encryption typically requires the encryption and decryption of data in fixed-size blocks. On the other hand, block cyphers are more commonly used for disk encryption to ensure data integrity and confidentiality.

37. (c) Among the options provided, the statement that streams ciphers are generally faster than block ciphers is true. Stream ciphers operate on data streams on a bit-by-bit or byte-by-byte basis, allowing for

efficient encryption or decryption. They have a more straightforward structure and require fewer computational operations, contributing to faster processing speed.

38. (b) Among the options, RC4 is a well-known and widely used key stream generator with stream ciphers. RC4 is a symmetric stream cipher that generates a pseudo-random key stream based on a secret key. This key stream is combined with the plaintext or cipher text using a bitwise XOR operation to produce the encrypted or decrypted data.

39. (a) Among the options provided, a disadvantage of stream ciphers is that they can be vulnerable to side-channel attacks. Side-channel attacks exploit information leaked through physical implementation characteristics of the cryptographic algorithm, such as power consumption, timing, electromagnetic emissions, or even sound. These attacks can reveal secret information, including the key in stream ciphers.

40. (d) Among the options provided, a common use case for stream ciphers is real-time video and audio stream encryption. Stream ciphers are well-suited for scenarios where data is continuously transmitted or processed in real-time, such as streaming media. Stream ciphers can encrypt the data stream on a bit-by-bit or byte-by-byte basis, ensuring the confidentiality and integrity of the transmitted video or audio content.

41. (c) GCM (Galois/Counter Mode) is known for its ability to provide confidentiality and integrity. GCM is a mode of operation for block ciphers that combines the counter mode (CTR) with additional authentication and integrity checks techniques. It uses a unique nonce and counter for each data block, providing confidentiality through encryption and integrity through an authentication tag.

42. (b) The Electronic Codebook (ECB) mode is the most susceptible to a data integrity attack among the options. ECB mode operates by dividing the plaintext into fixed-size blocks and encrypting each block independently using the same encryption key. Each plaintext block is encrypted into a corresponding cipher text block. However, the problem with ECB mode is that if the same plaintext block occurs multiple times in the message, it will produce the same cipher text block each time. This characteristic makes it easier for an attacker to modify or tamper with the cipher text by replacing one cipher text block with another without detection. Since the encryption and decryption process is block-wise and independent, any changes to the cipher text blocks will not affect the integrity of the overall message.

43. (c) The Counter (CTR) mode of operation is known for its parallelizability among the given options. CTR mode works by encrypting a counter value with a block cipher, then XORing the resulting cipher text with the plaintext to produce the final cipher text. The counter value is incremented for each block of data being encrypted. The parallelizability of CTR mode stems from the fact that each data block can be encrypted independently. Since the encryption of each block does not depend on the previous block, multiple blocks can be encrypted concurrently or in parallel. This property allows for efficient and parallel processing, which can be advantageous in scenarios where encryption and decryption must be performed on a large amount of data.

44. (d) The block cipher operation most commonly used for disk encryption is XTS (XEX-based Tweaked Codebook Mode with Cipher-Text Stealing). XTS mode is specifically designed for disk encryption and protects confidentiality and integrity. It is a specialized mode that addresses the unique requirements of disk storage, such as the ability to perform random access operations on the encrypted data.

45. (b) CBC mode operates by XORing each plaintext block with the previous cipher text block before encryption. CBC mode requires an initialization vector (IV) to ensure uniqueness in the encryption

process. The IV is an input parameter combined with the first plaintext block before encryption. The IV is typically a random value and needs to be unique for each encryption operation.

46. (d) The block cipher mode of operation that uses feedback to ensure the key stream is generated randomly is OFB (Output Feedback) mode. In OFB mode, the encryption process generates a key stream independently of the plaintext. The key stream is generated by encrypting an initialization vector (IV) with the encryption key. This key stream is then XORed with plaintext to produce the cipher text. The key stream generation does not depend on the plaintext or the previous cipher text blocks.

47. (a) Among the given options, the block cipher operation mode susceptible to a replay attack is ECB (Electronic Codebook) mode.

48. (c) CTR mode encrypts a counter value with the encryption key to generate a key stream. This key stream is then XORed with plaintext to produce the cipher text. The key feature of CTR mode is that each plaintext block is encrypted independently, allowing for parallel processing.

49. (c) CTR mode encrypts a counter value with the encryption key to generate a key stream. The counter value is incremented for each block of data being encrypted. The generated key stream is XORed with plaintext to produce the corresponding cipher text.

50. (b) End-user devices, such as computers, smartphones, tablets, and other devices used by individuals or organizations, are where symmetric encryption is commonly implemented. These devices perform encryption and decryption operations to secure data at the user level.

51. (b) The main advantage of using symmetric encryption devices on end-user devices is high performance.

52. (c) Network gateways connect different networks and are responsible for routing and filtering network traffic. While symmetric encryption can be implemented on network gateways for securing data in transit, it may introduce limitations in terms of scalability.

53. (a) Servers, especially those used in enterprise or data centre environments, often have specialized hardware components that provide hardware acceleration for symmetric encryption operations. These hardware accelerators, such as cryptographic coprocessors or dedicated cryptographic modules, are designed to offload the computational burden of encryption and decryption from the server's main CPU.

54. (c) Cloud servers. In a distributed environment, where computing resources and services are distributed across multiple locations or data centres, cloud servers offer several advantages for symmetric encryption.

55. (d) In a cloud environment, the location of symmetric encryption devices depends on the use case, so the correct answer is that it depends on the use case.

56. (a) High performance. Mainframe computers are known for their robust computing power and high-performance capabilities. They often have specialized hardware components and optimized architectures that allow for efficient execution of computationally intensive tasks, such as symmetric encryption and decryption.

57. (d) The type of device typically used to provide hardware-based symmetric encryption capabilities for storage devices is Solid-state drives (SSDs). Solid-state drives, also known as SSDs, are storage devices that use flash memory to store data. Many modern SSDs include hardware-based encryption capabilities

built into the drive itself. These hardware encryption features allow for the encryption and decryption of data directly on the drive, providing a transparent and efficient encryption solution for the stored data.

58. (b) A limitation of using symmetric encryption devices located on smartphones is Limited key size. Although powerful and versatile, smartphones may have limitations regarding the maximum key size they can support for symmetric encryption algorithms. Symmetric encryption algorithms typically operate with fixed-length keys, and certain smartphones may have limitations on the maximum key size they can handle.

59. (c) In large-scale data centres, the preferred location for symmetric encryption devices is Cloud servers. Large-scale data centres often utilize cloud server infrastructure to host and manage their computing resources.

60. (b) When using symmetric key encryption, the key used for encryption and decryption must be securely shared between the communicating parties. Exchanging keys in person is a widely used method to achieve secure key distribution in scenarios where it is feasible. Exchanging keys in person involves physically meeting and sharing the key securely, ensuring that only the intended recipients can access the key. This approach minimizes the risk of interception or unauthorized access to the key during transmission over insecure channels.

61. (d) The requirement for secure key distribution not listed among the given options is "Availability."

62. (a,c) The protocols commonly used for secure key distribution over an insecure network are SSL/TLS (Secure Socket Layer/Transport Layer Security) and IPsec (Internet Protocol Security).

63. (d) An example of a key distribution center (KDC) is a Kerberos server.

64. (d) Among the given options, the disadvantage of key distribution using symmetric key encryption that is not valid is that Symmetric key encryption is computationally expensive.

65. (d) Key Escrow is a method in which keys are distributed and stored in a hierarchical structure. In this approach, keys are typically divided into different levels, with higher-level keys providing access to lower-level keys. This hierarchical distribution allows efficient management and control of keys in large systems or organizations.

66. (a) Among the given options, an advantage of key distribution using public-key encryption is that the need for secure key distribution is eliminated. With public-key encryption, each participant has a pair of keys consisting of a public key and a private key. The public key can be freely distributed, while the private key is kept secret. This eliminates the need for a secure channel to distribute the encryption key since anyone can access the public key without compromising the system's security.

67. (a) Among the options provided, a disadvantage of key distribution using public-key encryption is that it requires a large amount of computation. Public-key encryption algorithms typically involve more complex mathematical operations than symmetric encryption algorithms. As a result, the computational overhead for key distribution using public-key encryption can be higher, especially for large-scale deployments or situations requiring frequent key exchanges.

68. (b) A Key Exchange Protocol distributes keys securely over an unsecured channel. Key Exchange Protocols are cryptographic protocols that allow two or more parties to securely establish a shared secret key over an unsecured communication channel. These protocols ensure that even if an adversary eavesdrops on the communication or intercepts the messages, they cannot obtain the shared secret key.

69. (a) The technique used to derive multiple keys from a shared secret key is a Key Derivation Function (KDF). A Key Derivation Function takes an input, usually a shared secret key or a master key, and applies a deterministic process to derive one or more derived keys. These derived keys can be used for different purposes, such as encryption, authentication, or key diversification.

The page was left intentionally blank.

Chapter 8
Key Distribution

This chapter includes questions from the following topics:
- Key Distribution.
- Symmetric Encryption.
- Asymmetric Encryption.
- Diffie-Hellman Key Exchange.
- Key Distribution Centre (KDC).
- Kerberos.
- X.509 Certificate.
- Public Key Infrastructure.

---

1. **What is key distribution in cryptography?**
   a. The process of generating encryption keys.
   b. The process of securely delivering encryption keys to authorized parties.
   c. The process of decrypting cipher text.
   d. The process of exchanging public keys.

2. **Which key distribution method requires a trusted third party?**
   a. Symmetric key distribution.
   b. Asymmetric key distribution.
   c. Diffie-Hellman key exchange.
   d. Key escrow.

3. **Which key distribution method uses a pair of mathematically related keys?**
   a. Symmetric key distribution.
   b. Asymmetric key distribution.
   c. Diffie-Hellman key exchange.
   d. Key escrow.

4. **How many keys are shared between the sender and receiver in a symmetric key distribution scheme?**
   a. One.
   b. Two.
   c. Three.
   d. It varies depending on the encryption algorithm.

5. **Which key distribution method is vulnerable to the man-in-the-middle attack?**
   a. Symmetric key distribution.
   b. Asymmetric key distribution.
   c. Diffie-Hellman key exchange.
   d. Key escrow.

6. **Which key distribution method provides forward secrecy?**
   a. Symmetric key distribution.
   b. Asymmetric key distribution.

    c. Diffie-Hellman key exchange.

    d. Key escrow.

7. **Which key distribution method is computationally more expensive?**

    a. Symmetric key distribution.

    b. Asymmetric key distribution.

    c. Diffie-Hellman key exchange.

    d. Key escrow.

8. **Which key distribution method is commonly used in SSL/TLS protocols?**

    a. Symmetric key distribution.

    b. Asymmetric key distribution.

    c. Diffie-Hellman key exchange.

    d. Key escrow.

9. **Which key distribution method uses a public-private key pair?**

    a. Symmetric key distribution.

    b. Asymmetric key distribution.

    c. Diffie-Hellman key exchange.

    d. Key escrow.

10. **Which key distribution method requires secure initial key exchange?**

    a. Symmetric key distribution.

    b. Asymmetric key distribution.

    c. Diffie-Hellman key exchange.

    d. Key escrow.

11. **What is symmetric key distribution in cryptography?**

    a. The process of generating symmetric encryption keys.

    b. The process of securely delivering symmetric encryption keys to authorized parties.

    c. The process of the decrypting cipher text using symmetric encryption.

    d. The process of exchanging public keys in a symmetric encryption scheme.

12. **How many keys are shared between the sender and receiver in symmetric key distribution?**

    a. One.

    b. Two.

    c. Three.

    d. It varies depending on the encryption algorithm.

13. **Which symmetric encryption algorithm is widely used for secure symmetric key distribution?**

    a. DES (Data Encryption Standard).

    b. RSA (Rivest-Shamir-Adleman).

    c. AES (Advanced Encryption Standard).

    d. Diffie-Hellman.

14. **Which key distribution method involves physically exchanging encryption keys?**

    a. Key exchange over a secure channel.

    b. Key exchange via email.

    c. Key exchange using public-key cryptography.

    d. Key exchange using key escrow.

15. **Which key distribution method is vulnerable to interception if not adequately secured during transmission?**
    a. Key exchange over a secure channel.
    b. Key exchange via email.
    c. Key exchange using public-key cryptography.
    d. Key exchange using key escrow.

16. **Which technique is commonly used to distribute symmetric encryption keys securely?**
    a. Password-based key derivation.
    b. Key wrapping.
    c. Key agreement protocols.
    d. Key escrow.

17. **Which symmetric encryption mode is suitable for distributing large amounts of data securely?**
    a. Electronic Codebook (ECB) mode.
    b. Cipher Block Chaining (CBC) mode.
    c. Counter (CTR) mode.
    d. Output Feedback (OFB) mode.

18. **Which technique uses a trusted third party to distribute symmetric encryption keys securely?**
    a. Key exchange over a secure channel.
    b. Key exchange via email.
    c. Key escrow.
    d. Key agreement protocols.

19. **Which key distribution method is unsuitable for distributing symmetric encryption keys over an untrusted network?**
    a. Key exchange over a secure channel.
    b. Key exchange via email.
    c. Key exchange using public-key cryptography.
    d. Key wrapping.

20. **Which key distribution method requires the sender and receiver to share a standard secret key in advance?**
    a. Key exchange over a secure channel.
    b. Key exchange via email.
    c. Key exchange using public-key cryptography.
    d. Key agreement protocols.

21. **What is Kerberos?**
    a. A symmetric encryption algorithm.
    b. A network authentication protocol.
    c. A digital signature scheme.
    d. A key distribution centre.

22. **Kerberos provides a solution for which security problem?**
    a. Confidentiality.

    b.   Integrity.

    c.   Authentication.

    d.   Availability.

23. What is the primary function of the Key Distribution Centre (KDC) in Kerberos?

    a.   Generate encryption keys.

    b.   Authenticate users and issue tickets.

    c.   Decrypt cipher text.

    d.   Establish secure network connections.

24. Which of the following entities is not involved in the Kerberos protocol?

    a.   Client.

    b.   Server.

    c.   Ticket Granting Server (TGS).

    d.   Certificate Authority (CA).

25. Which encryption algorithm is commonly used in Kerberos for encrypting authentication messages?

    a.   DES (Data Encryption Standard).

    b.   RSA (Rivest-Shamir-Adleman).

    c.   AES (Advanced Encryption Standard).

    d.   Diffie-Hellman.

26. What is a ticket in the context of Kerberos?

    a.   A digital certificate.

    b.   A secret encryption key.

    c.   A time-limited authentication token.

    d.   A hash function output.

27. In Kerberos, what is the purpose of the TGT (Ticket Granting Ticket)?

    a.   To request access to a specific service.

    b.   To authenticate the client to the KDC.

    c.   To request a session key for communication with the server.

    d.   To verify the integrity of the authentication messages.

28. Which protocol is used by clients to request a TGT from the KDC in Kerberos?

    a.   LDAP (Lightweight Directory Access Protocol).

    b.   TCP/IP (Transmission Control Protocol/Internet Protocol).

    c.   HTTP (Hypertext Transfer Protocol).

    d.   AS (Authentication Service).

29. Which component in Kerberos is responsible for verifying the server's authenticity during the ticket-granting process?

    a.   Client.

    b.   KDC.

    c.   TGS.

    d.   Certificate Authority (CA).

30. Which key is shared between the client and the TGS in Kerberos?

    a.   Session key.

    b.   Master key.

    c.   Ticket-granting key.

    d.   Service key.

31. What is the key distribution in asymmetric encryption?
    a.   The process of generating encryption keys.
    b.   The process of securely delivering encryption keys to authorized parties.
    c.   The process of decrypting cipher text.
    d.   The process of exchanging public keys.

32. Which key distribution method uses a pair of mathematically related keys?
    a.   Symmetric key distribution.
    b.   Asymmetric key distribution.
    c.   Diffie-Hellman key exchange.
    d.   Key escrow.

33. Which key distribution method requires a trusted third party?
    a.   Symmetric key distribution.
    b.   Asymmetric key distribution.
    c.   Diffie-Hellman key exchange.
    d.   Key escrow.

34. Which key distribution method uses a public-private key pair?
    a.   Symmetric key distribution.
    b.   Asymmetric key distribution.
    c.   Diffie-Hellman key exchange.
    d.   Key escrow.

35. In asymmetric key distribution, which key is used for encryption?
    a.   Public key.
    b.   Private Key.
    c.   Session key.
    d.   Master key.

36. In asymmetric key distribution, which key is used for decryption?
    a.   Public key.
    b.   Private Key.
    c.   Session key.
    d.   Master key.

37. Which asymmetric encryption algorithm is commonly used for secure key distribution?
    a.   DES (Data Encryption Standard).
    b.   RSA (Rivest-Shamir-Adleman).
    c.   AES (Advanced Encryption Standard).
    d.   Diffie-Hellman.

38. **Which key distribution method provides forward secrecy?**
    a. Symmetric key distribution.
    b. Asymmetric key distribution.
    c. Diffie-Hellman key exchange.
    d. Key escrow.

39. **Which key distribution method is computationally more expensive?**
    a. Symmetric key distribution.
    b. Asymmetric key distribution.
    c. Diffie-Hellman key exchange.
    d. Key escrow.

40. **Which key distribution method is commonly used in digital signatures and SSL/TLS protocols?**
    a. Symmetric key distribution.
    b. Asymmetric key distribution.
    c. Diffie-Hellman key exchange.
    d. Key escrow.

41. **What is an X.509 certificate?**
    a. A digital signature algorithm.
    b. A network encryption protocol.
    c. A format for public key certificates.
    d. A secure hash function.

42. **Which cryptographic standard is commonly used to create X.509 certificates?**
    a. RSA (Rivest-Shamir-Adleman).
    b. DES (Data Encryption Standard).
    c. AES (Advanced Encryption Standard).
    d. SHA (Secure Hash Algorithm).

43. **What information does an X.509 certificate typically contain?**
    a. The public key, private key, and encryption algorithm.
    b. The digital signature, symmetric key, and expiration date.
    c. Subject's identity, public key, and issuer's signature.
    d. IP address, MAC address, and domain name.

44. **Which component of an X.509 certificate verifies the integrity of the certificate?**
    a. Public key.
    b. Private Key.
    c. Digital signature.
    d. Encryption algorithm.

45. **What is the purpose of the issuer in an X.509 certificate?**
    a. To verify the identity of the subject.
    b. To issue the certificate and sign it with the issuer's private key.
    c. To encrypt the certificate using the issuer's public key.
    d. To revoke the certificate if necessary.

46. Which file format is commonly used to store X.509 certificates?
   a. PEM (Privacy-Enhanced Mail).
   b. XML (eXtensible Markup Language).
   c. JSON (JavaScript Object Notation).
   d. TXT (Plain Text).

47. Which protocol is commonly used for distributing and managing X.509 certificates?
   a. SSL (Secure Sockets Layer).
   b. SSH (Secure Shell).
   c. LDAP (Lightweight Directory Access Protocol).
   d. HTTP (Hypertext Transfer Protocol).

48. How is the validity period of an X.509 certificate specified?
   a. By the subject's private key.
   b. By the issuer's public key.
   c. The certificate's digital signature.
   d. By the certificate's "notBefore" and "notAfter" fields.

49. Which X.509 certificate extension provides information about the certificate's intended usage?
   a. Key Usage extension.
   b. Subject Alternative Name extension.
   c. Basic Constraints extension.
   d. Authority Key Identifier extension.

50. Which entity is responsible for validating the trustworthiness of an X.509 certificate?
   a. Certificate Authority (CA).
   b. Subject.
   c. Issuer.
   d. Public key infrastructure (PKI).

51. What is Public Key Infrastructure (PKI)?
   a. A network security protocol.
   b. A cryptographic algorithm for key exchange.
   c. A framework for managing digital certificates and encryption keys.
   d. A protocol for secure file transfer.

52. What is the primary purpose of a Certificate Authority (CA) in a PKI?
   a. To issue digital certificates.
   b. To encrypt data transmissions.
   c. To manage public and private keys.
   d. To authenticate users.

53. Which component in a PKI is responsible for verifying the identity of certificate holders?
   a. Certificate Revocation List (CRL).
   b. Registration Authority (RA).
   c. Certification Practice Statement (CPS).
   d. Certificate Signing Request (CSR).

54. What is the role of a Registration Authority (RA) in a PKI?

a. To issue digital certificates.
b. To revoke digital certificates.
c. To validate and authenticate certificate requests.
d. To manage public and private keys.

55. Which cryptographic algorithm is commonly used for generating and managing digital certificates in a PKI?
a. RSA (Rivest-Shamir-Adleman).
b. AES (Advanced Encryption Standard).
c. SHA (Secure Hash Algorithm).
d. Diffie-Hellman.

56. What is a Certificate Revocation List (CRL) in a PKI?
a. A list of trusted certificate authorities.
b. A list of revoked or expired digital certificates.
c. A list of public keys for encryption.
d. A list of digital signatures for authentication.

57. What is the purpose of a Certificate Signing Request (CSR) in a PKI?
a. To request a digital certificate from a CA.
b. To encrypt data using a public key.
c. To generate a private key for encryption.
d. To authenticate users in a network.

58. Which protocol is commonly used for secure communication between a client and a Certificate Authority (CA) in a PKI?
a. SSL (Secure Sockets Layer).
b. SSH (Secure Shell).
c. HTTPS (Hypertext Transfer Protocol Secure).
d. LDAP (Lightweight Directory Access Protocol).

59. What is the role of a Certification Practice Statement (CPS) in a PKI?
a. To specify the technical details of certificate management.
b. To establish trust between certificate authorities.
c. To define the cryptographic algorithms used in the PKI.
d. To authenticate users in a network.

60. What is the purpose of a Certificate Policy (CP) in a PKI?
a. To define the rules and procedures for certificate issuance and management.
b. To encrypt data using a public key.
c. To establish trust between certificate authorities.
d. To authenticate users in a network.

Answer Key

1. (b) The process of securely delivering encryption keys to authorized parties. Key distribution is a critical aspect of cryptography because the encryption system's security can be compromised without a secure method of delivering encryption keys to the intended recipients. It involves ensuring that only authorized parties receive the necessary keys to encrypt and decrypt information, thus maintaining the confidentiality and integrity of the communication.

2. (d) Key escrow involves using a trusted third party, an escrow agent, to store a copy of encryption keys securely. This is typically done for legal or regulatory compliance or in cases where authorities may need access to encrypted data. The trusted third party holds the keys in escrow and can release them under specific circumstances, such as with a court order. This method is often used when maintaining access to encrypted data is necessary, even if the original vital holders are unavailable or unwilling to cooperate.

3. (b) Asymmetric key distribution. In asymmetric cryptography (also known as public-key cryptography), there is a pair of mathematically related keys: public and private keys. The public key can be freely distributed to others, while the private key is kept secret. Data encrypted with the public key can only be decrypted using the corresponding private key and vice versa. This pair of keys forms the basis for secure communication and digital signatures in asymmetric cryptography.

4. (a) In a symmetric key distribution scheme, only one key is typically shared between the sender and receiver. So, the answer is one.

5. (c) The Diffie-Hellman key exchange is vulnerable to a man-in-the-middle attack if an attacker intercepts the communication between two parties and establishes separate, secret key exchanges with each party, effectively acting as a "middleman" between them. This allows the attacker to decrypt and potentially modify the communication without the knowledge of the two legitimate parties. Additional security measures, such as digital signatures or authentication, may be necessary to mitigate this vulnerability when using Diffie-Hellman key exchange.

6. (c) Diffie-Hellman key exchange. Forward secrecy, also known as perfect forward secrecy (PFS), is a property of key exchange protocols like Diffie-Hellman. It ensures that even if an attacker compromises a party's private key at a later time, it cannot retroactively decrypt previously recorded encrypted communication. In Diffie-Hellman key exchange, the exchanged keys are temporary and used only for a specific session, which means that compromising a long-term private key does not compromise the secrecy of past sessions. This property enhances security when the long-term private key may be compromised.

7. (b) Asymmetric key distribution. Asymmetric cryptography (public-key cryptography) is generally more computationally expensive than symmetric cryptography. The operations involving asymmetric keys, such as encryption and decryption, digital signatures, and key generation, require significantly more computational resources than symmetric cryptography. This is because asymmetric algorithms use longer key lengths and involve complex mathematical operations. Symmetric key distribution, on the other hand, is computationally less expensive because it uses shorter keys and more straightforward encryption and decryption processes.

8. (a) Symmetric key distribution. In SSL/TLS, symmetric and asymmetric cryptography is used. Initially, an asymmetric key exchange (such as RSA or Elliptic Curve Diffie-Hellman) is used to exchange a temporary symmetric key securely. Once this symmetric key is established, it is used for the bulk encryption and decryption of data during the session. This combination of symmetric and asymmetric cryptography provides security and efficiency in SSL/TLS protocols.

9. (b) Asymmetric key distribution. A public-private key pair is used in asymmetric cryptography (public-key cryptography). The public key is openly shared with others and is used for encryption or verifying digital signatures, while the private key is kept secret and is used for decryption or generating digital signatures.

This pair of keys is fundamental to asymmetric cryptography and provides the foundation for secure communication and authentication.

10. (a) In symmetric key distribution, the challenge lies in securely exchanging the initial symmetric key between communicating parties. Since both parties use the same key for encryption and decryption, the key must be securely shared at the beginning of the communication to prevent interception or compromise by malicious actors. Once the initial symmetric key is securely exchanged, it can be used for secure communication, but the key exchange process is critical in ensuring the system's overall security.

11. (b) Symmetric key distribution in cryptography refers to securely delivering symmetric encryption keys to authorized parties. The same key is used for encryption and decryption in symmetric key cryptography. Distributing this symmetric encryption key securely to the intended recipients is a crucial aspect of ensuring the confidentiality and integrity of data in a communication or encryption system.

12. (a) In symmetric key distribution, only one key is typically shared between the sender and receiver. So, the answer is one.

13. (c) The symmetric encryption algorithm widely used for secure symmetric key distribution is AES (Advanced Encryption Standard). AES is a widely adopted and recognized symmetric encryption algorithm for various encryption and data protection purposes, including securely distributing symmetric encryption keys. It provides high security and efficiency, making it a popular choice for securing data and communication channels.

14. (a) The key distribution method that involves physically exchanging encryption keys is Key exchange over a secure channel. The physical key exchange typically involves the secure transfer of encryption keys through a trusted and secure means, such as delivering the keys in person, using a secure courier service, or transmitting the keys via a hardware token or device. This method ensures the confidentiality and integrity of the keys during their transfer.

15. (b) Key exchange via email is The key distribution method that is vulnerable to interception if not adequately secured during transmission. Email communication is typically not considered a secure channel for exchanging encryption keys unless additional encryption or security measures, such as public-key cryptography or secure email protocols, are employed. Without proper encryption and security precautions, email-based key exchange can be intercepted by malicious actors, compromising the security of the keys and the data they protect.

16. (b) Key wrapping is commonly used to distribute symmetric encryption keys securely. Key wrapping is a method where a symmetric encryption key is wrapped (encrypted) using another encryption key, typically an asymmetric encryption key (public key). The wrapped key can then be securely transmitted or stored, and only the authorized recipient with the corresponding private key can unwrap (decrypt) it to obtain the original symmetric encryption key. This process ensures the confidentiality and integrity of the symmetric key during distribution and is commonly used in various cryptographic protocols and systems.

17. (c) The symmetric encryption mode that is suitable for distributing large amounts of data securely is Counter (CTR) mode. Counter (CTR) mode is often preferred for encrypting large amounts of data because it can parallelize the encryption process, making it more efficient for processing data in blocks or streams. It transforms a block cipher into a stream cipher, allowing for the independent encryption of individual blocks of data, which is well-suited for situations where data transmission or storage involves large volumes of information. It also provides good security when used correctly.

18. (c) The technique that uses a trusted third party to distribute symmetric encryption keys securely is Key escrow. Key escrow involves a trusted third party holding copies of encryption keys, typically for access recovery or legal requirements. While it does not directly distribute keys between communicating parties, it stores keys securely and can release them to authorized parties when needed. This approach is often used when a trusted entity is required to facilitate key distribution and management.

19. (b) The key distribution method unsuitable for distributing symmetric encryption keys over an untrusted network is Key exchange via email. Sending symmetric encryption keys via email is unsuitable for secure distribution over an untrusted network because email communication is generally not secure by default. Emails can be intercepted or compromised during transmission, potentially exposing the encryption keys and compromising the security of the data they protect. Other methods like key exchange over a secure channel, public-key cryptography, or key wrapping should be used to distribute symmetric encryption keys securely.

20. (a) Key exchange over a secure channel is The key distribution method that requires the sender and receiver to share a standard secret key in advance. In a key exchange over a secure channel, the sender and receiver must share a secret key in advance through a secure means. This secret key is used to authenticate and secure the communication channel during the key exchange process. Once the secure channel is established, the parties can securely exchange additional keys, such as symmetric encryption keys, as needed for secure communication.

21. (b) Kerberos is a network authentication protocol. Kerberos is a widely used network authentication protocol that allows users and systems to prove their identities securely over a non-secure network, such as the Internet or an internal network. It uses a trusted third-party server called a Key Distribution Center (KDC) to authenticate users and provide them with temporary authentication tokens (tickets) that can be used to access network resources without transmitting passwords over the network. Corporate networks commonly use it to provide secure authentication and access control.

22. (c) Kerberos provides an authentication solution. Kerberos is primarily designed to address the authentication aspect of security. It ensures that users and systems can authenticate themselves securely to access network resources without transmitting sensitive authentication credentials, such as passwords, over the network. While authentication is its primary focus, Kerberos indirectly contributes to integrity and confidentiality by helping establish secure authentication sessions.

23. (b) The primary function of the Key Distribution Center (KDC) in Kerberos is to authenticate users and issue tickets. The KDC in Kerberos is responsible for authenticating users, verifying their identities, and issuing authentication tokens (tickets) that can be used to access network resources securely without revealing sensitive authentication information like passwords. The KDC plays a central role in the Kerberos authentication process by providing these tickets to users and services within the network.

24. (d) The entity not directly involved in the Kerberos protocol is the Certificate Authority (CA). In the Kerberos protocol, the primary entities involved are the client, the server, and the Ticket Granting Server (TGS). These entities work together to enable secure authentication and access to network resources. While Certificate Authorities (CAs) are crucial in other authentication and security systems, they are not part of the core Kerberos protocol. Kerberos relies on its authentication mechanisms and does not use X.509 certificates issued by CAs.

25. (a) The encryption algorithm commonly used in Kerberos for encrypting authentication messages is DES (Data Encryption Standard). However, it is essential to note that modern implementations of Kerberos may use more robust encryption algorithms like AES (Advanced Encryption Standard) for improved security. DES was the original encryption algorithm used in Kerberos, but more modern encryption methods like AES have surpassed its security.

26. (c) In the context of Kerberos, a ticket is A time-limited authentication token. A Kerberos ticket is a time-limited authentication token that proves a user's identity to network services and grants access to those services for a specific period of time. It contains information such as the user's identity, a session key, and a timestamp, and it is used to facilitate secure authentication and communication between the client and the server within a Kerberos-protected network environment.

27. (c) The purpose of the TGT (Ticket Granting Ticket) in Kerberos is to request a session key for communication with the server. The TGT is obtained from the Ticket Granting Server (TGS) during the initial authentication process. It allows the client to request session keys for accessing specific network services from the TGS without having to re-authenticate with the Authentication Server (AS) every time. The TGT is presented to the TGS when requesting access to services, and it serves as the basis for obtaining session keys to secure communication with those services.

28. (d) In Kerberos, clients use the AS (Authentication Service) protocol to request a TGT (Ticket Granting Ticket) from the Key Distribution Center (KDC). So, the answer is AS (Authentication Service).

29. (c) The component in Kerberos responsible for verifying the server's authenticity during the ticket-granting process is TGS (Ticket Granting Server). The TGS ensures the server's authenticity by checking the server's ticket and authentication information. It verifies that the server requesting access to a specific service is legitimate before granting access and providing session keys for secure communication. This helps prevent attacks where an unauthorized server attempts to impersonate a legitimate one.

30. (c) The key shared between the client and the TGS (Ticket Granting Server) in Kerberos is the Ticket-granting key. The client and the TGS share a ticket-granting key used to encrypt and decrypt authentication messages and tickets during the ticket-granting process. This key is used to request and obtain service tickets from the TGS, allowing the client to access various network services securely.

31. (d) The key distribution in asymmetric encryption is exchanging public keys. In asymmetric encryption, the key distribution process typically involves exchanging public keys between users or parties. These public keys encrypt messages that can only be decrypted by the corresponding private keys held by the recipients. The secure exchange of public keys is a crucial part of asymmetric cryptography to enable secure communication between parties who may not have prior knowledge of each other's keys.

32. (b) The key distribution method that uses a pair of mathematically related keys is Asymmetric key distribution. In asymmetric encryption, there is a pair of keys: a public key and a private key. These keys are mathematically related, so data encrypted with one key can only be decrypted using the other. This pair of keys forms the foundation of asymmetric cryptography, enabling secure communication and digital signatures.

33. (b) The key distribution method that requires a trusted third party is asymmetric key distribution. In asymmetric key distribution, a trusted third party known as a Certificate Authority (CA) is often involved in verifying and certifying the public keys of users or entities. The CA's role is to vouch for the authenticity of public keys, helping to establish trust in the keys used for encryption and authentication.

This is commonly seen in public key infrastructure (PKI) systems where CAs issue digital certificates that bind public keys to specific identities.

34. (b) The key distribution method using a public-private key pair is asymmetric. In asymmetric encryption (also known as public-key cryptography), a pair of mathematically related keys is used: public and private keys. The public key is openly shared, while the private key is kept secret. Data encrypted with the public key can only be decrypted with the corresponding private key and vice versa. This pair of keys is fundamental to asymmetric cryptography and is used for secure communication, digital signatures, and various authentication purposes.

35. (a) In asymmetric key distribution, the public key is used for encryption. Data encrypted with the public key can only be decrypted using the corresponding private key, which is kept secret. This property is fundamental to asymmetric cryptography, enabling secure communication where anyone can encrypt a message using the recipient's public key, but only the recipient with the private key can decrypt and access the original data.

36. (b) In asymmetric key distribution, the private key is decrypted. Data encrypted using the corresponding public key can only be decrypted using the private key, which is kept secret by the key's owner. This is a fundamental characteristic of asymmetric cryptography, where the public key is used for encryption, and the private key is used for decryption and other security-related operations like digital signatures.

37. (b) The asymmetric encryption algorithm commonly used for secure key distribution is RSA (Rivest-Shamir-Adleman). RSA is widely used for various cryptographic purposes, including secure key distribution, digital signatures, and encryption of symmetric keys during the initial phases of secure communication. It is well-suited for key exchange and secure communication between parties without previously shared keys or established trust.

38. (c) The key distribution method that provides forward secrecy is the Diffie-Hellman key exchange. Forward secrecy, also known as perfect forward secrecy (PFS), is a property of key exchange protocols like Diffie-Hellman. It ensures that even if an attacker compromises a party's private key at a later time, they cannot retroactively decrypt previously recorded encrypted communication. Diffie-Hellman key exchange generates a new session key for each communication session, and this key is not derived from the long-term private keys, enhancing security by providing forward secrecy.

39. (b) The key distribution method that is computationally more expensive is asymmetric key distribution. Asymmetric key distribution involves public-key cryptography and is generally more computationally expensive than symmetric key distribution. Asymmetric encryption and decryption operations are typically more computationally intensive than symmetric cryptography because they involve longer key lengths and complex mathematical operations. In contrast, symmetric key distribution uses shorter keys and more straightforward encryption and decryption processes, making it computationally less expensive.

40. (b) The key distribution method commonly used in digital signatures and SSL/TLS (Secure Sockets Layer/Transport Layer Security) protocols is asymmetric key distribution. In digital signatures and SSL/TLS, asymmetric key distribution (public-key cryptography) plays a crucial role in verifying the authenticity of digital signatures, authenticating servers and clients, and establishing secure communication channels. Asymmetric cryptography is used to securely exchange session keys and verify the identities of parties involved in secure transactions, enhancing the security of these protocols.

41. (c) An X.509 certificate is a format for public key certificates. X.509 is a widely used standard format for public key certificates. These certificates include information about a public key's owner and the associated public key itself, and they are used for various purposes, such as authentication, digital signatures, and secure communication. X.509 certificates are crucial in many security protocols, including SSL/TLS for secure web browsing and email encryption with S/MIME.

42. (a) The cryptographic standard commonly used to create X.509 certificates is RSA (Rivest-Shamir-Adleman). RSA is a widely used asymmetric encryption algorithm often used for key pair generation and digital signatures in X.509 certificates. It allows for secure key exchange, authentication, and digital signature verification in various security protocols that rely on X.509 certificates, such as SSL/TLS, for secure web browsing.

43. (c) An X.509 certificate typically contains the Subject's identity, public key, and issuer's signature. The key components of an X.509 certificate include the identity of the certificate holder (the Subject), the Subject's public key, and the digital signature of the certificate issuer (the Certificate Authority or CA). This information is crucial for verifying the certificate holder's authenticity and ensuring the certificate's integrity. X.509 certificates may include other attributes and extensions, such as the certificate's expiration date and intended usage.

44. (c) The component of an X.509 certificate that verifies the certificate's integrity is a digital signature. The digital signature in an X.509 certificate is created using the private key of the certificate issuer (Certificate Authority or CA) and can be used to verify that the certificate has not been tampered with and that the trusted CA indeed issued it. It ensures the integrity and authenticity of the certificate.

45. (b) The purpose of the issuer in an X.509 certificate is to issue the certificate and sign it with the issuer's private key. The issuer of an X.509 certificate is typically a Certificate Authority (CA) responsible for verifying the identity of the certificate subject, generating the certificate, and signing it with the CA's private key. This digital signature allows others to verify the authenticity and integrity of the certificate, ensuring that a trusted authority indeed issued it.

46. (a) The file format that is commonly used to store X.509 certificates is PEM (Privacy-Enhanced Mail). PEM (Privacy-Enhanced Mail) is a widely adopted file format for storing cryptographic objects, including X.509 certificates. It uses ASCII encoding and typically has file extensions like ".pem" or ".crt." It is commonly used in security protocols and systems for storing and exchanging certificates and private keys.

47. (c) The protocol commonly used for distributing and managing X.509 certificates is LDAP (Lightweight Directory Access Protocol). LDAP is frequently used for directory services and can store and retrieve X.509 certificates in directories. It provides a structured and organized way to manage and query certificates, making it suitable for public key infrastructures (PKIs) and certificate management systems. While SSL (Secure Sockets Layer) and HTTP (Hypertext Transfer Protocol) can be used for transmitting certificates, LDAP is more commonly associated with certificate management in directory services.

48. (d) The validity period of an X.509 certificate is specified by the certificate's "notBefore" and "notAfter" fields. So, the correct answer is by the certificate's "notBefore" and "notAfter" fields. These fields indicate the start and end dates and times during which the certificate is considered valid. Any attempt to use the certificate outside this specified time range will invalidate authentication and other cryptographic operations. The validity period is an essential aspect of certificate management and security.

49. (a) The X.509 certificate extension that provides information about the certificate's intended usage is the Key Usage extension. The Key Usage extension specifies the purposes for which the public key in the certificate can be used, such as digital signatures, key encipherment, data encipherment, etc. This extension helps determine the roles and permissions associated with the certificate and ensures it is used appropriately for its intended purpose.

50. (a) The entity responsible for validating the trustworthiness of an X.509 certificate is Certificate Authority (CA). Certificate Authorities are trusted entities in a Public Key Infrastructure (PKI) that issue and sign X.509 certificates. The CA's role includes verifying the identity of the certificate subject (the certified entity), signing the certificate with its private key, and maintaining the infrastructure necessary for others to validate and trust certificates issued by that CA. The trustworthiness of a certificate is primarily determined by the trust in the CA that issued it.

51. (c) Public Key Infrastructure (PKI) is a framework for managing digital certificates and encryption keys. PKI is a comprehensive system with policies, processes, hardware, software, and standards for managing digital certificates and encryption keys. It provides the infrastructure for secure communication, authentication, digital signatures, and other cryptographic functions in various applications and systems. PKI is widely used to secure network communications, web browsing, and email encryption. It enables the secure distribution and management of public keys and digital certificates, establishing trust and ensuring the confidentiality and integrity of data.

52. (a) The primary purpose of a Certificate Authority (CA) in a Public Key Infrastructure (PKI) is to issue digital certificates. A Certificate Authority (CA) is responsible for verifying the identity of entities (such as individuals, devices, or servers), issuing digital certificates that bind the entity's public key to their identity, and signing those certificates with the CA's private key. These digital certificates are used for authentication, encryption, digital signatures, and other security purposes within a PKI. The CA is central to establishing trust in secure communications' digital identities and keys.

53. (b) The component in a Public Key Infrastructure (PKI) that is responsible for verifying the identity of certificate holders is the Registration Authority (RA). The Registration Authority (RA) acts as an entity that verifies the identity of individuals or entities before forwarding certificate requests to the Certificate Authority (CA) for certificate issuance. The RA plays a crucial role in a PKI's vetting and authentication process, ensuring that certificate holders are who they claim to be before certificates are issued.

54. (c) The role of a Registration Authority (RA) in a Public Key Infrastructure (PKI) is to validate and authenticate certificate requests. The RA is responsible for verifying the identity of individuals or entities requesting digital certificates. It ensures that certificate requests are legitimate and that the information provided by the requestor matches the identity of the certified entity. Once the RA validates and authenticates the request, it forwards it to the Certificate Authority (CA) for issuance. This two-step process helps establish trust in the certificates issued within the PKI.

55. (a) The cryptographic algorithm that is commonly used for generating and managing digital certificates in a Public Key Infrastructure (PKI) is RSA (Rivest-Shamir-Adleman). RSA is widely used for generating the key pairs (public and private keys) that form the basis of digital certificates in PKI. The public key is included in the certificate, and the private key is used for various security functions, such as digital signatures and decryption. While other cryptographic algorithms like ECC (Elliptic Curve Cryptography) are also used in some PKIs, RSA remains a prevalent choice for key pair generation and certificate management.

56. (b) A Certificate Revocation List (CRL) in a Public Key Infrastructure (PKI) is a list of revoked or expired digital certificates. A CRL is a list maintained by a Certificate Authority (CA) that contains information about digital certificates revoked before expiration. These certificates may be revoked for various reasons, such as compromise of the private key associated with the certificate, the certificate holder's request, or other security concerns. The CRL allows relying parties to check whether a certificate presented for authentication or encryption has been revoked, indicating that it should not be trusted for secure communications.

57. (a) The purpose of a Certificate Signing Request (CSR) in a Public Key Infrastructure (PKI) is to request a digital certificate from a Certificate Authority (CA). A CSR is a formal request submitted by an entity (such as a server or individual) to a CA to obtain a digital certificate. It includes the entity's public key and information about the entity, which the CA uses to create the digital certificate. The CA signs the certificate, thus validating the entity's identity and binding the public key to that identity. The certificate can then be used for various security purposes, including authentication and encryption.

58. (c) The protocol that is commonly used for secure communication between a client and a Certificate Authority (CA) in a Public Key Infrastructure (PKI) is HTTPS (Hypertext Transfer Protocol Secure). HTTPS is an extension of the HTTP protocol, but it incorporates SSL/TLS (Secure Sockets Layer/Transport Layer Security) to encrypt and secure the communication between the client and the server. When interacting with a CA, using HTTPS ensures the confidentiality and integrity of the data exchanged during the certificate request and issuance process, enhancing the security of the PKI.

59. (a) The role of a Certification Practice Statement (CPS) in a Public Key Infrastructure (PKI) is to specify the technical details of certificate management. A CPS is a document outlining the practices and procedures a Certificate Authority (CA) or a Certification Service Provider (CSP) follows in managing digital certificates within a PKI. It provides detailed information about how certificates are issued, revoked, renewed, and managed. It specifies technical details, operational processes, security measures, and legal aspects related to the PKI. A CPS is essential for establishing trust and ensuring the PKI operates securely and by industry standards and regulations.

60. (a) The purpose of a Certificate Policy (CP) in a Public Key Infrastructure (PKI) is to define the rules and procedures for certificate issuance and management. A Certificate Policy (CP) is a high-level document that outlines the rules, practices, and standards governing the issuance, use, and management of digital certificates within a PKI. It defines the policies and procedures that Certificate Authorities (CAs) and relying parties must follow when dealing with certificates. The CP helps ensure consistency, reliability, and security within the PKI by establishing a clear framework for certificate management.

Chapter 9
User Authentication and Authorization

This chapter includes questions from the following topics:
- User Authentication.
- Two-factor Authentication.
- Multi-factor Authentication.
- Policy-based Authentication.
- Password-based Attacks.

1. **What is the term used to describe the process of confirming the identity that a system entity has claimed?**
   a. Message authentication.
   b. User authentication.
   c. Biometric verification.
   d. Hash function verification.

2. **Which of the following is not considered an authenticating factor?**
   a. Something you know.
   b. Something you are.
   c. Something you have.
   d. Something you want.

3. **Which of the following options represents an example of two-factor authentication?**
   a. A password and a fingerprint scan.
   b. A username and a password.
   c. A security question and an answer.
   d. A smart card and a password.

4. **Which of the following options would be the most effective solution for enabling multi-factor authentication for the student login process at VRR Academy, which currently only requires a username and password to access vrracademy.com?**
   a. Require students to enter a cognitive password requirement (such as 'What is your dog's name?').
   b. Require students to enter a unique six-digit number sent to them by SMS after entering their username and password.
   c. Require students to create a unique PIN that is entered after their username and password are accepted.
   d. After logging in, students must choose an image as a secondary password.

5. **Please select the three factors utilized in multi-factor authentication from the following options (Select all that apply).**
   a. Something you have.
   b. Something you know.
   c. Someone you know.
   d. Something you can do.
   e. Something you are.

6. **Which of the following represents a legitimate type of authorization key used in modern cryptography**
   a. Public authorization key.
   b. Public ephemeral key authorization key.
   c. Asymmetric authorization keys.
   d. Symmetric authorization keys.

7. **Which of the following examples demonstrates two-factor authentication?**
   a. Hardware cryptographic tokens and biometrics.
   b. Biometrics and smart cards.
   c. Smart cards and hardware cryptographic tokens.
   d. All of the above.

8. **What is the biggest weakness of password-based authentication?**
   a. Passwords can be easily guessed.
   b. Passwords can be easily forgotten.
   c. Passwords can be easily stolen.
   d. Passwords can be easily cracked.

9. **Which of the following is not a standard method of password authentication?**
   a. Challenge-response authentication.
   b. Biometric authentication.
   c. One-time password authentication.
   d. Two-factor authentication.

10. **What is the difference between a salt and a hash in password authentication?**
    a. A salt adds random characters to a password before hashing it, while a hash is a one-way password encryption.
    b. A hash adds random characters to a password before hashing it, while a salt is a one-way password encryption.
    c. A salt is a one-way password encryption, while a hash adds random characters to a password before hashing it.
    d. A hash is one-way password encryption, while a salt adds random characters to a password before hashing it.

11. **What is the purpose of a password policy?**
    a. Ensure that all passwords are the same.
    b. Ensure that all passwords are unique.
    c. Ensure that all passwords are difficult to guess or crack.
    d. Ensure that all passwords are stored in plain text.

12. **What is the difference between a static and dynamic password in password-based authentication?**
    a. A static password remains the same, while a dynamic password changes each time.
    b. A static password changes each time, while a dynamic password remains the same.
    c. A static password is easy to guess, while a dynamic password is difficult.
    d. A static password is more secure than a dynamic password.

13. **Which of the following options describes security in e-commerce? (Select all that apply).**
    a. Authenticating messages received by an organization.
    b. Protecting an organization's data resources from unauthorized access.
    c. Preventing disasters from occurring.
    d. Safeguarding messages sent over the Internet from being read and understood by unauthorized individuals/organizations.

14. **Which of the following is an example of a multi-factor authentication system?**
    a. Password-based authentication using security questions.
    b. Biometric authentication using a fingerprint scanner.
    c. Smart card authentication using a PIN.
    d. Challenge-response authentication using a one-time password.

15. **Which of the following options is a safe and secure way to retrieve a password?**
    a. Ask the customer for their phone number and send the password via text message.
    b. Ask for the registered username and provide a link for password reset on the screen.
    c. Ask for the registered email or phone number and verify it against the database before providing a link for password reset on the screen.
    d. Ask for the username and send the password link to the registered email or phone number.

16. **Pick out the strongest password from the given lot.**
    a. Password
    b. asdfg12345
    c. P@33W@d
    d. xk3dC0mI@s

17. **What is the recommended method for secure password storage in modern systems?**
    a. Salted plain-text values of the password.
    b. Hashed values of the password.
    c. Plain-text passwords are stored in an encrypted database.
    d. Salted and hashed values of the password.

18. **Which of the following methods is the simplest way to change the default administrator password on 1000 workstations after a data breach?**
    a. Deploying a new group policy.
    b. Creating a new security group.
    c. Using the critical escrow process.
    d. Revoking the digital certificate.

19. **Which of the following is an example of two-factor authentication?**
    a. Username and password.
    b. Username and PIN.
    c. Thumbprint and password.
    d. Thumbprint and retina scan.

20. **In PKI, what concept is demonstrated when Company X trusts Company Y, Company Y trusts Company Z, and, as a result, Company X trusts Company Z?**
    a. Trust transitivity.
    b. Certificate authority hierarchy.

c. Public key cryptography.

d. Domain-based trust.

21. **VRR academy has implemented a new Group Policy that locks out any student account that enters their password incorrectly thrice. Once the student's account has been locked, he or she must wait 15 minutes before attempting to log in again. Which attack type is this mitigation method attempting to avert?**
    a. Privilege escalation.
    b. Brute force attack.
    c. Spoofing.
    d. Man-in-the-middle.

22. **During a penetration examination of your organization's network, the assessor discovered a spreadsheet with the passwords for various servers. Which of the four retrieved passwords is the weakest and should be changed first to increase the password's complexity?**
    a. P@$$w0rd
    b. Pa55w0rd
    c. P@$$W0RD
    d. pa55word

23. **What is the minimum number of characters that a password should have to prevent password-cracking attempts?**
    a. 7
    b. 8
    c. 9
    d. 10

24. **Checking whether a user can access a particular item can help prevent specific attacks. Which type of attack is this preventive measure most effective against?**
    a. Cross-site scripting (XSS).
    b. Security misconfiguration.
    c. Insecure Direct Object Reference.
    d. Injection.

25. **Which type of attack is possible when a computer system is accessed by a token and a four-digit PIN, with the token performing offline PIN verification?**
    a. Brute force.
    b. PIN guessing.
    c. Smurf.
    d. Spoofing.

26. **Which of the following is not an example of a token used in token-based authentication?**
    a. Smart card.
    b. One-time password token.
    c. Biometric token.
    d. All of the above.

27. **What type of token generates a new password for every authentication attempt?**
    a. Static token.

b. Dynamic token.
c. Hybrid token.
d. None of the above.

28. **Which of the following is not a benefit of using token-based authentication?**
    a. Reduced risk of password theft.
    b. Ease of use for end-users.
    c. Increased security compared to passwords alone.
    d. Flexibility in authentication methods.

29. **What type of token requires physical contact with a reader to initiate authentication?**
    a. Contactless token.
    b. Magnetic stripe token.
    c. Smart card token.
    d. Proximity token.

30. **Which of the following is not a factor that can impact the security of token-based authentication?**
    a. Strength of the token encryption algorithm.
    b. Security of the token storage device.
    c. Security of the token communication channel.
    d. Physical characteristics of the token user.

31. **Which protocol utilizes mutual authentication between the client and the server for security purposes?**
    a. RADIUS.
    b. Two-factor authentication.
    c. Secure LDAP.
    d. CHAP.

32. **Which two (2) of the following are among the advantages of Kerberos Authentication?**
    a. Delegated authentication.
    b. Distributed authentication.
    c. Single sign-on.
    d. Interoperability

33. **Which technologies rely upon the shared secret to protect communication between the file server and the RADIUS server during authentication?**
    a. RADIUS
    b. Kerberos
    c. PKI
    d. LDAP

34. **Which feature is exclusively supported by Kerberos and not by RADIUS?**
    a. Authentication services.
    b. Single sign-on capability.
    c. Ticket-based authentication.
    d. XML for cross-platform interoperability.

35. **Which attack is a brute-force hacking method that breaks into a password-protected computer or server by systematically entering every word in a dictionary as a password?**
    a. Dictionary attack.
    b. Rule-based dictionary attack.
    c. Online collection attack.
    d. Syllable collection attack.

36. **How do hackers take advantage of Rainbow Tables?**
    a. Match individual characters against their hashed values across a broad range of standard hashing algorithms.
    b. To coordinate a "full-spectrum" attack against a given target simultaneously.
    c. To decipher stolen passwords by looking up a hashed password and matching it to a string of clear text.
    d. To better understand the demographics of a target when constructing a phishing attack email.

37. **Which password-cracking technique requires significant resources to implement?**
    a. Proactive password checking.
    b. Reactive password checking.
    c. Computer-generated passwords.
    d. User-created passwords.

38. **What are the two broad categories of password-based authentication?**
    a. Fixed; variable.
    b. Time-stamped; fixed.
    c. Fixed; one-time.
    d. None of the above.

39. **For password management, which of the following ensures password strength?**
    a. Passwords with maximum key space, shorter passphrases, low entropy, and simple passphrases.
    b. Passwords with minimum key space, shorter passphrases, high entropy, and simple passphrases.
    c. Passwords with balanced key space, longer passphrases, high entropy, and complex passphrases.
    d. Passwords with most likely key space, longer passphrases, low entropy, and complex passphrases.

40. **When does proactive password checking take place?**
    a. After the user creates his/her password for the first time.
    b. When the user updates the password.
    c. Before the user selects the password.
    d. Upon successful registration of the user password.

41. **What makes a rainbow table attack more effective?**
    a. Large salt values are used.
    b. The password is not based on a dictionary word.
    c. The password has successfully passed the proactive checking.
    d. Numbers are used at the beginning of the password.

42. **In the electronic authentication process, who performs identity proofing?**
    a. Subscriber
    b. Registration authority.
    c. Applicant

    d.   Credential service provider.

43. Which of the following is not a factor affecting the security of remote user authentication?
    a.   Password strength.
    b.   Network security.
    c.   Location of the remote user.
    d.   Type of authentication mechanism used.

44. What is the primary purpose of a virtual private network (VPN) in remote user authentication?
    a.   To provide a secure connection between the remote user and the authentication server.
    b.   Encrypt the authentication data sent between the remote user and the authentication server.
    c.   To provide a remote user with a unique identifier for authentication purposes.
    d.   To provide the remote user with access to the local network resources.

45. Which of the following authentication factors is unique to remote user authentication?
    a.   Something the user knows.
    b.   Something the user has.
    c.   Something the user is.
    d.   Something the user does.
    e.   All of the above.

46. What is the purpose of a one-time password (OTP) in remote user authentication?
    a.   To provide an additional layer of security by requiring the user to enter a unique code generated for each authentication attempt.
    b.   To prevent unauthorised access, the user must enter a password that changes every hour.
    c.   To simplify the authentication process by allowing the user to use the same password for multiple sessions.
    d.   d. To reduce the risk of password theft by requiring the user to enter a password sent to their mobile device.

47. For identity management, which of the following requires multi-factor authentication?
    a.   User-to-host architecture.
    b.   Peer-to-peer architecture.
    c.   Client host-to-server architecture.
    d.   Trusted third-party architecture.

48. One of the password vulnerabilities is exploiting multiple password uses. What is meant by multiple password uses?
    a.   Multiple passwords are used for multiple systems.
    b.   Multiple passwords are used for one system.
    c.   One password is used for multiple systems.
    d.   One password is used for one system.

49. Regarding password guessing and cracking threats, which of the following can help mitigate such threats?
    a.   Passwords with low entropy, larger salts, and smaller stretching.
    b.   Passwords with high entropy, smaller salts, and smaller stretching.
    c.   Passwords with high entropy, larger salts, and larger stretching.
    d.   Passwords with low entropy, smaller salts, and larger stretching.

50. What unique feature makes the smartcard so flexible to use?
   a. The use of a microprocessor and programmable memory.
   b. The high speeds at which it can operate.
   c. The ability to protect stored information.
   d. The capability of storing vast amounts of information per unit of area.

51. Why are traditional authentication methods not suitable for use in computer networks?
   a. They do not use cryptographic techniques.
   b. They do not permit high-speed data flow.
   c. They use passwords.
   d. They are incompatible with the Internet.

52. What type of password attack combines both brute force and dictionary attacks?
   a. Rule-based password attack.
   b. Hybrid password attack.
   c. Syllable password attack.
   d. Online password attack.

53. What is a rainbow table?
   a. A massive table of passwords is used for cracking passwords.
   b. A pre-calculated table for reversing cryptographic hash functions is typically used for cracking password hashes.
   c. A table of hash values pre-computed for all salts and passwords.
   d. A table of the secret password.

54. What are the two main steps in user authentication?
   a. Identification and verification.
   b. Availability and encryption.
   c. Encryption and verification.
   d. Identification and encryption.

55. Which of the following options does not serve as a means of user authentication?
   a. User Password.
   b. Hash algorithms.
   c. Symmetric encryption.
   d. Tokens

56. What is the term for authenticating a user based on physical characteristics?
   a. Physical authentication.
   b. Remote user authentication.
   c. Biometric authentication.
   d. Characteristic authentication.

57. What do you call the approach wherein the system periodically runs its password cracker to find guessable passwords?
   a. Proactive password checking.
   b. User-created password checking.
   c. Reactive password checking.
   d. Computer-generated password checking.

58. **Which of the following options has the drawback of poor acceptance by the user?**
    a. User-created passwords.
    b. Proactive password checking.
    c. Computer-generated password.
    d. Reactive password checking.

59. **What is the term for the process of retrieving passwords from the data that is stored in or transmitted by a computer system?**
    a. Password backup.
    b. Password recovery.
    c. Password management.
    d. Password cracking.

60. **Which of the following statements accurately describes a password?**
    a. The least expensive and most secure.
    b. The least expensive and least secure.
    c. The most expensive and least secure.
    d. The most expensive and most secure.

61. **What term describes smart card authentication?**
    a. Proof-by-knowledge.
    b. Proof-by-property.
    c. Proof-by-possession.
    d. Proof-of-concept.

62. **What does the term "token" refer to?**
    a. The knowledge possessed by an individual.
    b. A dynamic biometric characteristic.
    c. A static biometric characteristic.
    d. Something possessed by an individual

63. **Which authentication mechanism provides the strongest security among the following options?**
    a. Passwords
    b. Smart Cards.
    c. Biometrics
    d. Pattern Lock.

64. **What is the main disadvantage of using one-time passwords for authentication?**
    a. They are too complex for users to remember.
    b. They are not secure enough for high-risk systems.
    c. They can be easily intercepted and used by attackers.
    d. They require additional hardware or software to generate the passwords.

65. **Which of the following is a drawback of using security questions for authentication?**
    a. The answers can be easily guessed or obtained through social engineering.
    b. They require users to remember complex passwords or phrases.
    c. They can only be used for online authentication.
    d. Most modern authentication systems do not support them.

66. **Which of the following is an advantage of using smart cards for authentication?**
    a. They can be easily replaced if lost or stolen.
    b. They do not require any additional hardware or software.
    c. They can be used for both online and offline authentication.
    d. They provide strong authentication without requiring user interaction.

67. **Which authentication method involves proving knowledge of a secret without transmitting it?**
    a. Password-based.
    b. Challenge-response.
    c. Both (a) and (b).
    d. Neither (a) nor (b).

68. **What type of attack is described where Mr Raja captures passwords from network traffic to use them for future attacks?**
    a. Dictionary attack.
    b. Brute-force attack.
    c. Social engineering attack.
    d. Replay attack.

69. **What is the name of the technique used by John's company to increase the security of their passwords, which involves adding a salt and cryptographic hash and running the process many times before storing the passwords?**
    a. Key stretching.
    b. Rainbow table.
    c. Salting.
    d. Collision resistance.

70. **What is remote user authentication?**
    a. The process of verifying a user's identity from a remote location.
    b. The process of granting remote access to users.
    c. The process of encrypting remote connections.
    d. The process of authenticating local users.

71. **Which of the following is NOT a commonly used remote user authentication method?**
    a. Password-based authentication.
    b. Biometric authentication.
    c. Token-based authentication.
    d. Physical key authentication.

72. **Which remote user authentication method involves the use of a unique physical device?**
    a. Password-based authentication.
    b. Biometric authentication.
    c. Token-based authentication.
    d. Certificate-based authentication.

73. **Which authentication factor relies on something the user knows?**
    a. Something the user has.
    b. Something the user is.
    c. Something the user does.

    d.   Something the user remembers.

74. Which authentication factor relies on something the user possesses?
    a.   Something the user knows.
    b.   Something the user is.
    c.   Something the user does.
    d.   Something the user has.

75. Which remote user authentication method uses a one-time password that changes periodically?
    a.   Password-based authentication.
    b.   Biometric authentication.
    c.   Token-based authentication.
    d.   Certificate-based authentication.

76. Which remote user authentication method relies on unique physiological or behavioural characteristics?
    a.   Password-based authentication.
    b.   Biometric authentication.
    c.   Token-based authentication.
    d.   Certificate-based authentication.

77. Which remote user authentication method uses digital certificates issued by a trusted authority?
    a.   Password-based authentication.
    b.   Biometric authentication.
    c.   Token-based authentication.
    d.   Certificate-based authentication.

78. Which authentication factor relies on something the user does?
    a.   Something the user knows.
    b.   Something the user has.
    c.   Something the user is.
    d.   Something the user remembers.

79. Which remote user authentication method is based on temporary access codes sent to a user's mobile device?
    a.   Password-based authentication.
    b.   Biometric authentication.
    c.   Token-based authentication.
    d.   Certificate-based authentication.

Answer Key

1.   (b) User Authentication. Authentication is the process of confirming the identity of a user, device, or any other entity attempting to access a system or resource. It involves verifying that the claimed identity of the entity is valid and that the entity has the necessary privileges to access the resource. In computer security, user authentication is the most common form of authentication, where a user provides a username and password to gain access to a system or application. However, there are other forms of authentication, such as biometric verification, where a user's unique physical characteristics, such as fingerprints, voice patterns, or iris scans, are used to confirm their identity.

2. (d) Something you want is not considered an authenticating factor in remote user authentication. The other options are commonly used as authenticating factors: Something you know: Examples include a password or a PIN. Something you are: Examples include biometric characteristics such as fingerprints or facial recognition. Something you have: Examples include physical devices like smart cards or tokens.

3. (a) A password and a fingerprint scan.

4. (b) The most effective solution for enabling multi-factor authentication for the student login process at VRR Academy would be (b) to require students to enter a unique six-digit number sent to them by SMS after entering their username and password. This is because it requires something the user has (their phone) and something they know (username and password). It also provides an additional layer of security by requiring a one-time code sent directly to the user's phone and cannot be guessed or intercepted by an attacker.

5. (a,b,e) The three factors utilized in multi-factor authentication are something you have, know, and are.

6. (c) A common type of authorization key used in modern cryptography is an asymmetric one consisting of a public and private key. The public key is used for encryption and can be freely distributed, while the private key is kept secret and used for decryption. On the other hand, Symmetric keys use the same key for encryption and decryption and are typically used for secure communication between two parties who share a secret key. The terms "public authorization key" and "public ephemeral key authorization key" do not have precise meanings in modern cryptography.

7. (a) Hardware cryptographic tokens and biometrics.

8. (c) The biggest weakness of password-based authentication is that passwords can be easily stolen through brute-force attacks, phishing scams, or other hacking methods.

9. (b) Biometric authentication is not a standard method of password authentication, as it relies on the user's physical characteristics (such as fingerprints or facial recognition) rather than a password.

10. (a) A salt adds random characters to a password before hashing it, while a hash is a one-way password encryption. In password authentication, a hash is a one-way function to transform a user's password into a fixed-size string of characters that cannot be reversed. If attackers gain access to the hashed password, they cannot quickly reverse it to recover the original password. A salt is a random string of characters added to a password before it is hashed. The purpose of a salt is to add randomness to the hashed password, making it more difficult for attackers to use pre-computed tables of hashed passwords (known as "rainbow tables") to crack passwords. So, a salt and a hash serve different purposes in password authentication, with the salt adding a layer of security to the hashing process.

11. (b,c) A password policy ensures that all passwords are unique and challenging to guess or crack. Therefore, options (b) and (c) are correct. Option (a) is incorrect because having all passwords be the same would be a security risk. Option (d) is also incorrect because storing passwords in plain text is a security risk and not recommended. A password policy ensures that all passwords are created and managed securely to protect sensitive information and prevent unauthorized access. The policy may include guidelines on password complexity, length, expiration, and other related aspects. The policy may also guide the storage and management of passwords, such as prohibiting the storage of passwords in plain text or requiring multi-factor authentication. A password policy aims to promote good password hygiene and reduce the risk of security breaches.

12. (a) A static password remains the same, while a dynamic password changes each time. A static password is a fixed sequence of characters that remains the same every time the user logs in, while a dynamic password changes each time and is generated by a special device or algorithm. Dynamic passwords, or one-time passwords (OTPs), are often used for two-factor authentication. They provide an extra layer of security because even if an attacker were to obtain the password somehow, it would no longer be valid after a short period of time.

13. (a,b,d) a. Authenticating messages received by an organization. b. Protecting an organization's data resources from unauthorized access. d. Safeguarding messages sent over the Internet from being read and understood by unauthorized individuals/organizations.

14. (b) Biometric authentication using a fingerprint scanner is an example of a multi-factor authentication system since it typically requires both something you know (e.g., a PIN or password) and something you have (e.g., a fingerprint) to authenticate.

15. (c). Ask for the registered email or phone number and verify it against the database before providing a link for password reset on the screen. This is a safe and secure way to retrieve a password. This ensures that the person requesting the password reset is the legitimate account owner, not someone attempting to gain unauthorized access.

16. (d) The strong password from the given options is d. xk3dC0mI@s, as it is a longer password with a mix of uppercase and lowercase letters, numbers, and symbols, making it harder to guess or crack.

17. (d) The recommended method for secure password storage in modern systems is to use salted and hashed values of the password.

18. (a) Deploying a new group policy is the simplest way to change the default administrator password on 1000 workstations after a data breach. A new group policy can be quickly pushed out to all workstations to change the default administrator password to a new, secure password. This is a more efficient solution than manually changing each password, which would be time-consuming and prone to errors. Creating a new security group, using the critical escrow process, and revoking the digital certificate are unrelated to changing passwords on workstations.

19. (c) Thumbprint and password are examples of two-factor authentication.

20. (a) Trust transitivity. In Public Key Infrastructure (PKI), trust transitivity refers to the idea that if Company A trusts Company B and Company B trusts Company C, then Company A can also trust Company C. This is possible due to PKI's hierarchical structure of certificate authorities (CAs). In PKI, digital certificates are issued by CAs, which are trusted entities that verify the identity of users or devices and issue digital certificates that contain their public keys. The public key is used to encrypt messages or data, and the private key is used to decrypt them. Each CA has its digital certificate, which a higher-level CA signs, called a root CA. All parties trust root CAs in the PKI system, and their digital certificates are pre-installed in web browsers and other software applications. CAs lower in the hierarchy chain are trusted because they have digital certificates signed by higher-level CAs, either directly or indirectly. Trust transitivity is achieved because if a user trusts the digital certificate of a CA higher in the chain, they can also trust the digital certificates of CAs lower in the chain as long as they can trace the trust path back to a trusted root CA.

21. (b) The mitigation method implemented by VRR Academy attempts to avert a brute force attack, where an attacker tries multiple combinations of usernames and passwords to gain unauthorized access to an account. By locking out the account after three failed attempts and implementing a waiting period, the academy makes it more difficult for an attacker to execute a brute-force attack successfully.

22. (d) Among the four passwords, the weakest password is "pa55word," as it consists of only lowercase letters and has no special characters or numbers. It is vulnerable to dictionary attacks, where an attacker uses a list of commonly used words to try and guess the password. To increase the password's complexity, it is recommended to use a combination of uppercase and lowercase letters, numbers, and special characters, such as in options (a), (b), and (c). However, it is essential to note that simply adding numbers and special characters to a weak password is not enough to make it secure, as attackers can still easily guess it is using specialized software. It is best to use unique, complex, and lengthy passwords that are difficult to guess.

23. (b) The recommended minimum number of characters for a password to prevent password-cracking attempts is 8. However, it is essential to note that longer passwords are generally more secure than shorter ones, so using a password even longer than eight characters is always recommended. In addition to using a longer password, it is also essential to use a combination of uppercase and lowercase letters, numbers, and special characters and to avoid using easily guessable information such as personal information or common dictionary words.

24. (c) The preventive measure of checking whether a user can access a particular item is most effective against Insecure Direct Object Reference (IDOR) attacks. In an IDOR attack, an attacker attempts to access an object, such as a file or database record, which they should not have access to by manipulating a parameter or URL. By checking whether a user is authorized to access a particular item, organizations can prevent attackers from accessing sensitive data or resources they are not supposed to. This can be achieved by implementing proper access controls, such as role-based access control (RBAC) or attribute-based access control (ABAC), and adequately validating user input to ensure that they can only access resources that they are authorized to.

25. (b) When a computer system is accessed by a token and a four-digit PIN, with the token performing offline PIN verification, the possible attack type is PIN guessing. PIN guessing is an attack where an attacker tries to guess a user's PIN by trying out different combinations of numbers until they find the correct one. In this scenario, an attacker could try to guess the four-digit PIN and use the token to verify whether it is correct. If the system does not have proper controls to prevent multiple failed attempts, such as locking the account after a certain number of failed attempts, it could be vulnerable to a PIN guessing attack. Brute force attacks, which involve trying out different combinations of usernames and passwords, are less likely in this scenario as the system uses a token for offline PIN verification. Smurf attacks and spoofing attacks are unrelated to this scenario.

26. (d) All options provided are examples of tokens that can be used in token-based authentication.

27. (b) The type of token that generates a new password for every authentication attempt is a dynamic token. A dynamic token, a one-time password (OTP) token, generates a new password every time the user logs in. This contrasts with a static token, which uses the same password for every login attempt. Dynamic tokens are a common way to implement two-factor authentication (2FA), which requires users to provide two forms of identification (e.g., a password and a dynamic token) to gain access to a system or resource. This helps to improve security by making it more difficult for attackers to gain unauthorized access, even if they have obtained a user's password through other means.

28. (d) The benefit of "Rigid authentication methods" is not associated with token-based authentication. Instead, token-based authentication provides flexibility in authentication methods, combining it with other authentication methods, such as biometrics, to provide additional security and flexibility in the authentication process.

29. (c) Smart card token. Smart card tokens require physical contact with a reader to initiate authentication. These tokens contain a microprocessor that stores and processes data, and they usually require the user to enter a PIN or biometric information to verify their identity.

30. (d) The physical characteristics of the token user are not a factor that can impact the security of token-based authentication. Factors that can impact the security of token-based authentication include the strength of the token encryption algorithm, the security of the token storage device, and the security of the token communication channel. These factors determine the overall security and effectiveness of the authentication system, and attackers can exploit any weakness in one of these areas to gain unauthorized access to the system.

31. (d) The CHAP (Challenge-Handshake Authentication Protocol) utilizes mutual authentication between the client and the server for security. CHAP is a widely used protocol for authenticating remote users and devices to network access servers, such as routers and switches. CHAP is a challenge-response authentication protocol that generates a random challenge value sent by the server to the client. The client then generates a response value using a cryptographic hash function that combines the challenge value with the client's password or secret key.

32. (a,b) a. Delegated authentication. b. Single sign-on.

33. (a) RADIUS. RADIUS stands for Remote Authentication Dial-In User Service and is a widely used protocol for network access authentication, authorization, and accounting (AAA) used by many organizations. It uses a shared secret, a password only known to the RADIUS server and the client, to secure the communication between the RADIUS server and the client during authentication. Kerberos also uses a shared secret, but it is used for mutual authentication between the client and server, not just for securing communication during authentication. PKI and LDAP are not directly related to share secrets for authentication.

34. (c) The feature Kerberos exclusively supports, not RADIUS or Diameter, is ticket-based authentication. Kerberos uses tickets to authenticate users to network services without transmitting their passwords across the network. This process involves three steps: authentication, ticket granting, and ticket validation. The ticket-based approach provides a more secure means of authentication because it eliminates the need to transmit sensitive user credentials over the network, reducing the risk of credential theft or interception by attackers. On the other hand, RADIUS and Diameter use a shared secret key to authenticate users and do not utilize ticket-based authentication.

35. (a) Dictionary attack.

36. (c) Hackers take advantage of Rainbow Tables by using precomputed tables of all possible plain-text values and their corresponding hashes to crack hashed passwords quickly. This involves looking up a hashed password and matching it to a string of clear text, thus revealing the original password. This method can be effective against weak passwords and hash functions with known vulnerabilities.

37. (a) The password-cracking technique that requires significant resources is proactive password checking. Proactive password checking involves checking passwords against a pre-computed table of password hashes or attempting to crack passwords using brute-force or dictionary attacks. These methods require significant computational resources, including high-end hardware and specialized software, to execute efficiently. In contrast, reactive password checking involves monitoring for and responding to failed login attempts in real time and does not require the same computational resources. Computer-generated and user-created passwords are not password-cracking techniques but methods for creating passwords.

38. (d) None of the above. The two broad categories of password-based authentication are: Static password-based authentication: This is the traditional form of authentication, where users must enter a fixed password or passphrase to access a system. Dynamic password-based authentication: In this method, a new password or passphrase is generated for every login attempt, and the password is valid for a limited time. This can include one-time passwords (OTP), time-based one-time passwords (TOTP), and other similar approaches.

39. (c) Passwords with a balanced key space, longer passphrases, high entropy, and complex passphrases can ensure password strength. A balanced key space ensures the passwords are complex and not easily guessable, while longer passphrases and high entropy strengthen the passwords. Complex passphrases can include upper and lower case letters, numbers, and special characters.

40. (c) Proactive password checking occurs before the user selects the password. It is a method of enforcing password policies by preventing users from choosing easily guessable or too-weak passwords. By conducting proactive password checking, administrators can improve the system's overall security by ensuring users create strong passwords that meet specific complexity requirements.

41. (b) A rainbow table attack is more effective when the password is not based on a dictionary word. This is because rainbow tables are pre-computed tables of hash values for possible plain-text passwords, usually based on dictionary words or commonly used passwords. If the password is not based on a dictionary word, the attacker will have more difficulty finding a matching hash value in the table, making the attack less effective. However, using large salt values can also make a rainbow table attack less effective by increasing the computational resources required to generate the table.

42. (b) A Registration authority typically performs identity proofing in the electronic authentication.

43. (c) The remote user's location is not a factor affecting the security of remote user authentication.

44. (a) The primary purpose of a virtual private network (VPN) in remote user authentication is to provide a secure connection between the remote user and the authentication server. By creating a secure tunnel, a VPN ensures that all data transmitted between the remote user and the authentication server is encrypted and secure. This helps prevent third parties' unauthorized access or interception of sensitive authentication information.

45. (e) All authentication factors (something the user knows, has, is, and does) can be used for remote user authentication. None of them are unique to remote user authentication.

46. (a) To provide an additional layer of security by requiring the user to enter a unique code generated for each authentication attempt.

47. (c) Client host-to-server architecture often requires multi-factor authentication for identity management.

48. (c) One password is used for multiple systems. Multiple password uses refer to using the same password for multiple systems or applications. This practice makes the password vulnerable to attacks, as compromising one system's password can lead to unauthorized access to other systems. Using unique and strong passwords for each system is generally recommended to minimize the risk of a successful attack.

49. (c) Passwords with high entropy, larger salts, and larger stretching can help mitigate password guessing and cracking threats. High entropy passwords are more difficult to guess or crack, while larger salts and stretching increase the computational cost and time required for attackers to crack the passwords using brute force attacks or rainbow table attacks.

50. (a) Using a microprocessor and programmable memory is the unique feature that makes the smartcard so flexible. Smartcards are credit card-sized devices with an embedded microprocessor and memory, enabling them to store and process information securely. This makes them ideal for various applications, including identification, authentication, and payment systems. The microprocessor allows the card to perform cryptographic operations, while the programmable memory allows the card to store and update information as needed.

51. (c) Traditional authentication methods, such as username and password, are unsuitable for computer networks because they are vulnerable to various attacks, such as password guessing, eavesdropping, and replay attacks. They cannot also provide strong authentication and protect against unauthorized access. Additionally, they do not use cryptographic techniques to protect data in transit and at rest. Therefore, modern authentication methods, such as multi-factor authentication, biometric authentication, and smart card authentication, are used in computer networks to provide more robust security and protection against various attacks.

52. (b) Hybrid password attack.

53. (b) A pre-calculated table for reversing cryptographic hash functions is typically used for cracking password hashes.

54. (a) The two main steps in user authentication are identification and verification.

55. (c) Symmetric encryption does not serve as a means of user authentication. Symmetric encryption is a technique used for encrypting and decrypting data, not for authenticating users.

56. (c) The term for authenticating a user based on physical characteristics is "biometric authentication."

57. (a) Proactive password checking.

58. (c) Computer-generated password. Computer-generated passwords are often long and complex, making them difficult to remember, which can lead to poor user acceptance.

59. (d) Password cracking.

60. (b) The least expensive and least secure.

61. (c) The term that describes smart card authentication is "Proof-by-possession."

62. (d) "Token" typically refers to an individual's physical device or information used for authentication. Examples of tokens include smart cards, USB keys, and one-time passwords.

63. (c) Among the given options, biometrics provides the most robust security as it uses an individual's unique physical or behavioural characteristics for authentication, which are difficult to forge or steal. Smart cards and pattern locks also provide vital security but can be lost or stolen, and their passwords or patterns can be cracked. Passwords are the weakest form of authentication among these options, as they can be easily guessed, cracked, or stolen.

64. (d) The main disadvantage of using one-time passwords for authentication is that they require additional hardware or software to generate the passwords, which can be inconvenient and costly for users.

65. (a) The answers can be easily guessed or obtained through social engineering.

66. (c) They can be used for both online and offline authentication.

67. (b) Challenge-response.

68. (d) The type of attack described is a "Replay attack."

69. (a) The technique John's company uses to increase the security of their passwords, which involves adding a salt and cryptographic hash and running the process many times before storing the passwords, is Key stretching. Key stretching is a security measure that repeatedly applies a cryptographic hash function (usually a slow one) to a password and a randomly generated salt. This process is performed multiple times to make it computationally expensive and time-consuming for attackers to crack the passwords using brute force or dictionary attacks.

70. (b) Remote user authentication verifies a user's identity from a remote location. It involves confirming the identity of a user attempting to access a system or network from a location that is not physically present at the organization's premises. Remote user authentication is commonly used when users need to access systems or resources over a network or the internet. Various authentication methods and protocols are used to validate remote users' identity securely.

71. (d) Physical key authentication. Physical key authentication is not a commonly used method for remote user authentication. While it is used for physical access control to buildings or rooms, it is not typically used for remote access to computer systems or networks. The other options (password-based authentication, biometric authentication, and token-based authentication) are more common methods for verifying the identity of remote users accessing digital resources.

72. (c) Token-based authentication. Token-based authentication involves using a unique physical device, often called a "token," to verify a user's identity. These tokens can take various forms, such as hardware tokens (like smart cards or USB tokens) or software tokens (usually generated by mobile apps). Users must possess the physical token or access the software token to authenticate themselves remotely. This method adds an extra layer of security beyond simple password-based authentication.

73. (d) Something the user remembers. Authentication factors that rely on something the user knows typically involve information that only the user should know, such as a password or a PIN (Personal Identification Number). This factor, often called "knowledge-based authentication, " is a common method for verifying a user's identity.

74. (d) Something the user has. Authentication factors that rely on something the user possesses typically involve physical objects or tokens, such as smart cards, security tokens, mobile devices, or cryptographic keys. These objects prove the user's identity by possessing the required item, a characteristic of "possession-based authentication."

75. (c) Token-based authentication. Token-based authentication often involves a one-time password (OTP) that changes periodically. Users are provided with a token, either hardware or software, that generates a new OTP at set intervals. When authenticating, the user must enter the current OTP, which is valid only for a short period of time, adding a layer of security compared to static passwords.

76. (b) Biometric authentication relies on individuals' unique physiological or behavioural characteristics to verify their identity. Examples of biometric traits include fingerprint scans, iris scans, facial recognition, voice recognition, and behavioural patterns like typing speed or mouse movement. These characteristics are unique to each person and are difficult to forge, making biometric authentication a secure method for remote user authentication.

77. (d) Certificate-based authentication relies on digital certificates issued by a trusted Certificate Authority (CA). These certificates bind a user's identity to a public key, and the authentication process involves presenting a valid certificate to prove identity. Certificate-based authentication is commonly used in secure communication protocols like SSL/TLS and is a strong method for remote user authentication, particularly in enterprise and government settings.

78. (c) Something the user does. Authentication factors that rely on something the user does involve actions or behaviours unique to the user. These may include typing patterns, mouse movements, or other behavioural biometrics. This category is known as "something the user does" or "behavioural authentication."

79. (c) Token-based authentication, specifically using mobile apps or devices, often involves generating and delivering temporary access codes (one-time passwords or OTPs) to a user's mobile device. These codes are used for authentication and are typically valid for a short period of time, enhancing security compared to static passwords. Mobile-based token authentication is a common method for securing remote access to various services and systems.

The page was left intentionally blank.

Chapter 10
Message Authentication

This chapter includes questions from the following topics:
- Message Authentication.
- Hashing Function.
- SHA Algorithm.
- Message Authentication Code.
- MD5 Hash Algorithm.
- HMAC.
- Digital Signature.

1. **What maximum message bit length can be used with the SHA-512 algorithm?**
   a. 2^{128}
   b. 2^{182}
   c. 2^{28}
   d. 2^{82}

2. **Which statement accurately describes the concept of hashing?**
   a. Confidentiality.
   b. Integrity.
   c. Availability.
   d. All of the above.

3. **What is the cryptographic attack that relies on a brute-force method to guess a targeted password by trying out all possible combinations until the correct one is discovered?**
   a. It is an offline attack.
   b. Spoofing attack.
   c. A brute force attack.
   d. Eavesdropping attack.

4. **If a 287-bit message is to be padded using the SHA algorithm, how many zeros are needed to complete the padding?**
   a. 145
   b. 160
   c. 97
   d. 159

5. **Among the following Message Authentication Codes (MAC), which one is not susceptible to length extension attacks?**
   a. HMAC-SHA.
   b. CBC-MAC.
   c. CMAC.
   d. Poly1305-AES.

6. **Which of the following is an irreversible one-way function?**
   a. DES
   b. SHA-1

   c.   RSA

   d.   AES

7. **What is the weakness of the MD5 hash function in message authentication?**
   a.   It has a fixed-length output.
   b.   It is resistant to collision attacks.
   c.   It is vulnerable to length extension attacks.
   d.   It provides perfect forward secrecy.

8. **Which of the following statements are true regarding hash values? (Select all that apply)**
   a.   Determining file size.
   b.   Filtering known suitable files from potentially suspicious data.
   c.   Reconstructing file fragments.
   d.   Validating that the original data has not changed.

9. **What is the term used to refer to protecting against unauthorized data modification?**
   a.   Confidentiality.
   b.   Integrity.
   c.   Authenticity.
   d.   Non-repudiation.

10. **What is the most effective technique to secure a password stored on a server and used for user authentication?**
   a.   Encrypting the server password with asymmetric keys.
   b.   Encrypting the server password with the user's private key.
   c.   Encrypting the server password with a public key.
   d.   Hashing the server password.

11. **Which of the following statements accurately describes the Hash function?**
   a.   Hashing provides integrity.
   b.   Maps data of arbitrary size to data of a fixed size.
   c.   Hashing makes data easy to reconstruct.
   d.   Protecting the data from unauthorized access.

12. **Which of the following options is not a tool for ensuring data integrity?**
   a.   Backups.
   b.   Physical protections.
   c.   Checksums.
   d.   Data correction codes.

13. **Which of the following message authentication protocols provides mutual authentication?**
   a.   HMAC.
   b.   TLS.
   c.   SAML.
   d.   Kerberos.

14. **VRR Academy has implemented a technique that involves adding a salt and cryptographic hash to their passwords and then running this process multiple times before storing them. What is this technique called?**

    a. Key stretching.
    b. Rainbow table.
    c. Salting.
    d. Collision resistance.

15. **What is the term used to describe verifying the steps taken to maintain evidence integrity?**
    a. Security Investigation.
    b. Chain of custody.
    c. Three As of investigation.
    d. Security policy.

16. **Which of the following methods can be used to prevent message replay attacks?**
    a. Using a nonce.
    b. Using a one-time pad.
    c. Using a hash function.
    d. Using a public key.

17. **Which of the following is an example of a hash-based Message Authentication Code (MAC)?**
    a. RSA
    b. AES
    c. HMAC
    d. PKCS#1

18. **Which of the following statements accurately describes a hashing function used for digital signature? (Select all that apply)**
    a. It must give a hashed message which is shorter than the original message
    b. It must be hardware-implementable
    c. Two different messages should not give the same hashed message
    d. is not essential for implementing a digital signature

19. **Which of the following is not a typical secure message authentication scheme requirement?**
    a. It should be computationally efficient.
    b. It should be able to authenticate messages of any length.
    c. It should be resistant to replay attacks.
    d. It should be resistant to preimage attacks.

20. **What is the method used by a sender to sign a hashed message?**
    a. His public key
    b. His private key
    c. Receiver's public key
    d. Receiver's private key

21. **What is the security property of a secure hash function used for message authentication?**
    a. It is collision-resistant.
    b. It is preimage-resistant.
    c. It is a trapdoor function.
    d. It is a one-way function.

22. **Which algorithm is used for verifying data integrity received from a remote user using a 128-bit hash?**
    a. Diffie-Hellman
    b. RSA (Rivest Shamir Adelman)
    c. MD5 (Message Digest 5)
    d. El Gamal

23. **What security criterion does hashing verify during the digital signature process?**
    a. Data integrity
    b. Non-repudiation
    c. Confidentiality
    d. Authentication

24. **What is the disadvantage of using symmetric key message authentication? (Select all that apply)**
    a. Key distribution is complex.
    b. The message length is limited.
    c. The key length must be longer than the message.
    d. The security of the system depends on the security of the key.

25. **What can be accomplished using digital signatures?**
    a. Encryption
    b. Availability
    c. Non-repudiation.
    d. Hashing

26. **What is not a concern of message authentication?**
    a. Validating the identity of the originator.
    b. Protecting the integrity of a message.
    c. Non-repudiation of origin.
    d. Non-repudiation of receipt.

27. **What is not a property of a secure Message Authentication Code (MAC)?**
    a. It should be easy to compute.
    b. It should be infeasible to forge a valid MAC.
    c. It should be infeasible to find a collision.
    d. It should be able to handle messages of arbitrary length.

28. **What are the proper criteria for a function to be considered a cryptographic hash function (h)? (Select all that apply)**
    a. We can find different data x and y where $h(x) = h(y)$.
    b. For a given data x where $h(x) = z$, we cannot find a data y different from x where $h(x) = h(y) = z$.
    c. For a given data x and a key k, it should be easy to compute $h(x) = z$ using the key k.
    d. For a given digest z, it is possible to reconstruct the data x where $h(x) = z$

29. **What is a true statement about hashing?**
    a. The original message can be retrieved from the hash if you have the encryption key.
    b. A weakness of hashing is that the hash is proportional in length to the original message.
    c. Hashing uses algorithms that are known as "one-way" functions.
    d. If two hashes differ only by a single character, you can infer that the original messages differ

very little.

30. **Which mechanism would assure the integrity of a message but not do much to assure confidentiality or availability?**
    a. Encrypting
    b. Hashing
    c. Audit logs
    d. Mirroring

31. **What is a true statement about Hash functions?**
    a. Hashes are becoming easier to reverse engineer since computers are becoming more powerful.
    b. The length of the hash string is proportional to the length of the input so that the approximate message length can be derived from a hash.
    c. Using hashing is an excellent way to ensure the confidentiality of your messages.
    d. Hashing is a reliable way to ensure the integrity of a message.

32. **Which of the following is not an example of a commonly used hash function for message authentication?**
    a. SHA-256
    b. MD5
    c. SHA-3
    d. AES

33. **Why would you make hash values of all the data on a system before moving or analyzing it?**
    a. To expose viruses or malware signatures in the data.
    b. Data analysis is primarily focused on what you learn from the hash values.
    c. To encrypt the original data so it cannot be further corrupted.
    d. To preserve the integrity of the original data.

34. **What is the binary value of OPAD used in the HMAC algorithm?**
    a. 01111100
    b. 01011100
    c. 10110110
    d. 00110110

35. **What is the size of the hash value/code produced by the MD5 algorithm?**
    a. 150
    b. 160
    c. 128
    d. 112

36. **What indicates that a digitally signed message has been altered during transmission?**
    a. The altered content has turned black.
    b. The digital signature could not be verified using the sender's public key.
    c. The message could not be opened.
    d. Introduction of some special symbols in the message.

37. **What does Mr Ali require from Mr Sam by email to ensure the source of information?**
    a. Sam should establish an SSH session to transfer the file rather than email it.

    b.   Sam should use PGP to encrypt the email.

    c.   Sam should digitally sign the mail.

    d.   Sam should use a hashing algorithm on the document and include the message digest in his email along with the document.

38. How many rounds of computation steps does the SHA-256 algorithm perform?
   a. 80
   b. 76
   c. 64
   d. 70

39. What type of function is a MAC concerning message authentication?
   a. One-to-many function.
   b. One-to-one function.
   c. Many-to-one function.
   d. One-to-many function.

40. What is the size of each data block in the SHA-512 algorithm?
   a. 1024
   b. 512
   c. 256
   d. 1248

41. What is the size of the output hash value produced by the SHA-1 algorithm?
   a. 256 bits.
   b. 160 bits.
   c. 180 bits.
   d. 128 bits.

42. Can you define what a Hash Function is?
   a. The hash function creates a small, flexible block of data.
   b. The hash function creates a small, fixed block of data.
   c. The hash function creates an encrypted block of data.
   d. None of the above.

43. How would you describe the property of a Hash function known as collision-free?
   a. It is computationally infeasible to find data mapping to a specific hash.
   b. It is computationally infeasible to produce digest from large-size inputs.
   c. It is computationally infeasible for two different inputs to result in the same digest.
   d. It is computationally infeasible to design an algorithm that inverts the hash function.

44. What is another term used for a Message Authentication Code?
   a. Keyed hash function.
   b. Message key hash function.
   c. Hash code.
   d. Key code.

45. When someone sends a message but denies sending it later, what is this an example of?
   a. Source repudiation.

b. Masquerading.
c. Content modification.
d. Destination repudiation.

46. Which technique can be used to ensure data integrity?
a. Hash Value.
b. Passwords.
c. Uninterruptible power supply.
d. Cypher Text

47. What assures the sender cannot deny having sent the message and the recipient cannot deny receiving it?
a. Repudiation
b. Non-repudiation.
c. Integrity
d. Authentication

48. Which scenario indicates that an unauthorized entity has altered a message?
a. The private key has been altered.
b. The message digest has been altered.
c. The message has been appropriately encrypted.
d. The public key has been altered.

49. What is the size of the hash value generated by the MD5 algorithm?
a. 128
b. 150
c. 160
d. 112

50. What is the most appropriate definition of a digital signature?
a. A method of transferring a handwritten signature to an electronic document.
b. A method to let the receiver of the message proves the source and integrity of a message.
c. A method to provide an electronic signature and encryption.
d. A method to encrypt confidential information.

51. Which of the following is not a necessary piece of evidence for non-repudiation of origin?
a. Identity of the originator.
b. Identity of the recipient.
c. Contents of the message.
d. Time of generation.

52. What technique is used to find the same hash value for two different inputs to expose any mathematical weakness in the hashing algorithm?
a. Brute force attacks.
b. Man-in-the-middle attacks.
c. Birthday attacks.
d. Tcpdump and Wireshark.

53. **What happens when two different messages produce the same hash value?**
    a. Duplicate key.
    b. Corrupt key.
    c. Collision.
    d. Message digests.

54. **What is meant by the term "message digest"?**
    a. A key pair is used to maintain integrity.
    b. A value or checksum.
    c. An encrypted email.
    d. A one-time pad.

55. **Which of the following provides a means of maintaining digital evidence for e-commerce transactions?**
    a. Integrity.
    b. Confidentiality.
    c. Non-repudiation.
    d. Availability.

56. **What is it called when a sender changes their identity and sends a message to a receiver?**
    a. Masquerading.
    b. Content modification.
    c. Timing modification.
    d. Source repudiation.

57. **What results from increasing the key field length in a cryptographic hash function?**
    a. Make the hash output longer.
    b. Encrypt the input message.
    c. Increase the difficulty of attacking.
    d. Store the length of the message used.

58. **When Ahmed receives an email from Khalid, what is the best way to ensure the email is authentic?**
    a. Encryption
    b. Digital signature.
    c. Firewall
    d. Hash code

59. **In non-repudiation, why would a sender send the hash of the message through a Trusted Third Party (TTP) instead of sending the actual message?**
    a. Because the content of the message is not essential.
    b. To preserve the confidentiality of the message.
    c. To prove the TTP has received the message.
    d. To make it difficult for the receiver to deny receiving the message.

60. What is used to create a digital signature?
   a.   The receiver's private key.
   b.   The sender's public key.
   c.   The sender's private key.
   d.   The receiver's public key.

61. What is the most critical non-repudiation of origin (NRO) feature between two parties? (Select all that apply)
   a.   Identity and contents are not protected.
   b.   Time stamping depends on the accuracy of the recipient's clock.
   c.   The sender needs encryption or hashing capability.
   d.   Trusted Third Party does archive.

62. What is the method shown in the diagram below, which illustrates non-repudiation of origin (NRO) involving three parties?
   a.   Trusted Third-Party Signature.
   b.   In-line Trusted Third Party.
   c.   Trusted Third Party Token.
   d.   Trusted Third Party Digest Signature.

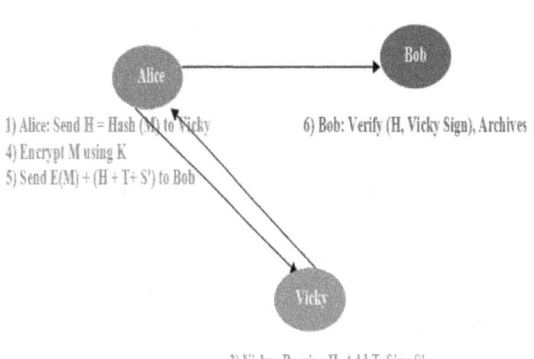

Answer key

1.   (d) The maximum message bit length used with the SHA-512 algorithm is 2^{128}, option (a). This means that the SHA-512 algorithm can handle messages up to 2^{128} bits in length, which is an incredibly large value. The SHA-512 algorithm is a hash function that produces a 512-bit hash value for a given input message. This hash value can then be used for various purposes, such as verifying the integrity of the message, providing a digital signature, or authenticating the message sender. The SHA-512 algorithm is considered very secure and widely used in many applications, including cryptography, digital signatures, and secure communications.

2.   (b) Integrity. Hashing converts input data (message) of arbitrary length into a fixed-size output value, usually a bit string of a specified length. The output value is referred to as the hash value or message digest. The primary purpose of hashing is to provide data integrity, i.e., ensuring that the data has not been altered or tampered with during transmission or storage. It does not provide confidentiality or availability.

3.   (c) A brute force attack, A brute force attack is a type of cryptographic attack where an attacker tries all possible combinations of characters, often starting with the simplest combinations, in an attempt to guess a password or decryption key. The attack aims to find the correct password or key to give the attacker access to the system or data they are trying to compromise. Brute force attacks are often used when the attacker has no other way to gain access to the system or data, and they can be time-consuming and resource-intensive. However, with powerful computers and password-cracking tools, brute-force attacks have become more common and can be successful in certain situations.

4.   (b) To pad a message using the SHA algorithm, the message is first appended with a 1-bit and then with some number of 0-bits until the message length is congruent to 448 modulo 512. Then, the length of the original message is appended as a 64-bit representation. In this case, the message length is 287 bits. So,

we need to append a 1-bit and then some 0-bits until the message length is congruent to 448 modulo 512. The number of 0 bits needed is 448 - (287 + 1) mod 512 = 160. Therefore, the answer is (b) 160.

5. (d) Poly1305-AES is not susceptible to length extension attacks, as it is designed to be used with specific block ciphers, such as AES. HMAC-SHA1, CBC-MAC, and CMAC are all susceptible to length extension attacks.

6. (b) SHA-1 is an irreversible one-way function.

7. (c) It is vulnerable to length extension attacks. Explanation: MD5 is a widely used cryptographic hash function that produces a fixed-length output of 128 bits. However, it is vulnerable to length extension attacks, where an attacker can append additional data to a hash value to create a new hash that appears to have been generated from a different message. This can lead to the creation of forged messages and the loss of data integrity. For this reason, using more secure hash functions such as SHA-256 or SHA-3 for message authentication is generally recommended.

8. (d) Validating that the original data has not changed. Hash values verify data integrity by generating a fixed-length unique string of characters, a digital fingerprint of the original data. Comparing the hash values of the original and the received data can determine whether the data has been altered or tampered with. Hash values are not used to determine file size, filter suitable files, reconstruct file fragments, or acquire images.

9. (b) Integrity protects data against unauthorized modification, deletion, or tampering. Data remains unchanged and unaltered during transmission or storage; any modification or alteration is detectable and traceable. Maintaining data integrity is essential for ensuring data accuracy, reliability, and consistency and protecting it from accidental or intentional damage. Integrity is often achieved through cryptographic hash functions, which generate fixed-length digital fingerprints of data that can be used to detect any changes or modifications. By comparing the hash value of the original data with the hash value of the received or stored data, integrity can be verified, and any tampering or alteration can be detected.

10. (d) The most effective technique to secure a password stored on a server and used for user authentication is hashing the server password. When a password is hashed, it is transformed into a fixed-length string of characters that is not easily reversible. The hashed password is stored on the server instead of the plain-text password. When a user logs in, the password they enter is hashed, and the result is compared to the hashed password stored on the server. If the two hashes match, the user is authenticated. Encrypting the server password with asymmetric keys or the user's private key is not recommended because they can decrypt the password if an attacker gains access to the private key. Encrypting the server password with a public key is also not recommended because anyone who has the public key can decrypt the password. Hashing is a one-way function, making it much more secure than encryption for password storage.

11. (b) Maps data of arbitrary size to fixed size data. A hash function is a mathematical function that takes in data of arbitrary size and outputs a fixed-size bit string called the hash value or message digest. Hashing is primarily used to ensure data integrity by verifying that a file or message has not been altered during transmission or storage. The hash function generates a unique fixed-length value representing the original data, and any change in the data, no matter how small, will result in a completely different hash value.

12. (b) While physical protections can help prevent damage or loss of data, they are not explicitly designed to ensure data integrity. The other options, backups, checksums, and data correction codes, are all tools used to help ensure data integrity.

13. (d) The message authentication protocol that provides mutual authentication is Kerberos. Kerberos is a network authentication protocol that uses a trusted third party to verify the identities of users and services on a network. It provides mutual authentication, where the client and the server authenticate each other's identities before communicating.

14. (a) The technique that VRR Academy has implemented is called key stretching. Key stretching is a method to make a cryptographic key derived from a password more secure by repeatedly applying a cryptographic hash function to the password, along with a randomly generated salt value. The number of times the hash function is applied is known as the iteration count or work factor. The higher the iteration count, the more secure the derived key becomes against brute-force attacks.

15. (b) The term used to verify the steps to maintain evidence integrity is "chain of custody." Chain of custody is a process used in legal and forensic investigations to document the chronological history of evidence, from the moment it is collected to the point of presentation in court. It involves tracking and documenting every individual who has handled the evidence and the date and time of each transfer. The chain of custody is important for maintaining the integrity of the evidence and ensuring that it can be admissible in court.

16. (a) The method that can be used to prevent message replay attacks is using a nonce. A nonce (number used once) is a random number generated by the sender that is included in the message. The receiver checks the nonce to ensure that the message has not been replayed. If the nonce is repeated, the receiver can identify it as a replay attack and discard the message.

17. (c) An example of a hash-based Message Authentication Code (MAC) is HMAC. HMAC (Hash-based Message Authentication Code) is a type of MAC that uses a cryptographic hash function to verify the integrity and authenticity of a message. It involves applying a secret key to a message and hashing the result using a cryptographic hash function, such as SHA-256 or SHA-512.

18. (c,d) The following statements accurately describe a hashing function used for digital signature: Two different messages should not give the same hashed message. This is known as the collision resistance property of a hashing function, and it is essential for ensuring that an attacker cannot forge a digital signature. It is not essential for implementing digital signatures but is often used as part of the process. A digital signature is created by combining a message with a private key, and the resulting signature can be verified using the corresponding public key. A hashing function can be used to reduce the size of the message before it is signed, making the process more efficient and secure.

19. (b) While a message authentication scheme should be able to handle messages of various lengths, it is not necessary for it to be able to authenticate messages of any length. In practice, there are often limits on the maximum message size that can be authenticated.

20. (b) The method a sender uses to sign a hashed message is his private key. A digital signature is created by combining a message with a private key, and the resulting signature can be verified using the corresponding public key. The sender uses his private key to sign the hashed message, which can be verified by anyone who has access to his public key. Therefore, option (b), "his private key," is the correct answer.

21. (a) A security property of a secure hash function used for message authentication is that it is collision-resistant. Collision resistance is a property of a hash function, which means it is computationally

infeasible to find two messages that produce the same hash value. This property is important for message authentication because it ensures that an attacker cannot create a fraudulent message with the same hash value as a legitimate one.

22. (c) The algorithm that is used for verifying data integrity received from a remote user using a 128-bit hash is MD5 (Message Digest 5). MD5 is a widely used hashing algorithm that produces a 128-bit hash value. It is commonly used for verifying the integrity of data received from a remote user and for other cryptographic applications such as password storage.

23. (a) Hashing verifies the data integrity criterion during the digital signature process. Data integrity ensures that the data has not been altered or tampered with during transmission. Hashing generates a fixed-length message digest or hash value of the data, which can be compared on the receiving end to verify that the data has not been modified in transit.

24. (a,d) The disadvantage of using symmetric key message authentication is that the system's security depends on the key's security. A symmetric key system uses the same key for encryption and decryption. If attackers access the key, they can decrypt the messages and compromise the system. Therefore, it is crucial to keep the key secret and secure. Other disadvantages of symmetric key message authentication include the difficulty of key distribution, especially for large networks, and the message length limitation due to the fixed key size. The key length does not need to be longer than the message in a symmetric key system, but it should be long enough to provide sufficient security.

25. (c) Non-repudiation can be accomplished using digital signatures. Digital signatures are a cryptographic mechanism used to provide authenticity and integrity of electronic documents and messages, and they can be used to ensure non-repudiation, which means that the message's sender cannot deny having sent it.

26. (d) Non-repudiation of receipt is not a concern of message authentication. Message authentication primarily concerns verifying the sender's identity and protecting the message's integrity. Non-repudiation of origin, which ensures that the sender cannot deny having sent the message, is also a concern of message authentication.

27. (a) It should be easy to compute and is not a property of a secure Message Authentication Code (MAC). A MAC is a cryptographic technique used to verify the authenticity and integrity of a message, and a secure MAC should be computationally infeasible to forge or find a collision and should be able to handle messages of arbitrary length. However, a secure MAC is not necessarily easy to compute, as it often involves complex cryptographic operations.

28. The correct options are: (a,b,d) a. We cannot find different data x and y where $h(x) = h(y)$. b. For a given data x where $h(x) = z$, we cannot find a data y different from x where $h(x) = h(y) = z$. d. For a given digest z, it should be infeasible to reconstruct the data x where $h(x) = z$.

29. (c) Hashing uses algorithms known as "one-way" functions, which is a true statement about hashing. One-way hash functions are designed to be easy to compute in one direction but difficult to reverse. Given a hash value, it should be challenging to determine the original input message. The other statements in the options are not true. The original message cannot be retrieved from the hash even with the encryption key; the length of the hash is typically fixed regardless of the message length, and small differences in the original messages can result in vastly different hash values.

30. (b) Hashing. Hashing is applying a mathematical function to a message to create a fixed-length output, known as a hash. This hash can be used to verify the integrity of the original message by comparing it to the hash of the received message. However, hashing does not provide any confidentiality or availability guarantees. Encrypting provides confidentiality, audit logs provide availability, and mirroring provides both availability and redundancy.

31. (d) Hashing is a reliable way to assure the integrity of a message. Hash functions are commonly used for message integrity as they take a message of any length and produce a fixed-length output, known as a hash or digest, representing the message. Even a small change in the input message would result in a vastly different hash output, making it easy to detect tampering with the original message. However, hashing alone does not assure confidentiality, as anyone with the original message can easily compute the hash.

32. (d) AES is not an example of a commonly used hash function for message authentication. It is a symmetric encryption algorithm for confidentiality, not generating message digests. The commonly used hash functions for message authentication are SHA-256, MD5, and SHA-3.

33. (d) To preserve the integrity of the original data. By creating hash values of all the data on a system before moving or analyzing it, you can compare the original data's hash values with the data's hash values after it has been moved or analyzed. If the hash values match, you can be confident that the data has not been altered or corrupted. This is a way to ensure the integrity of the original data.

34. (b) The binary value of OPAD used in the HMAC algorithm is b. 01011100.

35. (c) The size of the hash value/code produced by the MD5 algorithm is 128 bits.

36. (b) The digital signature could not be verified using the sender's public key, indicating that a digitally signed message was altered during transmission. When a message is digitally signed, the sender uses their private key to generate a signature appended to it. The receiver then uses the sender's public key to verify the signature. If the signature cannot be verified, the message has been altered or tampered with in some way during transmission.

37. (d) Sam should use a hashing algorithm on the document and include the message digest in his email along with the document. This would allow Mr Ali to verify the document's integrity by calculating its message digest using the same algorithm and comparing it with the one sent by Sam. However, it does not assure the sender's authenticity or the message's confidentiality. Mr Sam could use PGP to encrypt and digitally sign the email to ensure these.

38. (c) The SHA-256 algorithm performs 64 rounds of computation steps.

39. (b) One-to-one function. A MAC (Message Authentication Code) is a cryptographic technique that uses a secret key to generate a fixed-size message authentication code (MAC) from the original message. The MAC is a one-to-one function of the message and the secret key, meaning that the MAC value is always the same for a given message and key. Therefore, the MAC provides message authentication by verifying the integrity and authenticity of a message, ensuring that the message has not been tampered with or forged.

40. (a) The size of each data block in the SHA-512 algorithm is 1024 bits. Therefore, the correct answer is a. 1024.

41. (b) The size of the output hash value produced by the SHA-1 algorithm is 160 bits.

42. (b) The hash function creates a small, fixed data block. A hash function is a mathematical function that takes in an input (or "message") and produces a fixed-size, alphanumeric string of characters as output, which is referred to as a "hash value" or "hash code." Hash functions are commonly used in cryptography, computer security, and data analysis to verify data integrity, indexing, and search data. The hash function maps the input data to a fixed-size output, usually much smaller than the input data, making it easier to process and store. The hash function is designed to be a one-way function, meaning it is difficult (ideally impossible) to reverse-engineer the input data from the hash output. Additionally, any slight change in the input data should result in a significant change in the output hash value, making it helpful in detecting any unintended or malicious alterations to the data.

43. (c) It is computationally infeasible for two different inputs to result in the same digest.

44. (a) Keyed hash function.

45. (a) This is an example of source repudiation, where the sender denies sending the message even though it appears to have been sent from their account or device.

46. (a) Hash Value can be used to ensure data integrity.

47. (b) Non-repudiation assures that the sender cannot deny having sent the message, and the recipient cannot deny receiving it.

48. (b) The altered message digest indicates that an unauthorized entity has altered a message. The message digest is a hash value computed on the message, and any change to the message, intentional or unintentional, will result in a different digest. Hence, if the message digest has been altered, the message has been tampered with, and its integrity is compromised.

49. (a) The size of the hash value generated by the MD5 algorithm is 128 bits.

50. (b) A digital signature is a method to let the receiver of the message prove the source and integrity of a message. It is a cryptographic technique used to verify the authenticity of a digital message or document. It involves using a private key to sign a message, which anyone with access to the corresponding public key can verify. This allows the recipient to verify that it has not been altered in transit and that the claimed sender indeed sent it.

51. (b) Identity of the recipient. Non-repudiation of origin refers to the ability to prove that the sender of a message cannot deny having sent it. The necessary evidence for non-repudiation of origin is the originator's identity, the contents of the message, and the time of generation. The identity of the recipient is not relevant to non-repudiation of origin.

52. (c) Birthday attacks are used to find the same hash value for two different inputs to expose any mathematical weakness in the hashing algorithm. The attack is named after the birthday paradox, which states that in a group of 23 randomly chosen people, there is about a 50% chance that two have the same birthday. Similarly, in a hashing algorithm with a fixed output size, the probability of two different inputs producing the same hash value increases as the number of inputs hashed increases. This vulnerability can be exploited to generate collisions in the hash function, leading to security breaches.

53. (c) Collision. When two different messages produce the same hash value, it is called a collision. Hash functions are designed to be collision-resistant, meaning it is computationally infeasible to find two messages that produce the same hash value. However, collisions can still occur in practice, particularly if the hash function has weaknesses or vulnerabilities.

54. (b) "Message digest" refers to a value or checksum generated from a message using a hashing algorithm. The message digest is a fixed-length representation of the original message and is used to ensure the integrity of the message by detecting any changes that may have been made during transmission.

55. (c) Non-repudiation maintains digital evidence for e-commerce transactions, as it ensures that the sender cannot deny having sent the message, and the recipient cannot deny having received it. This helps establish the transaction's authenticity and integrity, essential for maintaining digital evidence. Integrity, confidentiality, and availability are important aspects of information security but do not directly address the issue of maintaining digital evidence in e-commerce transactions.

56. (a) Masquerading.

57. (c) Increasing the key field length in a cryptographic hash function would increase the difficulty of attacking the hash function. It would not necessarily make the hash output longer or encrypt the input message, but it could impact the storage requirements for the hash value.

58. (b) The best way to ensure an email is authentic when received from Khalid is by verifying the digital signature.

59. (d) To make it difficult for the receiver to deny receiving the message. By sending the hash of the message through a Trusted Third Party (TTP), the sender can provide proof that they sent a message with specific content to the receiver without revealing the content of the message itself. This makes it difficult for the receiver to deny receiving the message, as the TTP can provide evidence that the message was sent and received with specific content.

60. (c) The sender's private key creates a digital signature.

61. (b,c,d) b. Time stamping depends on the accuracy of the recipient's clock. c. The sender needs encryption or hashing capability. d. Trusted Third Party does archive.

62. (b) Based on the given options, the method shown in the diagram, which illustrates non-repudiation of origin (NRO) involving three parties, is a "Trusted Third-Party Signature."

The page was left intentionally blank.

Chapter 11
Biometric Security

This chapter includes questions from the following topics:

- Biometric Authentication.
- Two-Two-factor authentication.
- Multi-factor Authentication.
- Biometric Authentication.
- Behavioural Biometric Challenges.

1. **You want to grant access to network resources based on authenticating an individual's retina during a scan. Which security method uses a physical characteristic as a method of determining identity?**
   a. Smart card.
   b. I&A.
   c. Biometrics.
   d. CHAP.

2. **Which of the following is the most accurate biometric authentication?**
   a. Fingerprint.
   b. Handprint.
   c. Iris.
   d. Voice.

3. **What metric is used to evaluate biometric performance regarding the system's capacity to authenticate an authorized user by calculating the rate at which an unauthorized user is granted access by mistake?**
   a. False acceptance rate.
   b. False rejection rate.
   c. Crossover error rate.
   d. Failure to capture.

4. **Your bank just implemented 2-factor authentication. Before you can access your account, which two (2) pairs of factors would satisfy the "2-factor" criteria? (Select all that apply)**
   a. Your password and PIN.
   b. Your bank's ATM card and PIN.
   c. Your password and fingerprint scan.
   d. Voice recognition and face scan.
   e. Your fingerprint scan and face scan.

5. **Which of the following would be considered multi-factor authentication?**
   a. Username and password.
   b. Username and pin.
   c. Thumbprint and password.
   d. Thumbprint and retina scan.

6. **What is used to measure biometric performance to rate the system's ability to correctly authenticate an authorized user by measuring the rate that an unauthorized user is mistakenly permitted access?**
   a. False acceptance rate.
   b. False rejection rate.
   c. Crossover error rate.
   d. Failure to capture.

7. **Biometric authentication is based on the following:**
   a. Something you know.
   b. Something you have.
   c. Something you are.
   d. Something you do.

8. **Which of the following is not a commonly used biometric trait?**
   a. Fingerprint.
   b. Iris pattern.
   c. Voice recognition.
   d. Social security number.

9. **Biometric authentication provides which type of security factor?**
   a. Single-factor authentication.
   b. Two-factor authentication.
   c. Multi-factor authentication.
   d. Non-factor authentication.

10. **Which of the following is an advantage of biometric authentication?**
    a. Easy to share with others.
    b. Difficult to replicate.
    c. It can be easily forgotten.
    d. Requires additional hardware.

11. **Which biometric trait is based on the unique characteristics of a person's face?**
    a. Retina scan.
    b. Facial recognition.
    c. Hand geometry.
    d. Gait recognition.

12. **Biometric authentication is primarily used for what?**
    a. Physical access control.
    b. Online banking.
    c. Password recovery.
    d. Data encryption.

13. **Which biometric trait can be affected by changes in weight or ageing?**
    a. Fingerprint.
    b. Voice recognition.
    c. Iris pattern.
    d. Hand geometry.

14. **The accuracy of biometric authentication systems is typically measured using what?**
    a. False positives.
    b. False negatives.
    c. True positives.
    d. All of the above.

15. **Which biometric trait captures and analyses the unique patterns in a person's voice?**
    a. Fingerprint.
    b. Retina scan.
    c. Voice recognition.
    d. DNA analysis.

16. **Which of the following is a potential concern with biometric authentication?**
    a. Privacy issues.
    b. Low accuracy rates.
    c. Incompatibility with devices.
    d. Lack of user acceptance.

17. **Biometric authentication can be used for what?**
    a. Time and attendance tracking.
    b. Online shopping.
    c. Social media login.
    d. All of the above.

18. **Which of the following is a physiological biometric trait?**
    a. Signature.
    b. Typing rhythm.
    c. DNA analysis.
    d. PIN code.

19. **Which of the following is a behavioural biometric trait?**
    a. Face recognition.
    b. Hand geometry.
    c. Retina scan.
    d. Gait recognition.

20. **Which biometric trait is based on the unique characteristics of a person's hand?**
    a. Fingerprint.
    b. Retina scan.
    c. Hand geometry.
    d. Voice recognition.

21. **The process of converting a biometric trait into a digital representation is called what?**
    a. Encoding.
    b. Decoding.
    c. Encryption.
    d. Authentication.

22. **Which of the following is a commonly used biometric trait for mobile devices?**

    a.   Facial recognition.
    b.   Iris pattern.
    c.   Palm print.
    d.   All of the above.

23. What is biometric authentication?
    a.   Using personal information to authenticate a user.
    b.   Using physical characteristics to authenticate a user.
    c.   Using a password to authenticate a user.
    d.   Using a key to authenticate a user.

24. Which of the following is not a common biometric authentication method?
    a.   Fingerprint scanning.
    b.   Voice recognition.
    c.   Facial recognition.
    d.   Password protection.

25. What is the primary benefit of biometric authentication?
    a.   Convenience.
    b.   Security.
    c.   Speed.
    d.   Cost-effectiveness.

26. Which of the following is an example of behavioural biometrics?
    a.   Fingerprint scanning.
    b.   Voice recognition.
    c.   Facial recognition.
    d.   Keystroke dynamics.

27. Which of the following biometric authentication methods is the most widely used?
    a.   Fingerprint scanning.
    b.   Voice recognition.
    c.   Facial recognition.
    d.   Iris scanning.

28. Which of the following is not a common use case for biometric authentication?
    a.   Access control.
    b.   Time and attendance tracking.
    c.   Online shopping.
    d.   Border security.

29. Which of the following is a disadvantage of biometric authentication?
    a.   It is not secure.
    b.   It is expensive.
    c.   It can be intrusive.
    d.   It is not widely available.

30. Which of the following biometric characteristics is unique to each individual?
    a.   Face shape.

    b. Eye colour.
    c. Fingerprint.
    d. Hair colour.

31. Which of the following is an example of physiological biometrics?
    a. Signature recognition.
    b. Keystroke dynamics.
    c. Iris scanning.
    d. Voice recognition.

32. Which of the following is an example of a multimodal biometric system?
    a. Fingerprint and voice recognition.
    b. Facial and retina recognition.
    c. Iris and hand geometry recognition.
    d. All of the above.

33. Which of the following is a benefit of using biometric authentication in healthcare?
    a. Improved patient privacy.
    b. Reduced wait times.
    c. Lower costs.
    d. Increased access to care.

34. Which of the following is a disadvantage of using biometric authentication in healthcare?
    a. Lack of standardization.
    b. Limited availability.
    c. High cost.
    d. All of the above.

35. Which of the following is an example of a security risk associated with biometric authentication?
    a. Data theft.
    b. Identity theft.
    c. Social engineering.
    d. All of the above.

36. Which of the following is an example of a problematic biometric modality to spoof?
    a. Face recognition.
    b. Fingerprint scanning.
    c. Voice recognition.
    d. Keystroke dynamics.

37. Which of the following is a benefit of using biometric authentication in the workplace?
    a. Increased security.
    b. Reduced costs.
    c. Improved productivity.
    d. All of the above.

38. Which of the following is a disadvantage of using biometric authentication in the workplace?
    a. Low user acceptance.
    b. Limited availability.

    c.   Difficulty in integrating with existing systems.
    d.   All of the above.

39. **Which of the following is a challenge associated with using biometric authentication in mobile devices?**
    a.   Battery drain.
    b.   Low accuracy.
    c.   Limited processing.
    d.   All of the above.

40. **What is the purpose of using biometrics?**
    a.   To ensure confidentiality.
    b.   To maintain integrity.
    c.   To provide authentication.
    d.   To ensure availability.

41. **Which authentication method cannot be defeated using a brute force attack?**
    a.   Biometric.
    b.   Password.
    c.   Pattern.
    d.   PIN.

42. **During biometric identification, which of the following can result in slow system response times and increased expense?**
    a.   One-to-one matching.
    b.   One-to-many matching.
    c.   Many-to-one matching.
    d.   Many-to-many matching.

43. **What is the term used to describe the degree of difference between a biometric sample and a reference value returned by a biometric algorithm?**
    a.   Sensor Score.
    b.   Data Score.
    c.   Difference Score.
    d.   Live Score.

44. **What is the term for the automated process of identifying and encoding unique features from a biometric sample to create a template?**
    a.   Signature verification.
    b.   Verification.
    c.   Extraction.
    d.   Feature extraction.

45. **What is the term for collecting a biometric sample from an individual through a sensor?**
    a.   Capture or Submission.
    b.   Feature Extraction.
    c.   Iris recognition.
    d.   Recognition

46. Which of the following is not a factor that affects the strength of a biometric authentication system?
   a. The uniqueness of the biometric trait.
   b. The ability to spoof the trait.
   c. The precision of the sensor used to capture the trait.
   d. The computational power of the system used for recognition.

Answer Key

1. (c) Biometrics is a security method that uses physical characteristics, such as retina scans, fingerprints, or facial recognition, to determine an individual's identity. In this case, authenticating based on a retina scan would be considered a biometric authentication method.

2. (c) Iris recognition is considered one of the most accurate biometric authentication methods. The patterns in the eye's iris are unique to each individual and remain stable throughout a person's life. Iris recognition systems are highly accurate and less prone to false positives or negatives than biometric methods like fingerprints, handprints, or voice recognition.

3. (c) Crossover error rate. The metric used to evaluate biometric performance regarding the system's capacity to authenticate an authorized user by calculating the rate at which an unauthorized user is granted access by mistake is the "crossover error rate" (CER). The CER represents the point at which the false acceptance rate (FAR) and the false rejection rate (FRR) are equal, providing a balance between Security (FAR) and user convenience (FRR). Lower CER values indicate better overall biometric system performance.

4. (b) Your bank's ATM card and PIN. c. Your password and fingerprint scan. To satisfy the "2-factor" criteria for authentication, you must use two different factors from at least two categories: Something you know (Knowledge factors): Examples include passwords, PINs, or answers to security questions. Something you have (Possession factors): Examples include physical devices like ATM cards, smart cards, or mobile phones. Something you are (Biometric factors): Examples include fingerprint scans, voice recognition, or face scans. So, in this case, Option b combines Something you have (the bank's ATM card) and Something you know (the PIN). Option c combines Something You Know (the password) and Something You Are (the fingerprint scan). These combinations satisfy the "2-factor" criteria for authentication.

5. (c) Thumbprint and password. Multi-factor authentication (MFA) involves verifying a user's identity using two or more factors. In the options provided, Option c combines Something You Are (the thumbprint) and Something You Know (the password). This is an example of multi-factor authentication because it uses two different factors. The other options (a, b, and d) only involve a single factor each (Something you know or something you are) and do not constitute multi-factor authentication.

6. (a) False acceptance rate. The metric used to measure biometric performance regarding the system's ability to correctly authenticate an authorized user while measuring the rate at which an unauthorized user is mistakenly permitted access is the "false acceptance rate" (FAR). The FAR represents the percentage of authentication attempts by unauthorized users that are incorrectly accepted by the system, indicating a failure in security.

7. (c) Something you are. Biometric authentication is based on "something you are," which refers to an individual's unique physical or behavioural characteristics, such as fingerprints, retina scans, voice patterns, or facial features. These biometric traits are used to verify a person's identity. The other options

correspond to different authentication factors: "Something you know" refers to knowledge-based factors like passwords or PINs. "Something you have" refers to possession-based factors like smart cards or physical tokens. "Something you do" typically is not a primary authentication factor, but it can be considered in specific contexts, such as behavioral Biometrics, which involve actions like typing patterns or mouse movements.

8. (d) A social security number (SSN) is not a biometric trait. It is a form of personal identification issued by the government, but it does not fall under Biometrics. Common biometric traits include fingerprints, iris patterns, voice recognition, facial features, and others, unique physical or behavioral characteristics of an individual used for authentication and identification purposes. Social security numbers are typically used for administrative and legal purposes but are not biometric traits.

9. (c) Multi-factor authentication. Biometric authentication provides a form of multi-factor authentication (MFA) because it relies on an individual's unique physical or behavioral characteristics (Something you are) as one of the factors. MFA involves using two or more different factors to verify a user's identity, and biometric authentication can be one of those factors when combined with other factors like Something you know (e.g., a password) or Something you have (e.g., a smart card).

10. (b) Difficult to replicate. One of the advantages of biometric authentication is that it is difficult to replicate because it relies on an individual's unique physical or behavioral traits, such as fingerprints or iris patterns. Unlike passwords or PINs, which can be shared, forgotten, or stolen, biometric characteristics are inherently tied to the individual and are challenging to reproduce without physical access to the person.

11. (b) Facial recognition is a biometric trait based on the unique characteristics of a person's face. It involves analyzing an individual's facial features and patterns to verify their identity. This technology has become increasingly popular for authentication and identification purposes in various applications, including security systems and mobile devices.

12. (a) Physical access control. Biometric authentication is primarily used for physical access control, such as gaining access to secure areas, buildings, or devices. Security systems often use it to ensure that only authorized individuals are granted access to specific physical locations or resources. While it can also be used for other purposes like online banking or password recovery, its primary application is physical security.

13. (b) Voice recognition can be affected by changes in weight, ageing, illness, or other factors that can alter the sound and characteristics of a person's voice. This makes it less stable over time compared to other biometric traits like fingerprints or iris patterns, which tend to remain relatively consistent throughout an individual's life.

14. (d) All of the above. The accuracy of biometric authentication systems is typically measured using all options. False positives represent instances where the system incorrectly identifies an unauthorized person as an authorized user. False negatives represent instances where the system incorrectly rejects an authorized user, denying them access. True positives represent instances where the system correctly identifies an authorized user. These metrics help evaluate the performance of a biometric authentication system and are used to calculate essential statistics such as the False Acceptance Rate (FAR), False Rejection Rate (FRR), and the crossover error rate (CER).

15. (c) Voice recognition captures and analyzes the unique patterns in a person's voice to verify their identity. This biometric trait relies on distinct vocal characteristics, including pitch, tone, cadence, and other factors, to determine if the person is who they claim to be. It is commonly used in applications like voice-activated assistants, telephone-based authentication systems, and voice biometric authentication.

16. (a) Privacy issues. One of the potential concerns with biometric authentication is privacy issues. Biometric data, such as fingerprints or facial recognition scans, is highly personal and unique to each individual. Storing and handling this sensitive data can raise privacy concerns, mainly if it is not secured correctly or used without the individual's informed consent. There is a need for careful management and protection of biometric data to address these privacy concerns.

17. (d) All of the above. Biometric authentication can be used for various purposes, including time and attendance tracking in workplaces, online shopping for secure payment authorization, and logging into social media accounts, among many other applications. It offers a secure and convenient way to verify a person's identity in various contexts.

18. (c) DNA analysis is a physiological biometric trait. It involves studying and analyzing an individual's unique genetic makeup, a fundamental aspect of their physiology. Unlike the other options listed, Signature is a behavioral biometric trait because it depends on how a person signs their name, which can vary. Typing rhythm is also a behavioral biometric trait because it is based on how an individual types on a keyboard, which can change. PIN code is something you know, not a physiological trait.

19. (d) Gait recognition is a behavioral biometric trait. It involves analyzing an individual's walking pattern or gait as a means of identification. How a person walks is considered a behavioral characteristic because it is based on their unique movement and style, which can vary from person to person. The other options listed: Face recognition is based on the physical features of the face (a physiological trait). Hand geometry is also based on the physical characteristics of the hand (a physiological trait). Retina scan involves the unique patterns of blood vessels in the retina (a physiological trait).

20. (c) Hand geometry is the biometric trait based on a person's unique characteristics, including the hand's size and shape, length and width of fingers, and other physical features. This form of biometric authentication relies on the distinct aspects of an individual's hand to verify their identity.

21. (a) Encoding is converting a biometric trait into a digital representation. During this process, the unique characteristics of the biometric trait, such as a fingerprint or iris pattern, are converted into a format that can be stored and processed digitally for use in biometric authentication systems. This encoded data is then used for comparison and verification during authentication.

22. (d) All of the above. Facial recognition, iris pattern, and palm print recognition are commonly used biometric traits for mobile devices. These biometric authentication methods enhance the security and convenience of unlocking mobile devices and authorizing transactions. Users can often choose from multiple biometric options, depending on the capabilities of their specific mobile device.

23. (b) Using physical characteristics to authenticate a user. Biometric authentication uses an individual's unique physical or behavioral characteristics to verify their identity. This can include traits like fingerprints, iris patterns, facial features, and voice patterns. It is a highly secure form of authentication because it relies on something inherent to the individual that is difficult to fake or steal.

24. (d) Password protection is not a biometric authentication method. It is a traditional authentication method that relies on something the user knows (a password) rather than Something inherent to the user's physical or behavioral characteristics. In contrast, biometric authentication methods use an individual's unique physical or behavioral traits, such as fingerprints, voice patterns, or facial features, to verify their identity.

25. (b) The primary benefit of biometric authentication is security. Biometric traits are unique to each individual and are difficult to forge or steal, making biometric authentication methods highly secure. While they can also provide convenience and speed, the primary emphasis is enhancing security in various applications, such as access control, identity verification, and authentication.

26. (d) Keystroke dynamics is an example of behavioral Biometrics. It involves analyzing an individual's unique typing patterns and rhythm as they type on a keyboard. This behavioral trait can be used to verify a person's identity and is based on their distinct typing habits, such as keypress timing and speed. The other options listed: Fingerprint scanning is a physiological biometric trait. Voice recognition and facial recognition are also physiological biometric traits based on the physical characteristics of a person's voice and face.

27. (a) Fingerprint scanning is the most widely used biometric authentication method. Due to its accuracy and ease of use, have been adopted in various applications, including smartphones, access control systems, and border security. Fingerprint sensors are commonly found on many devices and have a long history of successful implementation for biometric authentication. While other methods like facial and voice recognition are also gaining popularity, fingerprint scanning remains the most prevalent.

28. (c) Online shopping. While biometric authentication can be used for various purposes, including access control, time and attendance tracking, and border security, it is not commonly used for online shopping. Online shopping typically relies on other forms of authentication, such as username and password, credit card information, and two-factor authentication methods like one-time passwords (OTP) or SMS verification. While Biometrics may become more prevalent in the future, it is not a common method for online shopping authentication as of my last knowledge update in September 2021.

29. (c) One of the disadvantages of biometric authentication is that it can be intrusive. Biometric methods often require collecting personal physical or behavioral data, such as fingerprints, iris scans, or facial recognition. Some individuals may find this process intrusive or uncomfortable, as it involves capturing and storing their biometric information. Additionally, privacy concerns can arise when biometric data is collected and stored, which can be seen as an intrusion into an individual's personal information.

30. (c) Among the options listed, fingerprints are unique to each individual. The ridge patterns and minutiae points on a person's fingerprint are highly distinct and remain consistent throughout their lifetime. This uniqueness and stability make fingerprints a commonly used biometric characteristic for identity verification and authentication.

31. (c) Iris scanning is an example of physiological Biometrics. It involves analyzing the unique patterns in the iris of a person's eye to verify their identity. The iris, the coloured part of the eye surrounding the pupil, has distinct patterns unique to each individual and remains stable over time. This makes it a reliable physiological biometric trait for authentication purposes.

32. (d) All of the above.

33. (a) One of the benefits of using biometric authentication in healthcare is improved patient privacy. Biometric authentication can help ensure that only authorized individuals can access patients' medical records and sensitive healthcare information. It adds an extra layer of security and reduces the risk of unauthorized access or data breaches, thus safeguarding patient privacy and confidentiality. While biometric authentication can have other potential benefits in healthcare, such as enhancing security and accuracy, the primary advantage in this context is often related to privacy and data protection.

34. (d) All of the above.

35. (d) All of the above.

36. (a) Face recognition. Face recognition can be a problematic biometric modality to spoof because, in some cases, it can be susceptible to spoofing attempts using photographs or 3D models of a person's face. While advanced facial recognition systems employ anti-spoofing techniques, such as requiring users to blink or move their heads, there are still potential vulnerabilities.

37. (d) All of the above.

38. (d) All of the above.

39. (a) Battery drain. One of the challenges associated with using biometric authentication in mobile devices is the potential for increased battery drain. Running biometric sensors and processing algorithms can consume additional power, reducing the battery life of mobile devices. Manufacturers and developers work to optimize these systems to minimize the impact on battery life, but it remains a consideration for mobile biometric authentication.

40. (c) The primary purpose of using Biometrics is to provide authentication. Biometric authentication relies on individuals' unique physical or behavioral characteristics to verify their identity and grant access to systems, devices, or physical locations. While Biometrics can contribute to security and help ensure confidentiality and integrity in various contexts, its primary role is to authenticate and confirm the identity of individuals.

41. (a) Biometric authentication methods, such as fingerprint scanning, iris recognition, or facial recognition, cannot be defeated using a brute force attack because they rely on individuals' unique physical or behavioral characteristics. These traits cannot be guessed or systematically tried in the same way that a brute force attack can be used to guess passwords, patterns, or PINs. Brute force attacks are ineffective against biometric authentication because they require replicating the biometric trait, which is extremely difficult to achieve.

42. (b) During biometric identification, one-to-many matching, or "1:N" matching, can result in slow system response times and increased expense. In this matching type, the system compares the presented biometric sample (e.g., a fingerprint) against an extensive database of enrolled biometric templates to find a match. This process can be computationally intensive, especially when dealing with a large number of enrolled templates, and it can lead to slower response times and increased hardware and processing requirements, which can be expensive to maintain and scale.

43. (c) The term used to describe the degree of difference between a biometric sample and a reference value returned by a biometric algorithm is typically called the "Difference Score." This score represents the level of similarity or dissimilarity between the presented biometric sample and the stored reference

template, and it plays a crucial role in determining whether the authentication or identification is successful.

44. (d) Feature extraction. The term for the automated process of identifying and encoding unique features from a biometric sample to create a template is "Feature extraction." This process involves identifying specific characteristics or patterns within the biometric sample, such as fingerprint ridge patterns or facial landmarks, and converting them into a digital template that can be stored and used for subsequent authentication or identification.

45. (a) The term for collecting a biometric sample from an individual through a sensor is often called "Capture" or "Submission." This is the initial step where the individual provides their biometric data, such as a fingerprint or iris scan, to the biometric system for further processing, feature extraction, and comparison with reference templates.

46. (d) The computational power of the system used for recognition is not a factor that affects the strength of a biometric authentication system. While computational power can influence the speed and efficiency of biometric recognition processes, it does not directly impact the fundamental strength of the system. The other factors listed, such as the uniqueness of the biometric trait, the ability to spoof the trait, and the precision of the sensor used to capture the trait, are all critical factors that can affect the strength and security of a biometric authentication system.

Chapter 12
Database Security

This chapter includes questions from the following topics:
- Database Security.
- SQL Injection.
- Statistical Database.
- Inference.
- Access Control Policy.
- Inference Countermeasure.

1. **One of the following is not an option when encrypting a database:**
   a. Encrypting the entire database.
   b. Only encrypting specific fields.
   c. Only encrypting specific records.
   d. Only encrypting queries.

2. **Raja conducts a vulnerability scan on one of his network's computers and discovers SQL injection vulnerability. Which of the following security controls is almost certainly absent from the network?**
   a. Transport Layer Security.
   b. Data Leak Prevention / Data Loss Prevention.
   c. Intrusion Detection System.
   d. Web Application Firewall.

3. **When a web application is vulnerable to an SQL injection but does not return error messages, it may still be susceptible to**
   a. SQL Injection.
   b. Blind SQL Injection.
   c. URL Injection.
   d. OS Command Injection.

4. **Pick out the information that should be leaked to the user upon some error.**
   a. Stack trace.
   b. The failed SQL Query.
   c. A failed Authorisation.
   d. Database Schema Details.

5. **In _____, the creator of a table grants and revokes access rights to the table.**
   a. Centralised administration.
   b. Decentralised administration.
   c. Ownership-based administration.
   d. Partnership administration.

6. **What are the classifications of distributed databases, data warehouses, big data, and file shares?**
   a. Data models.
   b. Data source types.

    c.   Database types.
    d.   Datacentre types.

7. **Which data source type is represented by Hadoop, MongoDB, and BigTable?**
    a.   Big data databases.
    b.   Data warehouses.
    c.   File Shares.
    d.   Distributed databases.

8. **What is the term for data that has been lost and cannot be recovered?**
    a.   Orphan data.
    b.   Raw data.
    c.   Backup data.
    d.   None of the above.

9. **Where would you go for help creating security benchmarks for your database if you watched the video Leveraging Security Industry Best Practices?**
    a.   Central Intelligence Agency (CIA).
    b.   Center for Internet Security (CIS).
    c.   Common Vulnerability and Exposures (CVE).
    d.   Department of Defense/Defence Information Systems Agency (DoD/DISA).

10. **How do people access data the majority of the time?**
    a.   Through a database client.
    b.   Directly from a hardened repository.
    c.   Through an application.
    d.   Directly from a database.

11. **Which of the following is an open-source database management system?**
    a.   Oracle Database
    b.   Microsoft SQL Server
    c.   MySQL
    d.   SAP Sybase

12. **What database name maintains user accounts and information about local users?**
    a.   Security Account Manager.
    b.   System Access Manager.
    c.   Security Access Manager.
    d.   System Account Manager.

13. **Raja has just installed the new database application on his server. He then uninstalls the sample configuration files, configures the application settings properly, and updates the software to the most recent version, following his company's policy. Which of the following best characterises Raja's recent actions?**
    a.   Patch management.
    b.   Input Validation.
    c.   Application hardening.
    d.   Vulnerability scanning.

14. **Which one of the following is an Open-source DBMS?**
    a. Oracle Database.
    b. Microsoft SQL Server.
    c. MySQL.
    d. SAP Sybase.

15. **What is the database that stores user accounts and local users' information?**
    a. Security Account Manager.
    b. System Access Manager.
    c. Security Access Manager.
    d. System Account Manager.

16. **An attacker submits hostile data through a Web page that stores it in a file, database, or other data store and depends on some other Web page or mid-tier application to use that hostile data in constructing an SQL statement.**
    a. Second-order SQL injection.
    b. SQL Injection.
    c. Blind SQL Injection.
    d. OS Command Injection.

17. **SQL Injection affects what?**
    a. Confidentiality.
    b. Integrity.
    c. Availability.
    d. All of the above.

18. **Which US government entity is a co-publisher of the Database Security Requirements Guide (SRG) in the video Leveraging Security Industry Best Practices?**
    a. Federal Bureau of Investigation (FBI).
    b. Department of Defense (DoD).
    c. Central Intelligence Agency (CIA).
    d. Center for Internet Security (CIS).

19. **Which of the following is used to attack databases and gain access to sensitive data from databases?**
    a. Inference.
    b. Encryption.
    c. Interruption.
    d. Modification.

20. **A hacker tailoring his actions based on the database errors the application displays is an example of which type of SQL Injection attack?**
    a. Error-based.
    b. UNION-based.
    c. Blind injection.
    d. Out of Band.

21. **An SQL injection is often used to attack what?**
    a. Small-scale machines such as Diebold ATMs.

    b.   Large-scale sequel databases such as those containing credit card information.

    c.   Servers running SQL databases similar to Hadoop or Hive.

    d.   Servers built on NoSQL.

22. **A SQL injection is _____.**
    a.   An inference technique.
    b.   A web hacking technique.
    c.   A monitoring system.
    d.   A secure database management system.

23. **What is the process of modifying SDB (Statistical Database) data to provide statistics that cannot be used to infer values for individual records when replying to a query?**
    a.   Query restriction.
    b.   Data perturbation.
    c.   Output perturbation.
    d.   Data encryption.

24. **A web application that is vulnerable to SQL injection but does not send error messages may still be vulnerable to**
    a.   SQL Injection.
    b.   Blind SQL Injection.
    c.   URL Injection.
    d.   OS Command Injection.

25. **An attacker sends hostile data to a Web page, which stores it in a file, database, or other data stores, and then relies on another Web page or mid-tier application to generate a SQL query using that hostile data.**
    a.   Second-order SQL injection.
    b.   SQL Injection.
    c.   Blind SQL Injection.
    d.   OS Command Injection.

26. **Choose the recommended action to take when handling inference during the query time of a database.**
    a.   Modify the database structure to isolate sensitive data.
    b.   Reject inference-based queries.
    c.   Encrypt the database in its entirety.
    d.   Accept all inquiries that may result in an inference.

27. **Which two (2) activities should be considered suspicious and warrant further investigation?**
    a.   An authorised user attempts to run SQL statements with invalid syntax.
    b.   Use of an Application ID from a hostname that is different from what has been specified by the application owner.
    c.   Use of an Application ID from an IP that is different from what has been specified by the application owner.
    d.   It takes an authorised user three attempts to enter the correct password.

28. **Understanding the following is not an option when encrypting queries, and the legitimate responses are known as:**

a. Inference.
b. Intrusion.
c. Access control.
d. Rejection.

29. **Which of the following describes a countermeasure which can be used to prevent an SQL injection attack?**
    a. The Web server service should be installed on the same system as the database so the system can be appropriately hardened.
    b. Use client-side input validation for user input.
    c. Use server-side input validation for user input.
    d. Applications should never use stored procedures.

30. _____ **are the contiguous block of memory used to store data**
    a. Stacks.
    b. Cache.
    c. Buffers.
    d. Arrays.

31. **Which of the following will not help detect buffer overflow vulnerability?**
    a. Examine the source code for strings declared as local variables in the function.
    b. Examine the source code for strings declared as global variables in methods.
    c. Force a large volume of data on an application.
    d. Check for improper use of standard functions.

32. **What is the memory area utilized by an application and allocated dynamically at runtime?**
    a. Heap.
    b. Buffer.
    c. Stack.
    d. Cache.

33. **Which of the following can be used to prevent an SQL injection attack?**
    a. Use dynamic SQL.
    b. Convert all single quotes to double quotes.
    c. Convert all double quotes to single quotes.
    d. Use error messages that provide specific information on the Web server.

34. **Which of the following involves plotting the tables in the database?**
    a. Database enumeration.
    b. Database scanning.
    c. Database foot printing.
    d. Table foot printing.

35. **Statistical query means what?**
    a. A query that fetches data from a statistics table.
    b. A query that produces a value calculated over a query set.
    c. A query that shows the individual data from a statistics table.
    d. A query that is used to encrypt the statistics table.

36. The type of attack shown in the below piece of code is _____.
    SELECT prodinfo FROM prodtable WHERE prodname = 'blah'; DROP TABLE prodinfo; --'
    a. XSS.
    b. CSRF.
    c. SQL Injection.
    d. Both (a) and (c).

37. The information transfer path by which unauthorized data is obtained is referred to as a(n) what?
    a. Distortion Channel.
    b. Inference Channel.
    c. Interface Channel.
    d. Information Channel.

38. Which of the following approaches protects Statistical Database from Inference attack?
    a. Query Set.
    b. Perturbation.
    c. Query Restriction.
    d. Both b and c.

39. Which of the following is used in the perturbation technique to secure the statistical database?
    a. Hash Function.
    b. Noise.
    c. Digital signature.
    d. Passwords.

40. The data in the _____ type of Statistical Database can be modified to produce statistics that cannot be used to infer values for individual records.
    a. Information Perturbation.
    b. Data Perturbation.
    c. Output Perturbation.
    d. Input perturbation.

41. Choose the command that can be used to manage access right in a database
    a. SELECT
    b. REFERENCES
    c. UPDATE
    d. REVOKE

42. Defending against data inference by restricting statistical queries to a database is known as what?
    a. Query rejection.
    b. Database encryption.
    c. Query restriction.
    d. Data perturbation.

43. Inference can be defined as _____.
    a. Extracting non-sensitive data from sensitive data.
    b. Extracting sensitive data from non-sensitive data.

    c.   Extracting non-sensitive data from other non-sensitive data.

    d.   Extracting sensitive data from other sensitive data.

44. **What type of Access Control Policy is used if only the administrator can give access rights to the various databases of the organization's departments?**
    a.   Ownership-based administration.
    b.   Centralised administration.
    c.   Decentralised administration.
    d.   Membership-based administration.

45. **"Only a small number of privileged users are allowed to GRANT and REVOKE access rights to a database"; this case is an example of _____.**
    a.   Ownership-based administration.
    b.   Decentralised administration.
    c.   Centralised administration.
    d.   The user-based administration.

46. **Salim owns a table in a database and has Grand and Revoke Access rights. If Salim can provide Grand and Revoke access rights to other users, the type of administration used is**
    a.   Centralised Administration.
    b.   Ownership-based administration.
    c.   Decentralised Administration.
    d.   The user-based administration.

47. **The process of performing authorized queries and deducing unauthorized information from a database is called as what?**
    a.   Interference.
    b.   Inference.
    c.   Reference.
    d.   Authorisation.

48. **A census database where only the statistical data is stored is an example of what?**
    a.   Pure Statistical database.
    b.   Ordinary database with statistical access.
    c.   Encrypted database.
    d.   Statistical Query.

49. **Which database command can be used to manage the access right?**
    a.   Grant.
    b.   Select.
    c.   Refer.
    d.   Rights.

50. **Which of the following can be used to protect your database against inference?**
    a.   Query Restriction.
    b.   Data Perturbation.
    c.   Output Perturbation.
    d.   All the above.

51. Grant and Revoke access rights means what?
   a.   Giving or removing access rights to/from a user.
   b.   Adding or deleting table data.
   c.   Creating or dropping a table.
   d.   Encrypting or decrypting a database.

52. Which of the following is true about Inference?
   a.   Getting sensitive data from non-sensitive data.
   b.   Getting non-sensitive data from sensitive data.
   c.   Getting sensitive data from non-sensitive data.
   d.   Getting non-sensitive data from non-sensitive data.

53. A manager decided that only the administrator should be able to give access rights to the various databases of the organization's departments. Which of the following access control policies is he using?
   a.   Decentralised administration.
   b.   Ownership-based administration.
   c.   Centralised administration.
   d.   Membership-based administration.

54. Assume there is a table named Student. Identify the correct syntax to revoke "update" from the user Tom.
   a.   REVOKE UPDATE ON ANY TABLE FROM Tom.
   b.   REVOKE UPDATE ON STUDENT FROM Tom.
   c.   REVOKE * ON ANY TABLE FROM Tom.
   d.   RE/VOKE UPDATE ON STUDENT TO Tom.

55. In a typical Database encryption model, which entity is responsible for transforming user queries into queries on encryption data?
   a.   Data Owner.
   b.   User.
   c.   Client.
   d.   Server.

56. Identify the commands used for Database Access Control.
   a.   Grant and Revoke.
   b.   Create a Table and Grant.
   c.   Create View and Create Table.
   d.   None of the above.

57. In what type of attack does the attacker attempt to send unauthorized commands to a back-end database through a web application?
   a.   CSRF.
   b.   SQL Injection.
   c.   Pass-the-hash.
   d.   Buffer overflow.

58. Identify the statement that is true regarding Inference.
   a.   Getting sensitive data from other sensitive data.

b. Getting non-sensitive data from sensitive data.
c. Getting sensitive data from non-sensitive data.
d. Getting non-sensitive data from other non-sensitive data.

59. **Ms. Shahana inspects her application logs and finds records indicating attackers may be attempting to use SQL injection attacks to access the database underlying her application. What is the most effective security control that Ms. Shahana can apply to address this risk?**
   a. Network firewall
   b. Input validation
   c. Application sandboxing
   d. Host firewall.

60. **Database Access Control refers to what?**
   a. Controlling physical access to the database server.
   b. Protecting the confidentiality of database backups.
   c. Managing user access and permissions to the database.
   d. Encrypting the database to prevent unauthorised access.

61. **The primary goal of Database Access Control is what?**
   a. Ensure data availability at all times.
   b. Prevent unauthorised access to the database.
   c. Optimise database performance.
   d. Simplify database administration tasks.

62. **Which of the following is not a standard component of Database Access Control?**
   a. User authentication.
   b. Role-based access control.
   c. Encryption algorithms.
   d. Audit logging.

63. **Role-based access control (RBAC) in databases involves what?**
   a. Assigning permissions directly to individual users.
   b. Assigning permissions to roles and then assigning roles to users.
   c. Assigning permissions to groups of users.
   d. Assigning permissions based on the user's geographic location.

64. **The "principle of least privilege" concept in Database Access Control means what?**
   a. Giving users the highest level of privileges to ensure productivity.
   b. Granting privileges based on the user's seniority in the organisation.
   c. Giving users the minimum level of privileges necessary to perform their tasks.
   d. Granting privileges based on the user's job title.

65. **How SQL injection attacks can be mitigated?**
   a. Using robust encryption algorithms.
   b. Implementing firewall rules on the database server.
   c. Applying input validation and parameterised queries.
   d. Granting all users read-only access to the database.

66. **Which of the following is an example of a database access control mechanism?**
    a.   Access control lists (ACLs).
    b.   Intrusion detection systems (IDS).
    c.   Virtual private networks (VPNs).
    d.   Public key infrastructure (PKI).

67. **Database auditing involves what?**
    a.   Monitoring and recording user activities and access attempts.
    b.   Encrypting the database to protect sensitive information.
    c.   Backing up the database regularly.
    d.   Optimising query performance for faster data retrieval.

68. **Which of the following is not a commonly used database authentication method?**
    a.   Username and password.
    b.   Biometric authentication.
    c.   Single sign-on (SSO).
    d.   Data encryption.

69. **The process of granting or revoking access privileges to a user in a database is typically managed by whom?**
    a.   The database administrator (DBA).
    b.   The network administrator.
    c.   The system architect.
    d.   The application developer.

70. **What does Database inference refer to?**
    a.   The process of extracting information from a database.
    b.   The process of inferring relationships between database tables.
    c.   The process of determining the database schema.
    d.   The process of querying a database using inference rules.

71. **In database inference, unauthorized users can access sensitive information through what?**
    a.   Guessing the correct query parameters.
    b.   Exploiting vulnerabilities in the database management system.
    c.   Analysing patterns and relationships in the available data.
    d.   Accessing the database during off-peak hours.

72. **The main objective of database inference attacks is what?**
    a.   Modify or delete data in the database.
    b.   Gain unauthorised access to the database server.
    c.   Extract confidential information indirectly from the database.
    d.   Overload the database with excessive queries.

73. **The primary countermeasure against database inference attacks is what?**
    a.   Implementing robust access control mechanisms.
    b.   Encrypting the entire database.
    c.   Regularly auditing and monitoring database activities.
    d.   Limiting the number of queries a user can execute.

74. Inference attacks based on database response timings involve what?
   a. Analysing the time taken by the database to respond to different queries.
   b. Exploiting timing vulnerabilities in the database management system.
   c. Analysing the metadata associated with the database tables.
   d. Executing queries during periods of high database activity.

75. The concept of "semantic security" in database inference refers to what?
   a. Ensuring that the database schema is correctly defined.
   b. Protecting the confidentiality of the database server.
   c. Implementing secure communication channels for database queries.
   d. Preventing unauthorised users from inferring sensitive information.

76. The "maximum entropy principle" is often used for what?
   a. Optimise database query performance.
   b. Determine the level of encryption applied to the database.
   c. Estimate the probability distribution of data in the database.
   d. Enhance the security of the database access control mechanisms.

77. How can Database inference attacks be mitigated?
   a. Applying data anonymization techniques.
   b. Increasing the complexity of the database query language.
   c. Limiting the number of records stored in the database.
   d. Disabling query logging in the database management system.

78. Database inference attacks are more likely to occur in what databases?
   a. Store only non-sensitive information.
   b. Have a small number of users with limited access privileges.
   c. Contains high volumes of diverse and interrelated data.
   d. Are isolated from external networks.

79. Database encryption refers to what?
   a. Encrypting the entire database system.
   b. Encrypting specific tables within the database.
   c. Encrypting individual rows or columns in the database.
   d. Encrypting database backups and transaction logs.

80. The primary goal of database encryption is what?
   a. Prevent unauthorised access to the database.
   b. Improve database query performance.
   c. Ensure data integrity in the database.
   d. Simplify database administration tasks.

81. In database encryption, encryption keys are typically stored where?
   a. Within the database tables.
   b. In a separate key management system.
   c. Within the application, accessing the database.
   d. In the database server configuration files.

82. Which of the following is not a standard encryption algorithm used in database encryption?

    a. Advanced Encryption Standard (AES).
    b. Data Encryption Standard (DES).
    c. Rivest Cipher (RC4).
    d. Blowfish.

83. Transparent Data Encryption (TDE) is a technique that encrypts what?
    a. Encrypts the entire database system.
    b. Encrypts specific tables within the database.
    c. Encrypts individual rows or columns in the database.
    d. Encrypts database backups and transaction logs.

84. In database encryption, data is decrypted when?
    a. Only when authorised users access it.
    b. Every time the database server restarts.
    c. Only during the backup and restore process.
    d. Automatically when it is written to the database.

85. Which of the following is a potential drawback of database encryption?
    a. Increased storage space requirements.
    b. Slower database query performance.
    c. Difficulty in managing encryption keys.
    d. All of the above.

86. In column-level database encryption, which data is typically encrypted?
    a. All data in the database.
    b. Sensitive data fields such as credit card numbers or social security numbers.
    c. Primary key fields.
    d. Metadata about the database structure.

87. Which of the following is a benefit of using database encryption?
    a. Compliance with data protection regulations.
    b. Enhanced database availability.
    c. Improved data compression ratios.
    d. Simplified database backup and restore processes.

88. Database encryption can be used with other security measures, such as what?
    a. Access control mechanisms.
    b. Intrusion detection systems (IDS).
    c. Network firewalls.
    d. All of the above.

Answer Key

1. (d) Only encrypting queries. When encrypting a database, you can typically choose to encrypt the entire database, specific fields (columns), or specific records (rows). Encrypting queries is not a common encryption option in database security. Queries are typically used to retrieve data from an already encrypted database, but the queries are not typically encrypted as part of the database encryption process.

2. (d) Web Application Firewall. SQL injection vulnerabilities typically involve exploiting weaknesses in web applications. A Web Application Firewall (WAF) is a security control designed to protect web

applications from attacks like SQL injection. If Raja discovered an SQL injection vulnerability, it suggests that the network lacks a Web Application Firewall or that the existing WAF is not correctly configured to detect and mitigate such vulnerabilities. The other options, Transport Layer Security (TLS), Data Leak Prevention (DLP), and Intrusion Detection Systems (IDS), may address other aspects of security but are not directly related to mitigating SQL injection vulnerabilities in web applications.

3. (b) Blind SQL Injection occurs when a web application is vulnerable to SQL injection but does not return error messages or display the results of the injected SQL queries directly. Instead, an attacker may need to infer the results of their injections based on the application's behaviour, such as differences in page responses or timing. This injection attack is more challenging to exploit than standard SQL injection but can still lead to data leakage and compromise if successfully executed.

4. (c) A failed Authorization. When an error occurs in a web application, it is generally not a good practice to leak sensitive information to the user. Among your options, a stack trace (option a) can contain technical details that may aid attackers. The failed SQL query (option b) should not be revealed to users as it can expose the database structure and potentially sensitive data. Database schema details (option d) should also be kept confidential. However, if an error occurs due to failed authorization (option c), it is reasonable to inform the user that their access is denied or that they do not have permission to perform a specific action. This is a security measure to protect sensitive data and resources.

5. (c) Ownership-based administration. In ownership-based administration, the owner or creator of a database table has the authority to grant or revoke access rights to that table. Database management systems often use this approach to control who can perform actions on specific database objects, such as tables.

6. (b) Data source types. Distributed databases, data warehouses, big data, and file shares are all different types of data sources or data storage solutions. They represent various ways data can be organized, stored, and managed, and they may use different data models and technologies depending on their specific purposes.

7. (a) Big data databases. Hadoop, MongoDB, and BigTable are examples of big data databases or storage solutions commonly used to handle large volumes of unstructured or semi-structured data in big data environments.

8. (a) Orphan data typically refers to data that has been lost or disconnected from its original context and cannot be quickly recovered or associated with its source or purpose.

9. (b) The Center for Internet Security (CIS) is a well-known organization that provides security best practices and benchmarks for various technologies, including databases. They offer valuable resources and guidelines for securing systems and databases based on industry best practices.

10. (c) Through an application. The majority of the time, people access data through applications. These applications interact with databases or data repositories to retrieve and manipulate the data on behalf of users. Users typically access data indirectly through these applications' interfaces rather than directly interacting with the database or repository.

11. (c) MySQL is an open-source database management system. Oracle Database, Microsoft SQL Server, and SAP Sybase are not open-source database systems; they are commercial database management systems.

12. (a) The Security Account Manager (SAM) is a database in Windows operating systems that maintains user accounts and information about local users. It stores password hashes and other security-related information for local user accounts.

13. (c) Application hardening. Raja's actions of uninstalling sample configuration files, configuring the application settings properly, and updating the software to the most recent version are all steps associated with application hardening. Application hardening involves securing and configuring software and applications to reduce their attack surface and make them more resistant to vulnerabilities and exploits. Patch management, input validation, and vulnerability scanning are related but distinct security practices.

14. (c) MySQL is an open-source database management system (DBMS). Oracle Database, Microsoft SQL Server, and SAP Sybase are not open-source DBMS but proprietary database systems.

15. (a) The Security Account Manager (SAM) database stores user accounts and local users' information on a Windows system.

16. (a) Second-order SQL injection, or stored SQL injection, occurs when an attacker submits malicious data to a web application stored in a database or other data store. The attack vector does not directly affect the application; instead, it impacts another part that relies on the stored malicious data, such as constructing an SQL statement.

17. (d) All of the above. SQL Injection can affect all three aspects of the CIA (Confidentiality, Integrity, and Availability) triad in information security. Depending on the specific attack and its consequences, it can lead to unauthorized access to data (confidentiality breach), unauthorized modification of data (integrity breach), and potentially even denial of service if it disrupts the normal functioning of a database or application (availability breach).

18. (b) Department of Defense (DoD). The Database Security Requirements Guide (SRG) mentioned in the video "Leveraging Security Industry Best Practices" is a document published by the Department of Defense (DoD) in the United States. This guide outlines security requirements and recommendations for securing databases used within the DoD and by defence contractors.

19. (a) Inference attacks are used to gain access to sensitive data from databases by making inferences from observed or accessible information, even if the sensitive data itself is not directly accessible. This type of attack involves using logical deductions or statistical analysis to infer information that should be protected. Encryption, interruption, and modification are not typically associated with inference attacks.

20. (a) In an error-based SQL Injection attack, the hacker exploits errors or exceptions generated by the database to gain information about the database structure and data. The attacker tailors their actions based on the error messages or responses received from the application, allowing them to extract information from the database.

21. (b) Large-scale sequel databases such as those containing credit card information. SQL injection attacks are commonly used to target large-scale SQL databases, especially those containing sensitive information such as credit card data, user credentials, or other valuable data. These attacks attempt to manipulate SQL queries to gain unauthorized access to the database or retrieve sensitive information.

22. (b) A web hacking technique. SQL injection is a web hacking technique that exploits vulnerabilities in web applications to manipulate SQL queries the database executes. It allows attackers to interact with a database and potentially gain unauthorized access or retrieve sensitive information.

23. (b) Data perturbation involves modifying the data in a statistical database (SDB) to provide statistics while protecting the individual record's confidentiality. It introduces noise or randomization into the data to prevent inference attacks on individual records. This technique maintains privacy when providing aggregated statistical information from sensitive datasets.

24. (b) Blind SQL Injection. Even if a web application does not send error messages in response to SQL injection attempts, it may still be vulnerable to blind SQL injection. Blind SQL injection is a type of SQL injection attack where the attacker can infer information about the database through the application's behaviour without directly seeing error messages. This attack relies on the attacker asking true/false questions to the database and determining the answers based on the application's responses.

25. (a) Second-order SQL injection is a type of SQL injection attack in which the attacker submits malicious input to a web application, which then stores that input and uses it to construct a SQL query in the future. The attack occurs when the web application does not properly validate or sanitize the stored data before using it in an SQL query, allowing the attacker to execute SQL injection later when the data is used in a query. This is sometimes called "delayed" or "second-order" SQL injection.

26. (b) Reject inference-based queries. When handling inference during the query time of a database, the recommended action is to reject inference-based queries. Inference attacks involve using statistical information and query responses to make educated guesses about sensitive data that may not be directly accessible. By rejecting such queries, you can mitigate the risk of exposing sensitive information through inference attacks.

27. (b) Use of an Application ID from a hostname that is different from what has been specified by the application owner. c. Use of an Application ID from an IP that is different from what has been specified by the application owner. Activities that involve deviations from specified configurations or attempted access from unapproved hostnames or IPs should be considered suspicious and warrant further investigation. These could indicate potential security breaches or unauthorized access attempts.

28. (c) Access control. When encrypting queries and ensuring the legitimate responses are known as part of query encryption, access control is not directly related. Instead, encryption protects the confidentiality of query contents and results, while access control determines who is authorized to execute queries and access the data. Inference and intrusion are related to security threats and detection, while rejection might refer to the action taken when a query does not meet specific criteria or security standards.

29. (c). Use server-side input validation for user input. To prevent SQL injection attacks, it is recommended to use server-side input validation for user input. This involves validating and sanitizing user inputs on the server before using them in SQL queries. This practice helps ensure that user inputs do not contain malicious SQL code that could be executed inappropriately.

30. (d) Arrays are contiguous blocks of memory used to store data elements of the same data type. They provide an efficient way to manage and access a memory collection of elements, such as integers or characters. Each element in an array is stored at a specific memory location, making it easy to access elements by their index.

31. (c). Force a large volume of data on an application. Detecting buffer overflow vulnerabilities typically involves examining the source code for potential issues, such as strings declared as local variables, global variables, or improper use of standard functions. Forcing a large volume of data onto an application is not a typical method for detecting buffer overflow vulnerabilities and may be ineffective in identifying such issues in the code. It is more important to analyze the code and identify potential vulnerabilities rather than relying on input volume to detect them.

32. (a) Heap. The memory area an application utilizes and allocates dynamically at runtime is typically called the "heap." It is where dynamic memory allocation occurs, and data can be allocated and deallocated as needed during program execution.

33. (a) Using dynamic SQL can help prevent SQL injection attacks because it allows you to parameterize SQL queries and safely pass user inputs without exposing them directly in the SQL statement. This can help protect against malicious SQL injection attempts.

34. (c) Database footprinting involves identifying and mapping the structure of a database, including its tables, columns, and relationships. It is often an initial step in the reconnaissance phase of a database security assessment.

35. (b) A query that produces a value calculated over a query set. Statistical queries are typically used to retrieve aggregated data or statistics from a database, such as calculating averages, counts, sums, or other statistical measures over a set of data. These queries provide summary information rather than detailed individual records.

36. (c) The type of attack shown in the given code is SQL Injection.

37. (b) The information transfer path by which unauthorized data is obtained is called an Inference Channel.

38. (d) To protect a Statistical Database from Inference attacks, both perturbation and query restriction methods are commonly used.

39. (b) In the perturbation technique used to secure a statistical database, noise is typically added to the data to introduce randomness and protect against inference attacks.

40. (c) The data in the Output Perturbation type of Statistical Database can be modified to produce statistics that cannot be used to infer values for individual records.

41. (d) REVOKE is The command used to manage access rights (specifically, to revoke access privileges) in a database.

42. (c) Defending against data inference by restricting statistical queries to a database is a Query restriction.

43. (b) Inference can be defined as Extracting sensitive data from non-sensitive data.

44. (b) Centralized administration is the type of Access Control Policy where only the administrator can give access rights to the various databases of the organization's departments.

45. (a) An example of Ownership-based administration is where only a few privileged users can GRANT and REVOKE access rights to a database.

46. (b) Ownership-based administration is used if Salim owns a table in a database and can GRANT and REVOKE access rights to other users.

47. (b) The process of performing authorized queries and deducing unauthorized information from a database is called inference.

48. (a) A census database where only the statistical data is stored is an example of a pure statistical database. In a pure statistical database, individual records or sensitive information is not stored; only aggregated statistical information is available.

49. (a) The database command used to manage access rights is GRANT.

50. (d) All the above can be used to protect your database against inference. Query Restriction, Data Perturbation, and Output Perturbation are all techniques commonly employed to safeguard a database against inference attacks and protect sensitive information.

51. (a) Grant and Revoke access rights means giving or removing access rights to/from a user.

52. (b) The true statement about inference is: Getting non-sensitive data from sensitive data.

53. (c) The manager is using the Centralized administration access control policy. In centralized administration, a central authority (administrator) controls access rights and permissions for various databases and users.

54. (b) The correct syntax to revoke "update" from the user Tom on the Student table would be REVOKE UPDATE ON STUDENT FROM Tom.

55. (c) In a typical Database encryption model, the Client is responsible for transforming user queries into queries on encrypted data.

56. (a) The commands used for Database Access Control are Grant and Revoke.

57. (b) The type of attack where the attacker attempts to send unauthorized commands to a back-end database through a web application is SQL Injection.

58. (b) The true statement regarding the inference is getting non-sensitive data from sensitive data.

59. (b) The most effective security control that Ms. Shahana can apply to address the risk of SQL injection attacks is Input validation. Input validation helps prevent malicious SQL injection by ensuring that user input is sanitized and only contains valid data, thus mitigating the risk of unauthorized access to the database through SQL injection attacks.

60. (c). Managing user access and permissions to the database. Database Access Control refers to managing and controlling user access and permissions to the database, ensuring that only authorized users have the appropriate data access level.

61. (b) The primary goal of Database Access Control is to prevent unauthorized access to the database. It aims to ensure that only authorized users can access and manipulate the database while preventing unauthorized access and maintaining data security.

62. (c). Encryption algorithms are not a standard Database Access Control component. While encryption is an important security measure, it typically falls under data protection and encryption practices rather than access control specifically. Access control components typically include user authentication, role-based access control, and audit logging.

63. (b) Assigning permissions to roles and then assigning roles to users. Role-based access control (RBAC) in databases involves creating roles, assigning permissions to those roles, and then assigning those roles to users. This approach simplifies access management and makes it more scalable, as permissions are assigned to roles rather than individual users.

64. (c) The "principle of least privilege" concept in Database Access Control means giving users the minimum privileges necessary to perform their tasks. This principle aims to restrict users' access rights to the minimum level required to complete their job responsibilities, reducing the potential for unauthorized access and limiting the potential damage from security breaches.

65. (c) SQL injection attacks can be mitigated by applying input validation and parameterized queries. Implementing proper input validation and using parameterized queries or prepared statements can help prevent SQL injection attacks by ensuring that user input is sanitized and not executed as part of SQL queries.

66. (a) Access control lists (ACLs) are an example of a database access control mechanism. Access control lists specify who is authorized to access certain resources or perform specific actions within a database or a system. They list the permissions associated with each user or entity.

67. (a) Monitoring and recording user activities and access attempts. Database auditing involves monitoring and recording user activities and access attempts to track who is accessing the database, their actions, and when they occur. This information is crucial for security and compliance purposes.

68. (d) Data encryption is not a commonly used database authentication method. Data encryption is a security measure used to protect the confidentiality of data, but it is not an authentication method in itself. Common authentication methods include username and password, biometric authentication, and single sign-on (SSO).

69. (a) The process of granting or revoking access privileges to a user in a database is typically managed by the database administrator (DBA). The DBA manages and administers the database, including user access and permissions.

70. (a) The process of extracting information from a database. Database inference refers to deducing or extracting sensitive or unauthorized information from a database by analyzing the intentionally provided or available information.

71. (c) In database inference, unauthorized users can access sensitive information by analyzing patterns and relationships in the available data. This typically involves making inferences about sensitive data by

examining patterns and relationships in the data that may reveal information that was not intended to be disclosed.

72. (c) The main objective of database inference attacks is to extract confidential information indirectly from the database. These attacks aim to indirectly infer sensitive or confidential information from the database by exploiting patterns and relationships in the available data.

73. (a) Implementing robust access control mechanisms is The primary countermeasure against database inference attacks. Organizations can mitigate the risk of inference attacks by controlling and restricting access to sensitive data within the database. Properly configured access control mechanisms help prevent unauthorized access to data and limit what users can see and query, reducing the potential for inference attacks.

74. (a) Inference attacks based on database response timings involve Analyzing the time the database takes to respond to different queries. These attacks analyze the variations in response times to infer information about the data or database structure. By measuring the time it takes for the database to respond to queries, attackers may gain insights into the underlying data, even if they do not have direct access to it.

75. (d) The concept of "semantic security" in database inference refers to Preventing unauthorized users from inferring sensitive information. Semantic security in this context means ensuring that sensitive information cannot be inferred from the information released by the database. It focuses on protecting data confidentiality even when attackers access partial or indirect information from the database.

76. (c) The "maximum entropy principle" is often used to estimate the probability distribution of data in the database. This principle is used in various fields, including statistics and information theory, to estimate probability distributions when limited information is available. In the context of databases, it can be used to estimate the distribution of data to protect against inference attacks while preserving data utility.

77. (a) Data anonymization techniques can mitigate database inference attacks. Data anonymization involves altering or masking data to make it more difficult for attackers to infer sensitive information. Generalization, suppression, and noise injection can help protect against inference attacks while preserving data utility.

78. (c) Database inference attacks are more likely to occur in databases that contain high volumes of diverse and interrelated data. Inference attacks often rely on diverse data and relationships between different pieces of information within the database, which can be exploited to infer sensitive information indirectly.

79. (d) Encrypting database backups and transaction logs. Database encryption typically involves encrypting sensitive data, including backups and transaction logs, to protect the confidentiality of the data and ensure that it remains secure even if unauthorized access or breaches occur. While it is possible to encrypt specific tables, rows, or columns in a database, the primary focus is protecting the data, including backups and logs.

80. (a) The primary goal of database encryption is to prevent unauthorized access to the database. Database encryption is primarily implemented to protect the confidentiality of data and prevent unauthorized access to sensitive information stored in the database. It does not directly improve query performance,

ensure data integrity, or simplify database administration tasks, although it can be part of a broader security strategy that addresses these concerns.

81. (b) In database encryption, encryption keys are typically stored in a separate key management system. Storing encryption keys separately from the database provides an additional layer of security, ensuring that the encryption keys remain protected even if the database is compromised. Key management systems are designed to generate, store, and manage encryption keys securely.

82. (c). Rivest Cipher (RC4) is not a standard encryption algorithm used in database encryption. The other options (AES, DES, Blowfish) are well-known encryption algorithms used in various encryption applications, including database encryption. RC4, while once popular, is now considered less secure and is not commonly used for database encryption.

83. (a) Transparent Data Encryption (TDE) is a technique that encrypts the entire database system. TDE is designed to encrypt the entire database at the file level, including data files, log files, and backups, ensuring the data remains encrypted at rest and during transmission.

84. (a) In database encryption, data is typically decrypted only when authorized users access it. Data is decrypted on the fly when authorized users with the necessary decryption keys access the encrypted data. This allows authorized users to work with the data while keeping it encrypted when not in use.

85. (d) All of the above are potential drawbacks of database encryption.

86. (b) Sensitive data fields such as credit card or social security numbers are typically encrypted in column-level database encryption. This approach allows organizations to selectively encrypt only the sensitive data within specific columns rather than encrypting the entire database.

87. (a) Compliance with data protection regulations is a significant benefit of using database encryption. Encrypting sensitive data in a database helps organizations comply with data protection and privacy regulations by providing an additional layer of security to protect the confidentiality of the data.

88. (d) All of the above. Database encryption can be used in conjunction with other security measures such as access control mechanisms, intrusion detection systems (IDS), network firewalls, and more to create a layered security approach that protects data both at rest and during transmission while also controlling who can access the data and detecting and responding to security threats.

Chapter 13
Cloud Security

This chapter includes questions from the following topics:
- Cloud Security.
- Cloud Service Models.
- Service Level Agreement.
- Cloud Access Security Broker (CASB).
- Cloud Provider Certifications.
- Cloud Security as a Service (SECaaS).
- Security Information and Event Management (SIEM).
- Virtual Private Cloud (VPC).

---

1. **A high-value research company stores its data in a secure cloud. Later, it decides to collaborate with a university in research and allows the university to store and manipulate the research-related data on its cloud. Such a storage system can be categorized as what?**
   a. Private cloud - since only research-related data is stored.
   b. Community Cloud - since both universities and companies share the cloud space.
   c. Public Cloud - Since university research is public.
   d. All of the above.

2. **Which hosting infrastructures require the most various data sources to be managed by the company?**
   a. PaaS.
   b. On-Premises.
   c. SaaS.
   d. IaaS.

3. **A cloud service model is called in which the consumer provides applications/software to run in the cloud environment.**
   a. PaaS (Platform as a Service).
   b. SaaS (Software as a Service).
   c. Iaas (Infrastructure as a Service).
   d. Daas (Data as a Service).

4. **Which hosting settings require the most distinct data sources to be managed by the service provider?**
   a. IaaS.
   b. On-Premises.
   c. PaaS.
   d. SaaS.

5. **A Service Level Agreement on a cloud between the customer and Service provider gives what?**
   a. A performance guarantee of the cloud services.
   b. Explains the security policy in place.
   c. Software and Hardware compliance.

    d.   All of the above.

6. **Which form of Cloud computing combines both public and private clouds?**
    a.   Hybrid cloud.
    b.   Open cloud.
    c.   Universal cloud.
    d.   Mixed cloud.
    e.   Binary cloud.

7. **Choose all essential characteristics of a suitable cloud service. (Select all that apply)**
    a.   Broad network access.
    b.   Rapid elasticity.
    c.   On-demand self-service.
    d.   Pay-per-Use billing Model.
    e.   All of the above.

8. **Identify the definition of IaaS.**
    a.   The capability provided to the consumer is to provision processing, storage, networks, and other fundamental computing resources.
    b.   The capability provided to the consumer is to deploy onto the cloud infrastructure consumer-created or acquired applications created using programming languages and tools supported by the provider.
    c.   The capability provided to the consumer is to use the provider's applications running on a cloud infrastructure.
    d.   All of the Above

9. **Which could be rated as the biggest problem in adopting cloud service?**
    a.   Security.
    b.   Integration.
    c.   Customization.
    d.   Cost.

10. **Choose the desirable properties of a device accessing the cloud. (Select all that apply)**
    a.   Strong authentication mechanisms.
    b.   Strong isolation between applications.
    c.   Cryptographic functionality when traffic confidentiality is required.
    d.   All of the above.

11. **Which of these security parameters should be addressed for Data-in-Transit for Cloud?**
    a.   Confidentiality.
    b.   Integrity.
    c.   Availability.
    d.   All of the above.

12. **Which of these security parameters should be addressed at Data-at-rest in the Cloud?**
    a.   Confidentiality.
    b.   Integrity.
    c.   Availability.
    d.   All of the above.

13. **Identify the issue with availability in the cloud IS.**
    a. Fear of loss of data.
    b. Unknown if computation went correctly in the cloud.
    c. Denial of Service attack.
    d. Proper Scaling on demand.

14. **In the scale of data exposed, which of the following could be the maximum intensity phishing in a Multitenancy Cloud?**
    a. An employee in a client phished.
    b. A client A's all-employee phished.
    c. Cloud Administrator.
    d. The largest client in terms of employees' phished.

15. **Choose all false statements about an attacker trying to hack a cloud network. (Select all that apply)**
    a. He can determine where in the cloud infrastructure an instance is located.
    b. He cannot determine if two instances are co-residents on the same physical machine.
    c. Adversary launching instances cloud be co-resident with other user instances.
    d. None of the above.

16. **Which security concerns follow your workload even after being moved to the cloud?**
    a. Data security.
    b. Disaster Recovery/Business Continuity Planning.
    c. Identity and Access Management.
    d. Compliance.
    e. All of the above.

17. **Which Business Continuity test types do we relocate processes from the primary to the alternate location?**
    a. Checklist Review.
    b. Structured Walkthrough.
    c. Parallel Test.
    d. Full-Interruption.

18. **A Service Level Agreement (SLA) between a customer and a cloud service provider establishes**
    a. A performance guarantee of the cloud services.
    b. Explains the security policy in place.
    c. Software and Hardware compliance.
    d. All of the above.

19. **A corporation conducting high-value research securely saves its data in the cloud. Later on, it decided to collaborate on research with a university, allowing the university to store and change research-related data on its cloud. This type of storage system is classified as what?**
    a. Private cloud - since only research-related data is stored.
    b. Community Cloud - since both universities and companies share the cloud space.
    c. Public Cloud - Since university research is public
    d. All the above

20. **If data security is paramount, which cloud computing model should be evaluated first?**
    a. Hybrid cloud.
    b. Universal cloud.
    c. Public cloud.
    d. Private cloud.

21. **In which cloud service model can the consumer "provision" and "deploy and run"?**
    a. SaaS.
    b. PaaS.
    c. IaaS.
    d. CaaS.

22. **Which cloud delivery model is implemented by a single organization, enabling it to be implemented behind a firewall?**
    a. Private.
    b. Public.
    c. Community.
    d. Hybrid.

23. **Which cloud service model provides the consumer with the infrastructure to create and host applications?**
    a. SaaS.
    b. PaaS.
    c. IaaS.
    d. CaaS.

24. **Which cloud delivery model could be considered a pool of services and resources delivered across the Internet by a cloud provider?**
    a. Private.
    b. Public.
    c. Community.
    d. Hybrid.

25. **Which cloud service model allows the consumer to use applications provided by the cloud provider over the Internet?**
    a. SaaS.
    b. PaaS.
    c. IaaS.
    d. CaaS.

26. **Which cloud delivery model has an infrastructure shared by several organizations with shared interests and common IT needs?**
    a. Private.
    b. Public.
    c. Community.
    d. Hybrid.

27. **Which cloud delivery model could be considered an amalgamation of other delivery models?**
    a. Private.

    b. Public.
    c. Community.
    d. Hybrid.

28. **With which of the following subscription-based models is security more cost-effective than individuals or smaller corporations could ever get on their own?**
    a. SECaaS.
    b. PaaS.
    c. XaaS.
    d. WaaS.

29. **Which of the following are on-premise or cloud-based security policy enforcement points?**
    a. Feature slugs.
    b. Flood guards.
    c. VDI/VDEs.
    d. Cloud access security brokers.

30. **Which feature of cloud computing involves provisioning (or de-provisioning) resources dynamically as needed?**
    a. Multitenancy.
    b. Elasticity.
    c. CMDB.
    d. Sandboxing.

31. **What is the term for restricting an application to a safe/restricted resource area?**
    a. Multitenancy.
    b. Fencing.
    c. Securing.
    d. Sandboxing.

32. **Which of the following terms implies hosting data from more than one consumer on the same equipment?**
    a. Multitenancy.
    b. Duplexing.
    c. Bastioning.
    d. Fashioning.

33. **When going with a public cloud delivery model, who is accountable for the security and privacy of the outsourced service?**
    a. The cloud provider and the organization.
    b. The cloud provider.
    c. The organization.
    d. None of the above.

34. **When your servers become too busy, you can offload traffic to resources from a cloud provider. This is known as which of the following?**
    a. Latency.
    b. Cloud bursting.
    c. Multitenancy.

    d.   Peaking.

35. What protocol is used by technologies for load balancing/prioritizing traffic?
    a.   ESX
    b.   QoS
    c.   IBJ
    d.   IFNC

36. What is Cloud Security?
    a.   Security measures for physical data centres.
    b.   Security Measures for cloud service providers.
    c.   Security measures for protecting data and applications in the cloud.
    d.   Security measures for network infrastructure.

37. Which of the following is a key concern in Cloud Security?
    a.   Availability.
    b.   Performance.
    c.   Scalability.
    d.   Data privacy.

38. What is the Shared Responsibility Model in Cloud Security?
    a.   A model where the cloud service provider is solely responsible for the security.
    b.   A model where the customer is solely responsible for the security.
    c.   A model where both the cloud service provider and the customer have shared security responsibilities.
    d.   A model where security is outsourced to a third-party provider.

39. Which encryption method is commonly used to protect data in transit in the cloud?
    a.   DES (Data Encryption Standard).
    b.   RSA (Rivest-Shamir-Adleman).
    c.   AES (Advanced Encryption Standard).
    d.   HMAC (Hash-based Message Authentication Code).

40. What is the purpose of Identity and Access Management (IAM) in Cloud Security?
    a.   To ensure data integrity.
    b.   To protect against DDoS attacks.
    c.   To manage user identities and control access to cloud resources.
    d.   To monitor network traffic.

41. Which authentication factor is typically used in Multi-Factor Authentication (MFA) for cloud services?
    a.   Something you know.
    b.   Something you have.
    c.   Something you are.
    d.   All of the above.

42. What is a Virtual Private Cloud (VPC) in Cloud Security?
    a.   A cloud-based firewall.
    b.   A virtualized network environment with dedicated resources.

    c.   A cloud-based antivirus software.
    d.   A cloud-based intrusion detection system.

43. What is Data Loss Prevention (DLP) in Cloud Security?
    a.   A technique for encrypting data at rest.
    b.   A technique for monitoring and preventing the unauthorized transmission of sensitive data.
    c.   A technique for preventing unauthorized access to cloud resources.
    d.   A technique for securing cloud network connections.

44. What is a Security Information and Event Management (SIEM) system in Cloud Security?
    a.   A system for managing cloud storage resources.
    b.   A system for monitoring and analyzing security events and logs in real time.
    c.   A system for encrypting cloud data.
    d.   A system for managing cloud virtual machines.

45. What is Data Encryption at Rest in Cloud Security?
    a.   A technique for encrypting data during transmission over the network.
    b.   A technique for encrypting data stored in cloud storage.
    c.   A technique for encrypting data in the cloud provider's infrastructure.
    d.   A technique for encrypting data on end-user devices.

46. What is the principle of least privilege in Cloud Security?
    a.   Granting users the maximum level of permissions in the cloud environment.
    b.   Granting users only the privileges necessary to perform their tasks.
    c.   Granting users unrestricted access to cloud resources.
    d.   Granting users administrative access to the cloud provider's infrastructure.

47. What is a Security Group in Cloud Security?
    a.   A group of users with administrative access to the cloud provider's infrastructure.
    b.   A group of users with elevated privileges in the cloud environment.
    c.   A virtual firewall that controls inbound and outbound traffic for cloud resources.
    d.   A virtual network that isolates cloud resources from the Internet.

48. Which of the following is a common security risk in cloud computing?
    a.   Limited scalability.
    b.   Data redundancy.
    c.   Vendor lock-in.
    d.   Physical access control.

49. What is the term used to describe the risk of unauthorized access to cloud data?
    a.   Data leakage.
    b.   Data loss.
    c.   Data breach.
    d.   Data encryption.

50. Which of the following is a countermeasure to mitigate the risk of data loss in the cloud?
    a.   Regular data backups.
    b.   Increased network bandwidth.
    c.   Strong password policies.

    d.   Redundant server infrastructure.

51. **What is the term used to describe the risk of cloud service unavailability?**
    a.   Data breach.
    b.   Data leakage.
    c.   Service disruption.
    d.   Service continuity.

52. **Which of the following is a countermeasure to mitigate the risk of service unavailability in the cloud?**
    a.   Decryption.
    b.   Load balancing.
    c.   Intrusion detection systems.
    d.   Firewall configuration.

53. **Which of the following is a security risk associated with cloud data storage?**
    a.   Insufficient network bandwidth.
    b.   Limited storage capacity.
    c.   Unauthorized data access.
    d.   Lack of data redundancy.

54. **Which of the following is a countermeasure to mitigate the risk of unauthorized data access in the cloud?**
    a.   Access control mechanisms.
    b.   Data compression techniques.
    c.   Data replication.
    d.   Network segmentation.

55. **What term is used to describe the risk of cloud provider data breaches?**
    a.   Insider threat.
    b.   Third-party risk.
    c.   Network vulnerability.
    d.   Encryption weakness.

56. **Which of the following is a countermeasure to mitigate the risk of cloud provider data breaches?**
    a.   Multi-factor authentication.
    b.   Regular software updates.
    c.   Data encryption.
    d.   Intrusion detection systems.

57. **What is the term used to describe the risk of data loss due to data centre outages or disasters?**
    a.   Data corruption.
    b.   Data leakage.
    c.   Data availability.
    d.   Data redundancy.

58. **What is data protection in the context of cloud computing?**

   a. Protecting physical servers in data centres.
   b. Protecting data from unauthorized access, loss, or corruption in the cloud.
   c. Protecting network infrastructure from cyber-attacks.
   d. Protecting cloud service providers from legal liabilities.

59. Which of the following is a data protection challenge in the cloud?
   a. Limited storage capacity.
   b. High network latency.
   c. Data encryption overhead.
   d. Vendor lock-in.

60. What is data encryption in the cloud?
   a. Encrypting cloud provider infrastructure.
   b. Encrypting data during transmission over the network.
   c. Encrypting data at rest in cloud storage.
   d. Encrypting data on end-user devices.

61. Which encryption key management approach gives the data owner complete control over the encryption keys?
   a. Cloud provider-managed key.
   b. User-managed key.
   c. Hardware security module (HSM).
   d. Key escrow.

62. What is data masking in the cloud?
   a. Replacing sensitive data with fictional data.
   b. Removing sensitive data from the cloud environment.
   c. Encrypting data during transmission over the network.
   d. Backing up data to multiple geographic locations.

63. What is data anonymization in the context of cloud data protection?
   a. Removing personal identifiers from data.
   b. Encrypting data at rest in cloud storage.
   c. Classifying data based on sensitivity levels.
   d. Limiting access to data based on user roles.

64. What is data backup and recovery in the cloud?
   a. Encrypting data at rest in cloud storage.
   b. Classifying data based on sensitivity levels.
   c. Creating copies of data for disaster recovery purposes.
   d. Preventing unauthorized access to cloud resources.

65. Which of the following is a common data protection regulation for cloud services?
   a. HIPAA (Health Insurance Portability and Accountability Act).
   b. GDPR (General Data Protection Regulation).
   c. PCI DSS (Payment Card Industry Data Security Standard).
   d. ISO/IEC 27001 (Information Security Management System).

66. What is the concept of data residency in cloud data protection?

    a. The physical location where cloud data is stored.
    b. The encryption algorithm is used to protect cloud data.
    c. The process of classifying data based on sensitivity levels.
    d. The frequency of data backups in the cloud.

67. What is Cloud Security as a Service (SECaaS)?
    a. A cloud-based antivirus software.
    b. A cloud service that provides security measures and tools.
    c. Cloud service for data storage and backup.
    d. Cloud service for network monitoring and analysis.

68. Which of the following is a benefit of using Cloud Security as a Service?
    a. Increased control over network infrastructure.
    b. Reduced need for internal security expertise.
    c. Enhanced physical security of data centres.
    d. Lower cost of cloud services.

69. What is the role of a Cloud Access Security Broker (CASB) in SECaaS?
    a. Securely authenticating users in the cloud environment.
    b. Monitoring and controlling access to cloud resources.
    c. Encrypting data during transmission over the network.
    d. Backing up data to multiple geographic locations.

70. Which of the following security services can be offered through SECaaS?
    a. Data encryption.
    b. Intrusion detection.
    c. Vulnerability scanning.
    d. All of the above.

71. Which security control is commonly provided by SECaaS to protect against Distributed Denial of Service (DDoS) attacks?
    a. Intrusion Prevention System (IPS).
    b. Virtual Private Network (VPN).
    c. Firewall.
    d. Web Application Firewall (WAF).

72. What is the purpose of Security Information and Event Management (SIEM) in SECaaS?
    a. Monitoring and analyzing security events and logs in real time.
    b. Encrypting data at rest in cloud storage.
    c. Preventing unauthorized access to cloud resources.
    d. Managing user identities and access control.

73. Which authentication method is commonly used in SECaaS for user access control?
    a. Single sign-on (SSO).
    b. Two-factor authentication (2FA).
    c. Public key infrastructure (PKI).
    d. Role-based access control (RBAC).

74. **What is the purpose of Security Orchestration, Automation, and Response (SOAR) in SECaaS?**
    a. Analyzing network traffic and detecting anomalies.
    b. Automating incident response and security operations.
    c. Encrypting data during transmission over the network.
    d. Managing cloud virtual machines.

75. **Which security compliance standard is commonly supported by SECaaS providers?**
    a. ISO/IEC 27001 (Information Security Management System).
    b. HIPAA (Health Insurance Portability and Accountability Act).
    c. PCI DSS (Payment Card Industry Data Security Standard).
    d. All of the above.

76. **What is the concept of elasticity in SECaaS?**
    a. The ability to scale security services based on demand.
    b. The encryption algorithm is used to protect cloud data.
    c. The process of classifying data based on sensitivity levels.
    d. The frequency of data backups in the cloud.

77. **What is a common concern related to data privacy in cloud computing?**
    a. Limited storage capacity.
    b. Vendor lock-in.
    c. Unauthorized data access.
    d. Lack of network bandwidth.

78. **What is data encryption in cloud computing?**
    a. Encrypting cloud provider infrastructure.
    b. Encrypting data during transmission over the network.
    c. Encrypting data at rest in cloud storage.
    d. Encrypting data on end-user devices.

79. **Which of the following is a security measure to address cloud data confidentiality?**
    a. Implementing strong password policies.
    b. Implementing intrusion detection systems.
    c. Implementing data classification and access controls.
    d. Implementing network load balancing.

80. **What is the purpose of cloud provider certifications and audits?**
    a. To guarantee data availability.
    b. To ensure data privacy.
    c. To verify compliance with security standards.
    d. To prevent unauthorized data access.

81. **What is the concept of cloud data segregation?**
    a. Separating cloud data based on its sensitivity level.
    b. Consolidating all cloud data into a single storage location.
    c. Merging cloud data with on-premises data.
    d. Storing cloud data in multiple geographic locations.

82. **What is the role of a Cloud Access Security Broker (CASB) in addressing cloud security concerns?**
    a. Monitoring and controlling access to cloud resources.
    b. Encrypting data during transmission over the network.
    c. Backing up data to multiple geographic locations.
    d. Managing cloud virtual machines.

83. **What is the importance of user awareness and education in cloud security?**
    a. It helps prevent unauthorized data access.
    b. It ensures regular data backups.
    c. It enables secure data encryption.
    d. It mitigates the risk of social engineering attacks.

84. **Which of the following is a best practice for securing cloud applications?**
    a. Regularly updating software and applying security patches.
    b. Storing sensitive data in clear text.
    c. Allowing unrestricted access to cloud resources.
    d. Sharing authentication credentials among users.

85. **What is the concept of continuous monitoring in cloud security?**
    a. Regularly reviewing and assessing the effectiveness of security controls.
    b. Storing backups of cloud data in multiple locations.
    c. Limiting access to cloud resources based on user roles.
    d. Encrypting data at rest in cloud storage.

Answer Key

1. (b) Community Cloud - since universities and companies share the cloud space. A community cloud is a computing environment where several organizations share infrastructure with common interests, such as research collaborations. In this scenario, the high-value research company and the university share the cloud infrastructure for research-related data, making it a community cloud.

2. (b) On-premises hosting infrastructure typically requires the company to manage various data sources themselves, including the hardware, software, and data storage, as everything is hosted within the company's physical premises. In contrast, with other hosting models like SaaS (Software as a Service), the service provider manages the infrastructure and data sources, reducing the burden on the company.

3. (a) PaaS (Platform as a Service). In the PaaS (Platform as a Service) cloud service model, the consumer provides applications or software to run in the cloud environment. PaaS provides a platform that includes the infrastructure and tools needed for developing, testing, and deploying applications, making it easier for developers to build and manage their software applications in the cloud.

4. (d) In the SaaS (Software as a Service) hosting setting, the service provider manages and hosts the application and its underlying infrastructure. Users access the software application through the Internet without worrying about managing data sources or infrastructure. This is why SaaS requires the most distinct data sources to be managed by the service provider, as everything related to the software application, including data storage and management, is typically handled by the SaaS provider.

5. (a) A performance guarantee of the cloud services. A Service Level Agreement (SLA) between the customer and the cloud service provider typically outlines the performance guarantees and expectations

for the cloud services. It defines metrics such as uptime, response times, and availability and specifies what level of service the customer can expect. While security policies and compliance may also be addressed in the SLA, its primary purpose is establishing performance-related terms and commitments.

6. (a) A hybrid cloud is a form of cloud computing that combines both public and private clouds, allowing data and applications to be shared between them. This approach offers greater flexibility and can help organizations leverage the benefits of both public and private clouds based on their specific needs and requirements.

7. (e) All of the above.

8. (a) The capability provided to the consumer is to provision processing, storage, networks, and other fundamental computing resources. This definition corresponds to the cloud computing model's infrastructure as a Service (IaaS).

9. (a) Security is often considered one of the biggest concerns and challenges in adopting cloud services, as it involves entrusting sensitive data and applications to third-party providers who may have different security measures and practices.

10. (d) All of the above. Desirable properties of a device accessing the cloud typically include robust authentication mechanisms, strong isolation between applications, and cryptographic functionality when traffic confidentiality is required. These properties help ensure the security and integrity of data and communications in the cloud environment.

11. (d) All of the above.

12. (d) All of the above.

13. (c) Availability issues in the cloud can be related to various factors, and one significant concern is the possibility of a Denial of Service (DoS) attack. A DoS attack can disrupt cloud services and make them temporarily or entirely unavailable for users, causing downtime and potential business disruptions. Proper scaling on demand (Option d) is a mechanism to address availability issues by ensuring resources can be allocated as needed to maintain service availability. Fear of data loss (Option a) and concerns about the correctness of computations (Option b) may be related to other aspects of cloud security but are not directly tied to availability issues caused by DoS attacks.

14. (c) Cloud Administrator. In a multitenancy cloud environment, the highest potential impact of a phishing attack in terms of the scale of data exposed would be if the cloud administrator's account is compromised. The cloud administrator typically has broad access and control over the entire cloud infrastructure, affecting all clients and their data. Phishing attacks targeting a cloud administrator could result in significant data exposure and potential security breaches across the entire cloud environment.

15. (a,b)

16. (e) All of the above. All the mentioned security concerns (data security, disaster recovery/business continuity planning, identity and access management, and compliance) can remain relevant and require attention even after moving workloads to the cloud. Cloud providers typically offer various tools and services to address these concerns, but organizations must implement and manage them effectively to ensure the security and compliance of their cloud-based workloads.

17. (c) In a Parallel Test, processes are relocated from the primary to the alternate location to ensure that the alternate location adequately supports the critical business functions and processes. This test is conducted to verify that the backup site or recovery environment can take over operations seamlessly in case of a disaster or interruption at the primary site.

18. (d) All of the above. A Service Level Agreement (SLA) between a customer and a cloud service provider can cover various aspects, including performance guarantees of the cloud services, security policies, and compliance with software and hardware requirements. Therefore, all the options listed are valid components that can be addressed in an SLA.

19. (b) Community Cloud - since universities and companies share the cloud space. In this scenario, where the corporation and the university share and collaborate on research-related data on the cloud, it aligns with the concept of a Community Cloud. A Community Cloud is a cloud infrastructure shared by several organizations or entities with similar interests or requirements, such as universities and corporations collaborating on research. It provides a more controlled and shared environment compared to a public cloud.

20. (d) Private cloud. When data security is paramount, the private cloud computing model should be evaluated first. A private cloud is typically used by a single organization and is hosted in a dedicated environment, providing greater control and security over data and resources. This makes it suitable for organizations with strict security and compliance requirements.

21. (b) In the Platform as a Service (PaaS) cloud service model, the consumer can "provision," "deploy," and "run" applications without worrying about the underlying infrastructure. PaaS provides a platform that includes tools and services for application development, making it easier for developers to focus on creating and deploying software applications.

22. (a) A private cloud is implemented by a single organization for its use and is typically located behind a firewall, providing dedicated and controlled access to cloud resources for that organization. It offers more control, privacy, and security than public or community clouds.

23. (b) Platform as a Service (PaaS) provides consumers with the infrastructure, tools, and services to develop, deploy, and host applications. It offers a platform for developers to build and manage their applications without worrying about the underlying infrastructure.

24. (b) The public cloud delivery model provides services and resources over the Internet by a cloud provider, making them accessible to a wide range of users or organizations.

25. (a) The SaaS (Software as a Service) cloud service model allows consumers to use software applications provided by the cloud provider over the Internet.

26. (c) The Community cloud delivery model is an infrastructure shared by several organizations with shared interests and common IT needs.

27. (d) The Hybrid cloud delivery model combines elements of private and public clouds, allowing data and applications to be shared between them.

28. (a) Security as a Service (SECaaS) is a subscription-based model that provides security services and solutions to organizations. It is often cost-effective because it allows organizations to access high-quality

security services and expertise that may be more affordable than trying to establish and maintain the same level of security on their own.

29. (d) Cloud access security brokers (CASBs) are security policy enforcement points that can be deployed both on-premises and in the cloud. They help organizations secure cloud services and applications by providing visibility, access control, and data protection features.

30. (b) Elasticity in cloud computing refers to the ability to dynamically provision and de-provision resources (such as computing power, storage, and network resources) to meet varying workloads and demands. It allows organizations to scale resources up or down as needed, which is one of the key advantages of cloud computing.

31. (d) Sandboxing is a security mechanism that restricts the actions of an application or software process within a controlled environment or "sandbox." This prevents it from accessing system resources and data that it should not have access to, reducing the risk of malicious behaviour or unauthorized access.

32. (a) Multitenancy is a cloud computing model where multiple customers (tenants) share the same physical hardware or infrastructure while maintaining isolation and separate instances of the software applications and data. It allows for efficient resource utilization and cost savings by serving multiple users on a single platform.

33. (a) The cloud provider and the organization. In a public cloud delivery model, both the cloud provider and the organization share responsibility for the security and privacy of the outsourced service. The cloud provider is responsible for the security of the underlying infrastructure and services they offer, while the organization is responsible for securing their applications, data, and configurations within the cloud environment. This shared responsibility is typically outlined in a Service Level Agreement (SLA) or similar contract between the two parties.

34. (b) Cloud bursting is offloading excess traffic or workload from your on-premises servers or private cloud to resources provided by a cloud provider when your servers become too busy. This allows organizations to handle peak or unexpected workloads without the need to provision and maintain additional on-premises infrastructure.

35. (b) Quality of Service (QoS) is a set of technologies and protocols used for load balancing and prioritizing network traffic to ensure that critical data or applications receive higher priority and better performance on a network. QoS helps manage and optimize network resources for different types of traffic, such as voice, video, and data.

36. (c) Security measures for protecting data and applications in the cloud. Cloud security refers to the practices, technologies, policies, and controls that protect data, applications, and infrastructure within a cloud computing environment. It encompasses measures to safeguard cloud-based resources from threats, unauthorized access, data breaches, and other security risks.

37. (d) Data privacy is a key concern in cloud security, as it involves protecting sensitive and confidential information from unauthorized access or disclosure when stored, processed, or transmitted in a cloud environment. Data privacy is essential to maintaining the trust and compliance of users and organizations utilizing cloud services.

38. (c) A model where the cloud service provider and the customer share security responsibilities. The Shared Responsibility Model in cloud security defines the division of security responsibilities between the cloud service provider and the customer. In this model, the provider is responsible for securing the underlying cloud infrastructure, while the customer is responsible for securing their data, applications, and configurations within the cloud environment. It is a shared effort to ensure comprehensive security.

39. (c) AES (Advanced Encryption Standard) is commonly used to protect data in transit in the cloud. It is a widely adopted encryption algorithm that provides robust security for data transmitted over networks and stored in the cloud.

40. (c) To manage user identities and control access to cloud resources. Identity and Access Management (IAM) in Cloud Security primarily focuses on managing user identities and controlling access to various cloud resources and services. It helps ensure that only authorized users can access specific cloud resources, enhancing security and reducing the risk of unauthorized access and data breaches.

41. (d). All of the above. Multi-factor authentication (MFA) typically combines multiple authentication factors for enhanced security. These factors can include something you know (e.g., a password), something you have (e.g., a mobile device or security token), and something you are (e.g., biometric data like fingerprint or facial recognition). Using multiple factors makes it more difficult for unauthorized users to access cloud services, improving security.

42. (b) A virtualized network environment with dedicated resources. A Virtual Private Cloud (VPC) is a network environment within a cloud provider's infrastructure that allows users to have their own isolated and private section of the cloud with dedicated resources such as virtual servers, storage, and networking. This isolation provides enhanced security and control over the cloud resources, making it suitable for organizations that require specific security measures and resource allocation.

43. (b) A technique for monitoring and preventing the unauthorized transmission of sensitive data. Data Loss Prevention (DLP) in Cloud Security refers to the tools, technologies, and policies used to monitor and prevent the unauthorized transmission or sharing of sensitive data within and outside an organization's network. It helps organizations protect their data from accidental leaks or intentional breaches by identifying and blocking the movement of sensitive information.

44. (b) A system for real-time monitoring and analyzing security events and logs. A Security Information and Event Management (SIEM) system in Cloud Security is a comprehensive solution for collecting, analyzing, and correlating security information and events from various sources within an organization's cloud environment. It helps organizations monitor their cloud infrastructure for security threats, detect anomalies, and respond to real-time security incidents. SIEM systems enhance cloud security by providing visibility into potential security issues and enabling rapid incident response.

45. (b) A technique for encrypting data stored in cloud storage. Data Encryption at Rest in Cloud Security refers to encrypting data stored in cloud storage services. This ensures that even if unauthorized access to the physical storage media occurs, the data remains protected because it is encrypted. Encryption at rest is an important security measure to safeguard sensitive data in cloud environments.

46. (b) Granting users only the privileges necessary to perform their tasks. The principle of least privilege in Cloud Security involves granting users or entities in a cloud environment only the minimum permissions and access rights necessary to perform their specific tasks or functions. This practice helps reduce the

potential for unauthorized access, data breaches, and security vulnerabilities by limiting privileges to what is required for legitimate purposes.

47. (c). A virtual firewall that controls inbound and outbound traffic for cloud resources. In Cloud Security, a Security Group is a virtual firewall that controls the network traffic to and from cloud resources. It acts as a set of inbound and outbound rules that define which network traffic is allowed or denied for specific resources within a cloud environment, such as virtual machines or instances. Security Groups help enhance network security and access control within the cloud infrastructure.

48. (c) Vendor lock-in is a common security risk in cloud computing. It refers to a situation where a cloud service provider's proprietary technologies and formats make it difficult or costly for customers to migrate their data and applications to another provider or back to an on-premises environment. This can create a security risk because it limits the customer's flexibility and control over their data and applications, potentially exposing them to vendor-specific vulnerabilities or issues.

49. (c) The term to describe the risk of unauthorized access to cloud data is a "data breach." A data breach occurs when sensitive or confidential data is accessed, disclosed, or exposed to unauthorized individuals or entities, potentially leading to data leakage or loss. Data breaches can have severe security and privacy implications and are a significant concern in cloud computing environments.

50. (a) Regular data backups are a countermeasure to mitigate the risk of data loss in the cloud. By frequently backing up data, organizations can ensure that they have copies of their data stored securely, which can be restored in the event of data loss due to various factors, including hardware failures, accidental deletion, or security breaches. This practice helps maintain data availability and reduces the impact of data loss incidents.

51. (c) The term used to describe the risk of cloud service unavailability is "service disruption." This refers to situations where cloud services become temporarily or permanently unavailable, leading to losing access to data and applications hosted in the cloud. Service disruptions can result from various factors, including hardware failures, network issues, cyber-attacks, or provider outages. Ensuring service continuity and minimizing disruptions is critical to cloud service management and security.

52. (b) Load balancing is a countermeasure to mitigate the risk of service unavailability in the cloud. Load balancing involves distributing incoming network traffic across multiple servers or resources to ensure that no single server becomes overloaded, thereby improving the availability and performance of services. This helps prevent service disruptions and enhances the overall resilience of cloud-based applications and resources.

53. (c) Unauthorized data access is a security risk associated with cloud data storage. It involves the risk of individuals or entities gaining unauthorized access to sensitive or confidential data stored in the cloud. Proper access controls, encryption, and other security measures are essential to mitigate this risk and ensure data privacy and security.

54. (a) Access control mechanisms mitigate the risk of unauthorized data access in the cloud. These mechanisms include user authentication, authorization, and permission settings to ensure that only authorized users can access specific data and resources in the cloud environment.

55. (b) The risk of cloud provider data breaches is often referred to as "third-party risk" because it involves the security and integrity of data entrusted to a third-party cloud service provider.

56. (c) Encrypting data before it is stored in the cloud can help mitigate the risk of cloud provider data breaches. It ensures the data remains encrypted and unreadable even if unauthorized access occurs without the appropriate decryption keys.

57. (c) The term used to describe the risk of data loss due to data centre outages or disasters is "data availability." It refers to the ability to access and use data when needed, and the risk involves situations where data becomes temporarily or permanently unavailable, such as during a data centre outage or a natural disaster.

58. (b) Protecting data from unauthorized access, loss, or corruption in the cloud. Data protection in the context of cloud computing refers to measures and practices aimed at safeguarding data stored, processed, or transmitted in cloud environments from unauthorized access, data loss, or data corruption. It involves security measures and strategies to ensure data confidentiality, integrity, and availability in the cloud.

59. (d) Vendor lock-in is a data protection challenge in the cloud because it can make it difficult for organizations to migrate their data and applications to another cloud provider or back to on-premises infrastructure if they change cloud providers. This can lead to concerns about data portability and maintaining control over one's data.

60. (c) Data encryption in the cloud refers to encrypting data stored in cloud storage services. This helps protect the data from unauthorized access in case of security breaches or other vulnerabilities.

61. (b) In a user-managed key approach, the data owner has complete control over the encryption keys, including their generation, storage, and management. This gives the data owner more control and autonomy in managing the security of their data in the cloud.

62. (a) Replacing sensitive data with fictional data. Data masking involves replacing sensitive or confidential data with fictional or scrambled data to protect the original data from unauthorized access or exposure. This technique is often used in non-production environments or during testing to maintain data privacy and security.

63. (a) Removing personal identifiers from data. Data anonymization involves removing or altering personal identifiers from data to protect individuals' privacy and make it challenging to trace data back to specific individuals. This technique is commonly used to de-identify sensitive data while preserving its utility for various analytical purposes.

64. (c). Creating copies of data for disaster recovery purposes. Data backup and recovery in the cloud involve creating copies of stored data to ensure that data can be recovered in case of data loss or disasters. These backups are essential for maintaining data availability and integrity.

65. (b) The General Data Protection Regulation (GDPR) is a common data protection regulation that applies to cloud services and aims to protect the privacy and personal data of individuals within the European Union (EU).

66. (a) The physical location where cloud data is stored. Data residency refers to where data is physically stored within a cloud infrastructure. It can affect data protection, legal compliance, and data privacy regulations.

67. (b) A cloud service that provides security measures and tools. Cloud Security as a Service (SECaaS) is a cloud-based service model that delivers various security measures and tools to protect cloud environments, applications, and data. As a cloud-based service, it offers security solutions such as firewall management, intrusion detection and prevention, identity and access management, encryption, and more.

68. (b) Reduced need for internal security expertise. One of the benefits of using Cloud Security as a Service (SECaaS) is that it can reduce the organization's need for internal security expertise. With SECaaS, the cloud service provider typically handles security measures, which can alleviate the burden on the organization's internal security team and reduce the requirement for specialized security skills within the organization. This allows the organization to focus on its core competencies while relying on the expertise of the cloud security provider.

69. (b) Monitoring and controlling access to cloud resources. A Cloud Access Security Broker (CASB) plays a crucial role in SECaaS by monitoring and controlling access to cloud resources. CASBs are intermediaries between an organization's on-premises infrastructure and cloud service providers. They provide security policy enforcement, data protection, and visibility into cloud usage. CASBs help organizations gain better control and security over their interactions with cloud services, including monitoring user activities, enforcing security policies, and protecting data as it moves between the organization and the cloud.

70. (d) All of the above. SECaaS (Security as a Service) can offer various security services, including data encryption, intrusion detection, vulnerability scanning, and many others. These services are provided through cloud-based solutions to enhance an organization's overall security posture and protect against various threats and vulnerabilities.

71. (d) A Web Application Firewall (WAF) is a common security control provided by SECaaS to protect against Distributed Denial of Service (DDoS) attacks explicitly targeting web applications. WAFs help filter and monitor incoming traffic to web applications, identifying and mitigating potential threats and attacks, including those associated with DDoS attacks.

72. (a) Monitoring and analyzing security events and logs in real-time. The primary purpose of Security Information and Event Management (SIEM) in SECaaS is to monitor and analyze security events and logs in real-time, providing insights into potential security threats and vulnerabilities within an organization's cloud environment. SIEM systems collect and correlate data from various sources to help identify and respond to security incidents effectively.

73. (b) Two-factor authentication (2FA) is commonly used in SECaaS for user access control to enhance security by requiring users to provide two different authentication factors before granting access to cloud resources. This typically involves something the user knows (e.g., a password) and something the user has (e.g., a mobile device for receiving one-time codes).

74. (b) Automating incident response and security operations. Security Orchestration, Automation, and Response (SOAR) in SECaaS primarily automates incident response and security operations. It helps security teams streamline processes, improve response times, and automate repetitive tasks for handling security incidents and alerts.

75. (d) All of the above. SECaaS providers commonly support various security compliance standards, including ISO/IEC 27001, HIPAA, and PCI DSS, depending on their offerings and the needs of their customers.

76. (a) The ability to scale security services based on demand. Elasticity in SECaaS refers to the capability to dynamically scale security services up or down based on the current demand or workload. This ensures that security resources can be adjusted to match the changing needs of an organization's cloud environment.

77. (c) Data privacy is a significant concern in cloud computing, and unauthorized data access is one of its primary risks. Organizations worry about the security of their data when it is stored in a cloud environment and whether unauthorized parties could access or misuse that data.

78. (c) Data encryption in cloud computing involves securing data that is stored in cloud storage by encrypting it. This ensures that even if someone gains access to the physical storage hardware, the data remains protected and unreadable without the encryption keys.

79. (c). Implementing data classification and access controls is a security measure that helps address cloud data confidentiality. This involves categorizing data based on sensitivity and implementing access controls to ensure only authorized users can access and view confidential data.

80. (c) To verify compliance with security standards. Cloud provider certifications and audits aim to verify and demonstrate compliance with security standards, regulations, and best practices. This helps ensure that the cloud provider's services meet the required security and privacy standards, which can build customer trust and provide data security and privacy assurance.

81. (a) Separating cloud data based on its sensitivity level. Cloud data segregation involves separating cloud data based on its sensitivity level or classification.

82. (a) Monitoring and controlling access to cloud resources. A Cloud Access Security Broker (CASB) plays a key role in addressing cloud security concerns by monitoring and controlling access to cloud resources. CASBs provide a centralized security platform that helps organizations enforce security policies, detect and respond to security threats, and ensure compliance in cloud environments. They act as intermediaries between cloud service providers and consumers, allowing for better visibility and control over cloud-related security issues.

83. (d) It mitigates the risk of social engineering attacks. User awareness and education are crucial in cloud security as they help mitigate the risk of social engineering attacks. Social engineering attacks rely on manipulating individuals into divulging confidential information or taking specific actions that compromise security. By educating users about the dangers of such attacks and how to recognize and respond to them, organizations can enhance their overall security posture in the cloud and protect sensitive data and resources.

84. (a) Regularly updating software and applying security patches is a best practice for securing cloud applications. This helps ensure that known vulnerabilities are addressed, reducing the risk of exploitation by attackers. Storing sensitive data in clear text, allowing unrestricted access, and sharing authentication credentials among users are all security risks, not best practices.

85. (a) Regularly reviewing and assessing the effectiveness of security controls. Continuous monitoring in cloud security involves regularly reviewing and assessing the effectiveness of security controls to ensure that they provide the intended protection and promptly identify and respond to any security incidents or vulnerabilities. This on-going process helps maintain the security posture of cloud environments.

Chapter 14
Data-Driven Fraud

This chapter includes questions from the following topics:
- Sensitive Data Exposure.
- Fraud Detection.
- Benford's Law.
- Data-Driven Approach.

1. **From the options, choose measures to prevent Sensitive Data Exposure. (Select all that apply)**
   a. Discarding/Deleting Sensitive data as soon as possible.
   b. Turning off auto-complete forms collecting sensitive data.
   c. Use of weak Cryptographic algorithm without proper key management.
   d. Data is stored in plain text for a long time.

2. **Which of the following is not a step in the deductive fraud detection approach?**
   a. Understanding the business or operations to be studied.
   b. Understanding what kinds of frauds could occur.
   c. Determining the most likely symptoms.
   d. Performing digital analysis of company databases.
   e. Gathering data about symptoms.

3. **Which of the following illustrates the proactive approach to fraud detection?**
   a. Using data-mining software to identify fraud.
   b. Using Benford's law to identify fraud.
   c. Locating accounting anomalies and investigating for possible fraud.
   d. Learning about the business or operations to be studied prior to investigating for fraud.

4. **Which of the following proactive fraud detection methods uses Benford's Law to detect fraud?**
   a. Commercial data-mining software.
   b. Digital analysis of company databases.
   c. Deductive fraud detection.
   d. None of the above.

5. **All of the following are symptoms of vendor fraud except:**
   a. Short shipping.
   b. Billing for goods not ordered or shipped.
   c. Providing poor-quality goods.
   d. All of the above are symptoms of vendor fraud.

6. **The data-driven method of fraud detection does not include which of the following characteristics?**
   a. Determining symptoms that the most likely frauds would generate.
   b. Understanding the business.
   c. Understanding and using Benford's law to analyze company databases.
   d. Understanding what kinds of frauds could occur.

7. **What is the principal disadvantage of using the data-driven approach?**
   a. It is more expensive than the traditional reactive approach.
   b. Limited when databases are large.
   c. This leads to excessive leads of possible fraud.
   d. None of the above.

8. **Each of the following is true about Benford's Law except:**
   a. Benford's law broadly identifies the possible existence of fraud but does not identify promising leads.
   b. Benford's law states that each digit (from 1 to 9) will be the first digit in a number approximately the same amount of times as every other.
   c. A significant advantage of using Benford's law to detect fraud is that it is the least expensive method to implement and use.
   d. Fraud perpetrators are less likely to learn that you are analyzing data according to Benford's law because it does not involve extensive data mining queries.

9. **Benford's law states that the most likely first digit of any randomly selected number will be which of the following?**
   a. 1
   b. 7
   c. 3
   d. 4

10. **One of the significant disadvantages of Benford's law in detecting fraud is what?**
   a. You know precisely what you are looking for.
   b. It is a reasonably expensive method to use.
   c. You have enormous amounts of information to sift through.
   d. It only broadly identifies the possible existence of fraud and can include non-fraud factors.

11. **In a data-driven investigation, putting yourself in the shoes of a criminal would be an example of what step?**
   a. Identify possible frauds that could exist.
   b. Investigate symptoms.
   c. Use technology to gather data.
   d. Understanding the business.

12. **Identify the true statement about detecting fraud through financial statements reports.**
   a. To perform horizontal analysis, convert the financial statement balances to total assets or gross sales percentages.
   b. Vertical analysis is the most direct method of focusing on changes from period to period.
   c. Before performing fraud analysis, all three types of financial statements need to be converted to change statements.
   d. Small frauds usually do not significantly affect the financial statement balance.

13. **A mathematical algorithm that predicts the percentage of the time each digit will appear in a sequence of numbers is what?**
   a. Inductive fraud detection.
   b. Deductive fraud detection.
   c. Benford's law.
   d. Horizontal analysis.

   e.   Vertical analysis.

14. **The following are all techniques for time trend analysis, except what?**
   a.   Graphing each case.
   b.   Regression analysis.
   c.   All of the above.
   d.   None of the above.

15. **Benford's law can help detect fraud by what?**
   a.   Establishing weaknesses in the accounting controls system.
   b.   Identifying accounting anomalies.
   c.   Identifying employees that are at high risk for fraud.
   d.   It shows attempts by fraudsters to make stolen amounts look random.

16. **Which is not one of the steps in the Proactive Fraud Detection process?**
   a.   Determine if actual fraud or other factors are causing the symptoms.
   b.   Understanding the business or operations to be studied.
   c.   Use databases and information systems to identify the fraud.
   d.   Understanding what kinds of frauds could occur (fraud exposures) in the operation.

17. **Which of the following backup methods will generally provide the fastest backup times?**
   a.   Full backup.
   b.   Incremental backup.
   c.   Differential backup.
   d.   Archival backup.

18. **Which data protection process provides prebuilt capabilities, mapped to specific regulations, to create the necessary resources to implement and demonstrate compliance with these regulations?**
   a.   Real-time alerting.
   b.   Blocking, masking and quarantining.
   c.   Active analytics.
   d.   Automated compliance support.

19. **Which two data-copying techniques are employed in the gathering of software data?**
   a.   Remote and local.
   b.   Local and logical.
   c.   Logical and physical.
   d.   Physical and compact.

20. **Which data protection process prevents a suspicious data request from being completed?**
   a.   Data risk analysis.
   b.   Data discovery.
   c.   Blocking, masking and quarantining.
   d.   Data classification.

21. **Which of the following are characteristics of acquisition files in a proprietary format? (Select all that apply)**
   a.   Can compress or not compress the acquisition data?

b. Can segment acquisition output files into larger volumes, allowing them to be archived to CD or DVD.
c. Case metadata can be added to the acquisition file, eliminating the need to keep track of any additional validation documentation or files.
d. Incorporates the hash algorithm for validation purposes.

22. **What information does a logical acquisition gather during an investigation?**
    a. Fragments of unallocated data in addition to the logically allocated data.
    b. Unallocated data only.
    c. Only specific files of interest to the case.
    d. A bit-for-bit copy.

23. **Which acquisition method should you use when creating a copy of a drive that contains whole-disk encryption?**
    a. Physical Disk Acquisition.
    b. Logical copying of a disk partition.
    c. Reconstructing file fragments.
    d. Spanish Inquisition Forensic Tools.

24. **Which of the following is not a factor in determining which data acquisition method to use?**
    a. Size of the source drive.
    b. What operating system is installed on the suspect computer?
    c. How long will the acquisition take?
    d. Where the disk evidence is located.

25. **When is it appropriate to use a shared data backup tool like Norton Ghost during a computing investigation?**
    a. The suspect computer cannot be taken offline for several hours but can be shut down long enough to switch disks with a Ghost backup.
    b. When the hard drive is over 2 GB.
    c. When the suspect computer uses RAID, it can be used with Ghost backup.
    d. As a more efficient alternative to a remote acquisition.

26. **Which aspect of computer evidence is the most critical?**
    a. Validation.
    b. Verification.
    c. Documentation.
    d. Analysis.

27. **What issues should you be aware of when conducting remote acquisitions?**
    a. Data transfer speeds.
    b. Access permissions over the network.
    c. Antivirus programs.
    d. All of the above.

Answer Key
1. (a,b) Discarding/Deleting Sensitive data as soon as possible and turning off auto-complete forms collecting sensitive data.

2. (d) In the deductive fraud detection approach, understanding the business or operations to be studied, understanding what kinds of frauds could occur, determining the most likely symptoms, and gathering data about symptoms are essential. However, "performing digital analysis of company databases" is not typically considered a step in the deductive fraud detection approach. Instead, digital analysis may be a part of the overall data analysis process, but it is not a distinct step in the deductive approach.

3. (d) Learning about the business or operations to be studied prior to investigating for fraud. The proactive approach to fraud detection involves learning about the business or operations to be studied before investigating for fraud. This approach emphasizes understanding the specific context and risks associated with the organization or industry to identify potential fraud schemes or vulnerabilities. It is a preventive approach aiming to proactively address fraud risks by implementing controls and strategies based on a deep understanding of the business environment. The other options (a, b, c) are more reactive approaches that involve data analysis and forensic techniques after fraud has occurred or is suspected.

4. (d) None of the above. Benford's Law is a statistical method used for fraud detection, but it is not typically associated with proactive methods like commercial data-mining software, digital analysis of company databases, or deductive fraud detection. Instead, it is used in data analysis and forensic accounting to identify anomalies or irregularities in numerical data sets that may indicate potential fraud. So, it is not part of proactive fraud detection methods but rather a technique for investigating data for signs of fraud.

5. (c) Providing poor-quality goods may not necessarily be a symptom of vendor fraud; it could simply indicate issues with product quality control or manufacturing processes. Vendor fraud typically involves fraudulent billing, short shipping, overcharging, or delivering goods that were not ordered or shipped with the intent to deceive and benefit financially. Poor-quality goods may be a separate issue related to product quality but may not necessarily indicate fraud by the vendor.

6. (c) While Benford's Law is a statistical method used in data analysis for fraud detection, it is not typically considered a characteristic of the data-driven method of fraud detection. The data-driven method generally involves analyzing large datasets and identifying patterns or anomalies that may indicate fraud. This can include understanding the business, determining likely fraud symptoms, and understanding potential fraud scenarios. However, Benford's Law is a specific analytical technique that may or may not be part of the data-driven method, depending on the context and the specific tools and approaches used.

7. (c) The principal disadvantage of using the data-driven approach to fraud detection is that it can generate a high volume of potential fraud leads or alerts, many of which may be false positives. This can overwhelm investigators and lead to significant time and resource costs as they sift through the alerts to identify actual instances of fraud. Therefore, managing and prioritizing the numerous leads generated by data-driven methods can be a challenge and a drawback of this approach.

8. (c) A significant advantage of using Benford's Law to detect fraud is that it is the least expensive method to implement and use. This statement is not entirely accurate. While Benford's Law is a statistical method that can be used for fraud detection, it is not necessarily the least expensive method to implement and use. The cost of implementing Benford's Law analysis can vary depending on factors such as the complexity of the data, the tools and software used, and the analysts' expertise. Additionally, other fraud detection methods may also have their associated costs. Therefore, the cost-effectiveness of Benford's Law compared to other methods can vary depending on the specific circumstances.

9. (a)

10. (d) It only broadly identifies the possible existence of fraud and can include non-fraud factors. One significant disadvantage of using Benford's Law in detecting fraud is that it only broadly identifies the possible existence of fraud by flagging anomalies in digit distributions. It does not provide specific details about the nature or source of fraud, and it can generate false positives by identifying anomalies that may not be related to fraud but are due to other factors or errors. Therefore, while it can be a helpful tool, it should be used with other investigative techniques for a more comprehensive fraud detection approach.

11. (a) Identify possible frauds that could exist. Putting yourself in the shoes of a criminal to think about possible fraud scenarios is part of the initial step of identifying possible frauds that could exist. It involves considering various fraud schemes and understanding how they might manifest in the data or business operations. This step helps investigators anticipate and recognize potential fraud indicators during the data-driven investigation process.

12. (b) Vertical analysis is the most direct method of focusing on changes from period to period. Vertical analysis, also known as common-size analysis, is a method used to analyze financial statements by expressing each line item as a percentage of a base item within the same period. This approach allows for a direct comparison of the proportions of different financial statement elements and helps identify changes from one period to another. It is a helpful method for understanding the relative composition of financial statements and detecting irregularities or trends.

13. (c) Benford's Law is a mathematical algorithm that predicts the percentage of the time each digit (from 1 to 9) will appear as the first digit in a sequence of naturally occurring numbers. It is used in data analysis and fraud detection to identify anomalies or irregularities in numerical datasets.

14. (d) None of the above. All of the mentioned techniques, including graphing each case and regression analysis, are techniques for time trend analysis. These methods are used to analyze data over time to identify patterns, trends, and anomalies, which can be valuable for fraud detection and data analysis.

15. (d) It shows attempts by fraudsters to make stolen amounts look random. Benford's Law can help detect fraud by revealing anomalies or irregularities in the distribution of first digits in numerical datasets. When fraudsters manipulate numbers to create fictitious transactions or embezzle funds, they may inadvertently deviate from the expected digit distribution according to Benford's Law. Detecting such deviations can indicate fraudulent activity, as it suggests an attempt to make stolen amounts appear random to avoid detection.

16. (c) Use databases and information systems to identify the fraud. The step "Use databases and information systems to identify the fraud" is not typically part of the Proactive Fraud Detection process. Proactive fraud detection usually involves understanding the business, identifying possible fraud exposures, determining the most likely symptoms, gathering data about those symptoms, and then investigating whether actual fraud or other factors are causing the symptoms. Using databases and information systems may be involved in the investigative process, but it is not a step in the initial proactive phase.

17. (a) A full backup involves copying all the data in a system or a particular data set at a specific time. It provides the fastest backup times because it captures everything, and there is no need to compare data or calculate differences as in the case of incremental and differential backups. However, complete backups can be time-consuming and require significant storage space compared to other backup methods.

18. (d) Automated compliance support uses prebuilt capabilities and tools mapped to specific regulations or compliance requirements. These tools help organizations create the necessary resources and processes to implement and demonstrate compliance with regulations effectively. It simplifies and streamlines the compliance process by automating various tasks and ensuring that the organization adheres to the required standards and regulations.

19. (c) Logical and physical. In the context of data copying techniques for software data, two common approaches are logical copying and physical copying. Logical copying involves copying data at a high level, such as copying files or database records, without necessarily replicating the underlying storage structure. On the other hand, physical copying involves copying data at a lower level, including duplicating the underlying storage structure, which may include disk blocks or storage volumes.

20. (c) Blocking, masking, and quarantining. The process of blocking, masking, and quarantining prevents a suspicious data request from being completed. It involves identifying potentially malicious or unauthorized data requests and blocking, masking, or quarantining the data to protect it from unauthorized access or misuse. This process is a part of data protection and security measures to safeguard sensitive information and prevent data breaches.

21. (a) Can compress or not compress the acquisition data? c. Case metadata can be added to the acquisition file, eliminating the need to keep track of any additional validation documentation or files. Acquisition files in a proprietary format can compress or not compress the acquisition data, and they often allow for the inclusion of case metadata within the file to simplify the management of additional validation documentation or files. The other options are not typically associated with proprietary acquisition file formats.

22. (a) Fragments of unallocated data and the logically allocated data. A logical acquisition gathers data from logically allocated storage areas, including specific files of interest to the case and fragments of unallocated data. This type of acquisition focuses on data accessible through the file system and does not involve a bit-for-bit copy of the entire storage device as a physical acquisition does.

23. (a) Physical Disk Acquisition. When dealing with a drive containing whole-disk encryption, performing a physical disk acquisition is typically necessary. This method involves creating a bit-for-bit copy of the entire storage device, including the encrypted data, to decrypt and analyze the data in a controlled environment. Logical copying of a disk partition or other methods may not provide access to the encrypted data. "Spanish Inquisition Forensic Tools" is not recognized in digital forensics.

24. (c) While the time it takes to perform a data acquisition can be a consideration, it is not a primary factor in determining which data acquisition method to use. The primary factors include the size of the source drive, the operating system on the suspect computer, and where the disk evidence is located. The choice of acquisition method is typically based on these factors and the specific requirements of the investigation rather than the time it takes to complete the acquisition.

25. (a) The suspect computer cannot be taken offline for several hours but can be shut down long enough to switch disks with a Ghost backup. A shared data backup tool like Norton Ghost is appropriate when the suspect computer cannot be taken offline for an extended period but can be briefly shut down to switch disks with a Ghost backup. This allows for creating a forensic copy of the data without extended downtime for the computer.

26. (c) Documentation is the most critical aspect of computer evidence because it provides a clear and well-documented record of how evidence was collected, preserved, and analyzed. This documentation is essential for establishing the integrity and admissibility of evidence in a legal or investigative context. Without proper documentation, the validity and credibility of the evidence can be called into question. Verification and validation are essential steps within the documentation process to ensure the accuracy and reliability of the evidence. Analysis, while crucial, relies on the foundation of well-documented and valid evidence.

27. (d) All of the above.

Chapter 15
Access Control

This chapter includes questions from the following topics:
- Access Control Principles.
- Subjects, Objects and Access Rights.
- Discretionary Access Control.
- UNIX File Access Control.
- Role-Based Access Control.
- Attribute-based Access Control.
- Identity, Credential and Access Management.

1. **Which of the following is not an access control?**
   a. Attribute-based Access Control (ABAC).
   b. Discretionary Access Control (DAC).
   c. Hash-Based Access Control (HBAC).
   d. History-of-Presence Based Access Control (HPBAC).

2. **In a Discretionary Access Control system, access rights are typically associated with which of the following?**
   a. Users or groups.
   b. Job titles or roles.
   c. Security clearances.
   d. IP addresses.

3. **Which of the following is a typical example of Discretionary Access Control implementation?**
   a. Role-based access control (RBAC) model.
   b. Mandatory access control (MAC) model.
   c. File permissions in a file system.
   d. Secure Sockets Layer (SSL) encryption.

4. **Access control based on a user's responsibilities is known as what?**
   a. DAC (Discretionary Access Control).
   b. MAC (Mandatory Access Control).
   c. RBAC (Role-based Access Control).
   d. SAC (Subject Access Control).

5. **A security designer concluded that the system contains three resources: files, printers, and mailboxes. The company is divided into four central departments, each performing a separate function: sales, marketing, management, and production. Each department requires a unique set of resources. Each user has his or her own workstation. Which roles should be defined to enable the RBAC (Role-Based Access Control) paradigm to function correctly?**
   a. File, printer, and mailbox roles.
   b. Allow access and deny access roles.
   c. Sales, marketing, management, and production roles.
   d. User and workstation roles.

6. Which of the following access control approaches include user authentication and data classification?
    a. MAC (Mandatory Access Control).
    b. SAC (Subject Access Control).
    c. DAC (Discretionary Access Control).
    d. RBAC (Role-Based Access Control).

7. What does the principle of least privilege require in terms of access control?
    a. Only processes are given the most restricted privileges.
    b. Every user or process is given the most restricted privileges.
    c. Users are subjects that receive clearance levels.
    d. Control permissions.

8. A need-to-know security policy would provide access based on which of the following criteria?
    a. Least privilege.
    b. Loss of privilege.
    c. Due cared.
    d. Escalation of privilege.

9. Users can access data or conduct actions they should not be allowed to do when access control checks are done incorrectly. This technique is known as What?
    a. Invalid Authorization.
    b. Missing Authorization.
    c. Non-existent Authorization.
    d. Incorrect Authorization.

10. Which Access control is divided into three categories?
    a. Discretionary access control.
    b. System access control.
    c. Mandatory access control.
    d. All of the above.

11. Which method of access control offers the highest level of security?
    a. RBAC.
    b. MAC.
    c. DAC.
    d. ABAC.

12. When access control checks are incorrectly applied, users can access data or perform actions they should not be allowed to perform. This method is called what?
    a. Invalid Authorization.
    b. Missing Authorization.
    c. Non-existent Authorization.
    d. Incorrect Authorization.

13. _____ grants or denies access to protected resources such as files, memory, etc.
    a. Discretionary access control.
    b. System access control.
    c. Mandatory access control.

    d.   All of the above.

14. **The Discretionary Access Control restricts access to objects based on what?**
    a.   The role of the subject is to access the object.
    b.   The role of the subject and the sensitivity of the information in those objects.
    c.   The identity of the subject trying to access the object.
    d.   The sensitivity of the information contained in those objects.

15. **In access control models, an object can be assigned with what?**
    a.   Security Service.
    b.   Security Clearance.
    c.   Security Classification.
    d.   Security Model.

16. **The concept of separation of duties refers to which of the following?**
    a.   Dividing access privileges among multiple users to prevent abuse of power.
    b.   Granting all access privileges to a single user for simplicity.
    c.   Assigning access privileges based on the user's physical location.
    d.   Restricting access privileges to specific days and times.

17. **Role-based access control (RBAC) is based on what?**
    a.   User's seniority within the organization.
    b.   User's job title or role within the organization.
    c.   User's geographic location.
    d.   User's level of technical expertise.

18. **Which access control method primarily concerns individuals' role in the organization?**
    a.   MAC
    b.   DAC
    c.   RBAC
    d.   STAC

19. **Granting access to a user based on how high up he is in an organization violates what basic security premise?**
    a.   The principle of unified access control.
    b.   The principle of least privileges.
    c.   Role-Based Access Control (RBAC).
    d.   The principle of top-down control.

20. **Mr Raja has access to materials because he works in her company's research division. He has access to more resources as a manager. Which access control system is most likely in use at her place of business?**
    a.   Mandatory Access Control (MAC).
    b.   Discretionary Access Control (DAC).
    c.   Hierarchical Access Control (HAC).
    d.   Role-Based Access Control (RBAC).

21. **What fundamental security principle is violated by granting access to a user based on his or her position within an organization?**

    a.   Role-Based Access Control (RBAC).
    b.   The principle of top-down control.
    c.   The principle of unified access control.
    d.   The principle of least privileges.

22. **What type of access control provides the most substantial level of protection?**
    a.   RBAC
    b.   MAC
    c.   DAC
    d.   ABAC

23. **Access control is a security mechanism that ensures what?**
    a.   Confidentiality
    b.   Integrity
    c.   Availability
    d.   All of the above.

24. **Mr Raja must grant access to any individual or group he wants to allow access to the files he owns. Which access control type is in use in Mr Raja's organization?**
    a.   Discretionary Access Control (DAC).
    b.   Role-Based Access Control (RBAC).
    c.   Hierarchical Access Control (HAC).
    d.   Mandatory Access Control (MAC).

25. **The principle of least privilege states what?**
    a.   Users should have the highest level of access privileges at all times.
    b.   Users should have the minimum access privileges necessary to perform their job functions.
    c.   Access privileges should be granted based on the user's job title.
    d.   Access privileges should be granted based on the user's seniority within the organization.

26. **Mandatory access control (MAC) is a security model that _____.**
    a.   Allows users to define their own access control rules.
    b.   Assigns access privileges based on the user's job title.
    c.   Assigns access privileges based on the classification of data and user clearances.
    d.   Grants access privileges to all users by default.

27. **Authentication is the process of what?**
    a.   Granting access to specific resources or information.
    b.   Verifying the identity of a user or entity.
    c.   Encrypting data during transmission.
    d.   Controlling access based on the user's job function.

28. **What does the principle of accountability state?**
    a.   Users should be responsible for their access control.
    b.   A central authority should manage access control.
    c.   Access control logs should be maintained to track user activities.
    d.   Access privileges should be reviewed annually.

29. **Biometric authentication is based on what?**

    a.   Something you know.
    b.   Something you have.
    c.   Something you are.
    d.   Something you do.

30. Access control lists (ACLs) are commonly used in what?
    a.   Physical security systems.
    b.   Network firewalls.
    c.   Intrusion detection systems.
    d.   Biometric authentication systems.

31. In the context of access control, a subject refers to what?
    a.   A user or entity that requests access to an object.
    b.   The object being accessed.
    c.   The access rights are assigned to an object.
    d.   The operating system manages access control.

32. An object in the context of access control refers to what?
    a.   A user or entity that requests access to a resource.
    b.   The access rights are assigned to a subject.
    c.   The operating system manages access control.
    d.   The resource being accessed.

33. Which of the following is an example of a subject in a computer system?
    a.   A file is stored on a hard drive.
    b.   A user account with login credentials.
    c.   A network router.
    d.   An application running on a server.

34. In the context of access control, access rights refer to what?
    a.   The permissions or privileges assigned to a subject for accessing an object.
    b.   The encryption keys are used to secure data transmission.
    c.   The hardware components are used to authenticate users.
    d.   The network protocols are used for secure communication.

35. Which term refers to granting or denying access rights to a subject for an object?
    a.   Authentication
    b.   Authorization
    c.   Encryption
    d.   Decryption

36. Role-based access control (RBAC) assigns access rights based on what?
    a.   User's job title or role within the organization.
    b.   User's level of technical expertise.
    c.   User's geographic location.
    d.   User's seniority within the organization.

37. Discretionary access control (DAC) allows which of the following?
    a.   The owner of an object determines access rights.

    b.   The operating system determines access rights based on predefined rules.

    c.   The network administrator determines access rights.

    d.   The subject requested access to determine access rights.

38. Mandatory access control (MAC) assigns access rights based on which of the following?

    a.   The owner of an object.

    b.   The subject's security clearance and the object's security classification.

    c.   The subject's job title.

    d.   The subject's seniority within the organization.

39. The Access Control lists (ACLs) are used for what?

    a.   Define and enforce access rights for subjects on objects.

    b.   Authenticate users and grant access rights.

    c.   Encrypt and decrypt data during transmission.

    d.   Monitor network traffic for security threats.

40. Discretionary Access Control (DAC) is based on what?

    a.   User's job title or role within the organization.

    b.   User's level of technical expertise.

    c.   User's geographic location.

    d.   User's seniority within the organization.

41. In DAC, access control decisions are made by whom?

    a.   The owner of the resource.

    b.   The system administrator.

    c.   The operating system.

    d.   The user is requesting access.

42. In DAC, access control is enforced through what?

    a.   Access control lists (ACLs).

    b.   Role-based access control (RBAC).

    c.   Mandatory access control (MAC).

    d.   Rule-based access control (RBAC).

43. The owner of a resource in DAC has the authority to do what?

    a.   Grant or deny access to the resource.

    b.   Assign security clearances to users.

    c.   Determine the security classification of the resource.

    d.   Control network traffic for the resource.

44. Which of the following is a limitation of DAC?

    a.   Lack of centralized control and uniformity.

    b.   Inability to support complex access control policies.

    c.   Difficulty in managing access rights for large systems.

    d.   All of the above.

45. In DAC, a user with read access to a file can typically do what?

    a.   Modify the file.

    b.   Delete the file.

c. Execute the file.
d. Only view the contents of the file.

46. In DAC, if a user grants access to a resource to another user, the second user becomes a _____.
a. Subject.
b. Object.
c. Owner.
d. Administrator.

47. Which of the following is the primary advantage of DAC?
a. Flexibility and simplicity in managing access control.
b. Granular control over access rights.
c. Centralized administration and control.
d. Strong resistance to insider attacks.

48. In UNIX, how the file permissions are represented?
a. Octal values.
b. Alphanumeric characters.
c. Binary values.
d. Hexadecimal values.

49. What are the three basic permissions in UNIX file access control?
a. Read, write, execute.
b. Open, close, modify.
c. Copy, paste, delete.
d. Edit, save, print.

50. In UNIX file permissions, the "r" permission allows which of the following?
a. Reading the file's contents.
b. Writing or modifying the file.
c. Executing or running the file.
d. Changing the ownership of the file.

51. In UNIX file permissions, the "w" permission allows which of the following?
a. Reading the file's contents.
b. Writing or modifying the file.
c. Executing or running the file.
d. Changing the ownership of the file.

52. In UNIX file permissions, the "x" permission allows which of the following?
a. Reading the file's contents.
b. Writing or modifying the file.
c. Executing or running the file.
d. Changing the ownership of the file.

53. Which command is used to change file permissions in UNIX?
a. Chmod
b. chown
c. chgrp

d.   ls

54. The numeric value 755 in UNIX file permissions means what?

a.   The owner has read, write, and execute permissions; the group and others have read and execute permissions.
b.   The owner has read and write permissions; the group has read permissions; others have no.
c.   Owner, group, and others have read and write permissions; no execute permissions.
d.   Owner, group, and others have read, write, and execute permissions.

55. Which command is used to change the ownership of a file in UNIX?

a.   chmod
b.   chown
c.   chgrp
d.   ls

56. Which command is used to change the group ownership of a file in UNIX?

a.   chmod
b.   chown
c.   chgrp
d.   ls

57. Which file stores the user and group information in UNIX?

a.   /etc/passwd
b.   /etc/shadow
c.   /etc/group
d.   /etc/permissions

58. In RBAC, access control decisions are made based on what?

a.   The user's identity.
b.   The permissions associated with a specific object.
c.   The user's assigned role or job function.
d.   The user's security clearance.

59. In RBAC, users are assigned with what?

a.   Individual access rights to each object.
b.   Roles that encompass a set of access rights.
c.   Security clearances for specific objects.
d.   Access control lists (ACLs) for each object.

60. Which of the following is a key benefit of RBAC?

a.   Simplifies access control administration.
b.   Provides fine-grained access control.
c.   Offers strong resistance against insider attacks.
d.   All of the above.

61. In RBAC, a user can be assigned with what?

a.   Multiple roles.
b.   Only one role.
c.   No roles.

    d.   A combination of roles and individual access rights.

62. The RBAC model includes which of the following entities?
    a.   Users, roles, and objects.
    b.   Users, groups, and permissions.
    c.   Users, sessions, and networks.
    d.   Users, tokens, and encryption keys.

63. Which RBAC component determines the permissions associated with each role?
    a.   Role hierarchy.
    b.   Role assignment.
    c.   Role authorization.
    d.   Role permissions.

64. In RBAC, how the role hierarchy can be defined?
    a.   The relationships between different roles.
    b.   The order in which permissions are assigned.
    c.   The duration of role assignments.
    d.   The locations where roles can be accessed.

65. Separation of duties (SoD) is a concept in RBAC that _____.
    a.   Ensures users can only perform specific tasks within their assigned role.
    b.   Prohibits users from having multiple roles simultaneously.
    c.   Restricts the number of roles assigned to each user.
    d.   Requires users to rotate their roles periodically.

Answer Key

1.   (c) Hash-Based Access Control (HBAC). This option is not a standard access control model. Hash-based techniques are commonly used in cryptography and data integrity, but they are not a well-known or widely used approach to access control in the same sense as ABAC or DAC.

2.   (a) Users or groups. Discretionary Access Control (DAC) is an access control model where the owner of a resource has the discretion to control access to that resource. In a DAC system, access rights are typically associated with individual users or groups of users. The resource owner can decide who gets access to the resource and what level of access is granted based on the user's identity or group membership. This is in contrast to other access control models like Role-Based Access Control (RBAC) or Attribute-Based Access Control (ABAC), which focus on roles, attributes, or other criteria for access control.

3.   (c) File permissions in a file system. File permissions in a file system are a typical example of Discretionary Access Control (DAC) implementation. In a DAC system, file owners can set access permissions on files and directories, determining who can access them and what actions they can perform. This aligns with the concept of discretionary control, where the owner of a resource has the discretion to manage access rights.

4.   (c) RBAC (Role-based Access Control). Role-based Access Control (RBAC) is an access control model that assigns permissions to users based on their roles and responsibilities within an organization. Users are associated with specific roles, and the permissions associated with those roles determine what actions

the user can perform. This approach simplifies access management by grouping users with similar responsibilities and granting them appropriate access rights.

5. (c) To enable the RBAC (Role-Based Access Control) paradigm to function correctly in this scenario, the roles that should be defined are Sales, marketing, management, and production.

6. (a) The access control approach that includes user authentication and data classification is MAC (Mandatory Access Control).

7. (b) Every user or process is given the most restricted privileges. The principle of least privilege (POLP) is a fundamental concept in access control and security. It states that a user, program, or process should be granted only the minimum access privileges necessary to perform their required functions. This approach reduces the potential impact of security breaches or vulnerabilities because even if a user or process is compromised, the damage they can inflict is limited by their restricted privileges.

8. (a) Least privilege. A need-to-know security policy ensures that individuals are granted access only to the information and resources necessary to perform their tasks. This principle is closely aligned with the concept of least privilege, which states that users should be given the minimum access privileges required to perform their roles effectively. The need-to-know policy helps reduce the risk of unauthorized access and data exposure by adhering to the principle of least privilege.

9. (b) Missing Authorization. Missing Authorization occurs when access control checks are not adequately implemented or are absent, allowing users to perform actions or access data they should not be authorized to. This can lead to security vulnerabilities and unauthorized access. Incorrect or inadequate access control mechanisms can result in missing authorization issues.

10. (d) All of the above.

11. (b) MAC (Mandatory Access Control). MAC offers the highest level of security among the listed options. In a MAC system, access decisions are based on system-enforced security labels or clearances, typically determined by an organization's security policies. MAC ensures strict control over data and resource access, reducing the risk of unauthorized access and data leakage. It is commonly used in environments with high-security requirements, such as government and military systems. While the other options (RBAC, DAC, ABAC) provide varying access control and security levels, MAC is often regarded as more stringent and capable of providing more robust security controls.

12. (b) Missing Authorization occurs when access control mechanisms are improperly implemented or absent, allowing users to perform actions or access data they should not be authorized to. This can lead to unauthorized access and security vulnerabilities. It is essential to ensure proper authorization checks are in place to prevent missing authorization issues.

13. (b) System access control is the mechanism that grants or denies access to protected resources such as files, memory, and other system-related components. It encompasses various access control models, including discretionary access control (DAC) and mandatory access control (MAC). System access control is critical to overall security, ensuring that only authorized users and processes can access and manipulate protected resources within a computer system.

14. (c) The identity of the subject trying to access the object. In Discretionary Access Control (DAC), access to objects is restricted based on the identity of the subject (user or process) attempting to access the

object. The object's owner can control access and grant or deny permissions to specific users or groups based on their identities. The options b and d are not entirely accurate descriptions of DAC. While the sensitivity of information might play a role in access control decisions, DAC primarily centres on the owner's discretion and the subject's identity rather than the subject's role or the sensitivity of the information.

15. (c) Security Classification. In access control models, objects (resources) can be assigned a security classification that represents the level of sensitivity or importance of the information contained within the object. This security classification is then used to determine access permissions and restrictions for subjects (users or processes) attempting to access the object. The security classification helps enforce proper access controls and ensures only authorized individuals or processes can interact with the object. The other options (a, b, and d) are not the primary attributes associated with assigning objects in access control models.

16. (a) Dividing access privileges among multiple users to prevent abuse of power. Separation of duties is a security principle that involves distributing tasks, responsibilities, and access privileges among multiple users to prevent a single individual from having unchecked control over critical operations. This helps reduce the risk of fraud, errors, and abuses of power. By requiring the collaboration of multiple individuals to complete specific actions, the organization creates a system of checks and balances that enhances security and accountability.

17. (b) User's job title or role within the organization. RBAC is an access control model that assigns permissions to users based on their defined roles or responsibilities within an organization. Users are grouped into roles associated with specific access rights to resources. This approach simplifies access management by linking permissions to roles rather than managing permissions per user.

18. (c) RBAC (Role-Based Access Control) is an access control method that focuses on assigning permissions based on the roles and responsibilities of individuals within an organization. Access decisions are made based on user roles, ensuring that individuals are granted appropriate access rights based on their specific functions. This approach simplifies access management and enhances security by organizing permissions according to well-defined roles.

19. (b) The principle of least privileges dictates that users should only be granted the minimum access privileges necessary to perform their specific tasks or roles. Granting access based solely on an individual's hierarchical position or seniority violates this principle, as it can lead to unnecessary access and potential misuse of privileges. Access should be based on job responsibilities and needs, not just organizational hierarchy.

20. (d) In a Role-Based Access Control (RBAC) system, access to resources is determined by the roles and responsibilities of users within an organization. Mr Raja's case reflects the characteristics of RBAC, where his access to resources is based on his roles, such as being part of the research division and a manager. RBAC provides a structured and efficient way to manage access permissions by associating roles with predefined access rights, allowing users varying access levels based on their positions and responsibilities.

21. (d) The principle of least privileges states that users should only be given the minimum access rights necessary to perform their specific tasks or roles. Granting access based solely on an individual's position within an organization can result in unnecessary privileges, potentially leading to misuse, data breaches, or unauthorized access. This violates the principle of least privileges by granting more access than required for the user's responsibilities.

22. (b) Mandatory Access Control (MAC) provides the most substantial level of protection among the options listed. In MAC, access decisions are based on system-enforced security labels or clearances, often determined by strict organizational policies and security classifications. MAC ensures that access is controlled at a granular level, reducing the risk of unauthorized access and providing a higher security level than other access control models.

23. (d) All of the above.

24. (a) In Discretionary Access Control (DAC), the owner of a resource (in this case, Mr. Raja) has the discretion to control access permissions and decide who is allowed access to the resources they own. Mr. Raja is responsible for granting access to individuals or groups as he sees fit. DAC gives the owner the authority to manage access to their resources.

25. (b) Users should have the minimum access privileges necessary to perform their job functions. The principle of least privilege (POLP) emphasizes that users should be granted only access rights and permissions to carry out their specific job tasks or roles. This approach reduces the risk of security breaches, unauthorized actions, and potential misuse of privileges, as users are restricted to the bare minimum access required to perform their responsibilities effectively.

26. (c) Assigns access privileges based on data classification and user clearances. In a Mandatory Access Control (MAC) security model, access decisions are determined by the security labels and clearances assigned to users and objects. The classification of data and the level of clearance held by users play a critical role in granting or denying access to resources. MAC is commonly used in environments with strict security requirements, such as government or military systems.

27. (b) Authentication is the process of confirming or verifying the identity of a user, system, or entity attempting to access a resource or system. It involves presenting credentials, such as a username and password, biometric information, or digital certificates, to prove that the user or entity is who they claim to be. The primary goal of authentication is to ensure that only authorized individuals or entities gain access to protected resources.

28. (c) The principle of accountability emphasizes the importance of tracking and recording user activities and actions within a system or network. Access control logs should be maintained to record who accessed what resources, when the access occurred, and what actions were performed. This helps establish a trail of accountability, enables auditability, and enhances security by allowing administrators to monitor and review user activities for suspicious or unauthorized behaviour.

29. (c) Biometric authentication relies on an individual's unique physical or behavioural characteristics, such as fingerprints, facial features, iris patterns, voiceprints, or other biologically distinctive traits. These characteristics are inherently linked to the person and are difficult to forge or reproduce, making them a reliable method for verifying identity. "Something you are" refers to the inherent biological or behavioural attributes set individuals apart.

30. (b) Access control lists (ACLs) are commonly used in network firewalls to control and manage traffic flow. An ACL is a set of rules that specifies what traffic is allowed or denied based on various criteria, such as source and destination IP addresses, port numbers, and protocols. ACLs help enforce security policies by allowing or restricting specific types of network communication, thereby enhancing network security and controlling access to resources.

31. (a) A user or entity that requests access to an object. In access control, a "subject" refers to a user or entity that requests access to an object. Access control systems manage and enforce access rights based on the permissions and privileges assigned to subjects (users or entities) when interacting with objects (resources or assets).

32. (d) An "object" refers to the resource or asset accessed or protected in access control. Access control systems manage and enforce access rights and permissions for subjects (users or entities) when interacting with objects (resources). The objects can include files, directories, devices, databases, and other resources that require access control to protect them from unauthorized access or modification.

33. (b) In a computer system, a user account with login credentials is an example of a subject. Subjects are typically users or entities interacting with the system and requesting access to resources or objects. A user account, represented by a username and password, is a common way for individuals to access and interact with a computer system, making it an example of a subject.

34. (a) In the context of access control, access rights refer to the permissions or privileges that are assigned to a subject (user or entity) for accessing an object (resource or asset). These access rights define what actions the subject is allowed or denied when interacting with the object. Access rights can include actions such as read, write, execute, delete, or modify, determining the level of access and control a subject has over the object.

35. (b) The term "Authorization" refers to the process of granting or denying access rights to a subject (user or entity) for an object (resource or asset). It involves determining what actions or operations the subject is allowed or not allowed to perform on the object based on their permissions and privileges. Authorization is a crucial component of access control, and it follows the authentication process, which verifies the subject's identity.

36. (a) User's job title or role within the organization. Role-based access control (RBAC) assigns access rights based on a user's job title or role within the organization. In RBAC, permissions and privileges are associated with specific roles, and users are assigned to these roles based on their job responsibilities. This approach simplifies access control by aligning permissions with organizational roles rather than individual user attributes like technical expertise, geographic location, or seniority. Users within the same role typically have similar access rights, which can be easier to manage and maintain.

37. (a) The owner of an object determines access rights. Discretionary access control (DAC) allows the owner of an object (typically a file or resource) to determine access rights and permissions for that object. In DAC, the owner has discretion over who can access and manipulate the object, including granting or denying access to other users or entities. This model gives the owner a high degree of control and flexibility but also places responsibility on them for managing access rights.

38. (b) The subject's security clearance and the object's security classification. Mandatory access control (MAC) assigns access rights based on the subject's security clearance and the object's security classification. In MAC, access is determined by security labels associated with both the subject (user or entity) and the object (resource or asset). The security labels represent the sensitivity and classification levels of subjects and objects. Access is granted if the subject's security clearance is equal to or greater than the object's security classification, following the principle of "need-to-know" and the hierarchy of security levels. This model is often used in government and military contexts to enforce strict data confidentiality and integrity requirements.

39. (a) Access Control Lists (ACLs) are used to define and enforce access rights for subjects (users or entities) on objects (resources or assets). ACLs specify who is allowed or denied access to an object and what actions they can perform on that object. They are commonly used in various operating systems and network devices to manage permissions and control access to files, directories, and other resources.

40. (a) Discretionary Access Control (DAC) is based on a user's job title or role. In DAC, access rights and permissions are determined by the owner or administrator of an object, and they are often associated with specific job titles or roles. Users are granted access to resources based on their roles, and the owner of an object can decide who has access and what level of access they are granted. This model allows for flexibility in access control but relies on individuals to make access decisions.

41. (a) The owner of the resource. In Discretionary Access Control (DAC), access control decisions are made by the owner of the resource or object. The owner can determine who is granted or denied access to the resource and each user or entity's level of access. This model empowers resource owners to manage access control for their resources, and it is commonly used in systems where resource ownership is well-defined.

42. (a) In Discretionary Access Control (DAC), access control is typically enforced through Access Control Lists (ACLs). ACLs are lists associated with resources that specify which users or groups have permission to access the resource and what specific actions they are allowed or denied. ACLs are a common mechanism for implementing DAC and are used to manage permissions and access rights for individual resources in many operating systems and applications.

43. (a) Grant or deny access to the resource. In Discretionary Access Control (DAC), the owner of a resource has the authority to grant or deny access to that resource. The owner can decide which users or entities are allowed to access the resource and what level of access they have, including read, write, execute, or delete permissions. This discretionary authority allows resource owners to control access to their resources based on their judgment and requirements.

44. (d) All of the above.

45. (d) Only view the contents of the file. In Discretionary Access Control (DAC), a user with read access to a file can typically only view the contents of the file. They are allowed to read or view the information within the file but are not granted permission to modify, delete, or execute the file. This level of access provides read-only access to the resource. Actions like modification, deletion, or execution require additional permissions or access rights.

46. (a) Subject. In Discretionary Access Control (DAC), if a user grants access to a resource to another user, the second user becomes a "subject." The first user, the owner or the one granting access, takes on the role of the owner or administrator in this context. The subject (second user) is the one who requests access to the resource and is subject to the access permissions and control determined by the owner or administrator.

47. (a) Flexibility and simplicity in managing access control. The primary advantage of Discretionary Access Control (DAC) is its flexibility and simplicity in managing access control. DAC allows resource owners to have a high degree of control over who can access their resources and their users' level of access. It is a straightforward model that aligns well with organizational roles and responsibilities, making it easy to implement and understand.

48. (a) Octal values. In UNIX and UNIX-like operating systems, file permissions are represented using octal values. These values use three octal digits to specify the permissions for the file's owner, the group, and others (everyone else). Each digit corresponds to a set of permissions (read, write, execute), and the combinations of these digits represent the permission settings for the file. For example, "755" might represent read, write, and execute permissions for the owner and read and execute permissions for the group and others.

49. (a) Read, write, execute.

50. (a) Reading the file's contents. In UNIX file permissions, the "r" permission (read permission) allows users to read or view the file's contents. It does not grant permission to modify or execute the file or allow changing the file ownership.

51. (b) Writing or modifying the file. In UNIX file permissions, the "w" permission (write permission) allows users to write to or modify the file's contents. It allows the user to make changes to the file, including creating new content, editing existing content, and deleting content. It does not grant permission to execute the file, read its contents, or change ownership.

52. (c) Executing or running the file. In UNIX file permissions, the "x" permission (execute permission) allows users to execute or run the file if it is an executable program or script. It allows the user to run the file as a program but does not grant permission to read or write its contents or change its ownership.

53. (a) The "chmod" command changes file permissions in UNIX and UNIX-like operating systems. It allows users to modify the read (r), write (w), and execute (x) permissions for files and directories. Users can control who can access, modify, or execute the file by specifying the desired permission settings and the target file or directory.

54. (a) The owner has read, write, and execute permissions; the group and others have read and execute permissions.

55. (b) The "chown" command changes a file or directory ownership in UNIX and UNIX-like operating systems. This command lets you change the owner and/or group associated with a file or directory. You can specify the new owner and group using the "chown" command.

56. (c) The "chgrp" command changes the group ownership of a file or directory in UNIX and UNIX-like operating systems. It allows you to modify the group associated with a particular file or directory without changing the owner. You can specify the new group using the "chgrp" command.

57. (a) /etc/passwd - In UNIX and UNIX-like operating systems, the "/etc/passwd" file stores user account information, including usernames, user IDs (UIDs), group IDs (GIDs), home directories, and login shells. It does not contain password information, typically stored in the "/etc/shadow" file for enhanced security. On the other hand, the "/etc/group" file stores information about user groups and their members.

58. (c) The user's assigned role or job function. In Role-Based Access Control (RBAC), access control decisions are made based on the user's assigned role or job function within the organization. Instead of making access decisions solely based on the user's identity or security clearance, RBAC defines roles corresponding to specific job responsibilities or functions. Users are then assigned to roles, each with a set of associated permissions. Access control decisions are based on the user's role and the permissions

associated with that role. This approach simplifies access management and ensures that users have the appropriate level of access based on their roles.

59. (b) In Role-Based Access Control (RBAC), users are assigned roles encompassing access rights or permissions. Rather than assigning individual access rights to each object for each user, RBAC simplifies access management by grouping users into roles, and each role is associated with a predefined set of permissions. Users are then assigned one or more roles based on their job responsibilities or functions within the organization. This approach makes it easier to manage access control and ensures that users with similar roles have consistent access to resources.

60. (a) Simplifies access control administration.

61. (a) Multiple roles. In Role-Based Access Control (RBAC), a user can be assigned multiple roles. This flexibility allows organizations to accommodate situations where users may have multiple job functions or responsibilities requiring different permissions. By assigning users multiple roles, RBAC ensures they have the appropriate access rights for all their relevant roles without requiring complex individual access rights assignments.

62. (a) Users, roles, and objects.

63. (d) In Role-Based Access Control (RBAC), the component that determines the permissions associated with each role is referred to as "Role permissions." Each role is associated with a predefined set of permissions or access rights that define what actions users in that role are allowed to perform on specific objects or resources. Role permissions specify the level of access control granted to users within the context of their assigned roles.

64. (a) In Role-Based Access Control (RBAC), the role hierarchy can be defined by specifying the relationships between different roles. The role hierarchy establishes the structure and dependencies among roles within the organization. It can include parent-child relationships, where specific roles inherit permissions or characteristics from higher-level roles. This hierarchical structure helps in organizing roles and managing access control more effectively.

65. (a) Ensures users can only perform specific tasks within their assigned role. Separation of duties (SoD) is a concept in Role-Based Access Control (RBAC) that ensures users can only perform specific tasks or actions within the scope of their assigned role. It helps prevent conflicts of interest and enhances security by enforcing restrictions on which combinations of tasks or permissions a single user can have. SoD is designed to reduce the risk of fraudulent or harmful activities by restricting users from having conflicting or sensitive combinations of access rights within their roles.